Narratives of Free Trade

Global Connections

School of Modern Languages and Cultures
The University of Hong Kong

Series General Editor: Dixon H.W. Wong

The Global Connections series explores the movement of ideas, people, technologies, capital and goods across national and regional borders. Books in the series reveal how these interconnections have the power to produce new global forms of cultures, politics, identities and economies. Seeking to explore the dynamics of change, the series includes both historical and contemporary topics. It focuses on interactions between the world's diverse cultures through the production of new interdisciplinary knowledge.

Forthcoming title

Europe and China: Strategic Partners or Rivals? edited by Roland Vogt

Narratives of Free Trade

The Commercial Cultures of Early US–China Relations

Edited by Kendall Johnson

香港大學出版社
Hong Kong University Press

Hong Kong University Press
14/F Hing Wai Centre
7 Tin Wan Praya Road
Aberdeen
Hong Kong
www.hkupress.org

ISBN 978-988-8083-53-4 (*Hardback*)
ISBN 978-988-8083-54-1 (*Paperback*)

British Library Cataloguing-in-Publication Data
A catalogue record for this book is available from the British Library.

10 9 8 7 6 5 4 3 2 1

Printed and bound by Kings Time Printing Press Ltd., Hong Kong, China

Contents

Acknowledgements

In June 2009, the American Studies Programme in the School of Modern Languages and Cultures at the University of Hong Kong worked with the Department of History at Sun Yat-sen University, the Instituto Cultural do Governo da R.A.E. de Macau, and the Hong Kong-America Center to invite a group of scholars to participate in a colloquium on the representation of free trade in narratives of early American and Chinese relations. The participants included Dr. Paul Bové (University of Pittsburgh), Dr. Max Cavitch (University of Pennsylvania), Dr. May Bo Ching (Sun Yat-sen University), Dr. John R. Haddad (Penn State University), Dr. Vincent Ho (University of Macao), Dr. Sibing He (Independent Scholar, Guangzhou), Dr. Yinghe Jiang (Sun Yat-sen University), Dr. Yeewan Koon (University of Hong Kong), Dr. Khun Eng Kuah-Pearce (University of Hong Kong), Dr. Joseph Abraham Levi (University of Hong Kong), Dr. Aili Li (Sun Yat-sen University), Dr. Rogério Miguel Puga (FCSH-Universidade Nova de Lisboa/FCT, Portugal), Dr. Paul A. Van Dyke (University of Macao), and Ms. Huang Yedan (University of Hong Kong). The moderators who generously contributed their time and insightful commentary were Dr. Wayne Cristaudo (Director of the European Studies Programme, University of Hong Kong), Professor Douglas Kerr (School of English, University of Hong Kong), and Dr. Pui Tak Lee (Centre for Asian Studies, University of Hong Kong).

The colloquium experience materialized through the hard work and planning of several people, including Dr. Dixon Wong (Head of the School of Modern Languages and Cultures at the University of Hong Kong), Marie Imelda Macleod (Director of the Arquivo Historico de Macau), Dr. May Bo Ching (Department of History, Sun Yat-sen University), and Dr. Glenn Shive (Director of the Hong Kong-America Center). For their intellectual energy and support of the events, deep appreciation goes to Professor Takeshi

Hamashita and Professor Liu Zhiwei (the School of Asia-Pacific Studies, Sun Yat-sen University), Professor Wu Yixiong (Department of History, Sun Yat-sen University), Professor Kam Louie (Dean of the Faculty of the Arts, University of Hong Kong), and to Dr. Vincent Wai-kit Ho (University of Macao). Thank you to Dr. Q. S. Tong (Head of School, School of English, University of Hong Kong) for additional support. For her expert administrative coordination, Ms. Christy M. Y. Ho of the University of Hong Kong deserves special thanks. The Fulbright Scholar Program and Swarthmore College provided the opportunity and resources to enable such gratifying international scholarly exchange. The suggestions of two anonymous readers from Hong Kong University Press greatly enhanced the manuscript. Finally, thank you to Michael Duckworth and Christopher Munn for their interest in and encouragement of this book.

Contributors

Paul A. Bové teaches English at the University of Pittsburgh where he is Distinguished Professor. Editor of *boundary 2*, an international journal of literature and culture, he is the author of the prize-winning 1986 study, *Intellectuals in Power* as well as several other major books in critical theory, American literature, modern literature, and poetics. His most recent book, *Poetry Against Torture*, is the result of a lecture series at the University of Hong Kong where Bové has regularly visited as a professor. The author of nearly 100 refereed articles, his most recent essay is "Misprisions of Utopia: Messianism, Apocalypse, and Allegory" in the *Field Day Anthology*. He is currently completing two books, *Art Against Allegory* and, for Harvard University Press, *Henry Adams and the Creative Love of Imagination*.

May-bo Ching is a professor of history in the Centre for Historical Anthropology at Sun Yat-sen University. Her major research interest is the social and cultural history of modern China. Her book *Regional Culture and National Identity: The Shaping of "Guangdong Culture" Since the Late Qing* (in Chinese) discusses changes in the articulation of regional identity against the rise of nationalism at the turn of nineteenth and twentieth centuries. Her current projects include a preliminary study of the introduction of natural history drawings and knowledge into China since the late eighteenth century and a social history of Cantonese opera from the 1860s to 1950s.

John R. Haddad currently teaches American Studies at Penn State Harrisburg, where he is an associate professor of American Studies and Literature. He holds a Ph.D. in American Studies from the University of Texas at Austin (2002). His book, *The Romance of China: Excursions to China in U.S. Culture, 1776–1876* (Columbia University Press, 2006) explores ways that

Americans learned about and constructed China in the eighteenth and nineteenth centuries.

Sibing He received his Ph.D. in US diplomatic history from Miami University and his research interests are in the areas of Sino-US relations, overseas Chinese studies and international relations in space exploration and utilization. He is currently serving as guest professor at the Center for the Studies of Overseas Chinese Culture, Huaqiao University in Quanzhou, China.

Yedan Huang is a Ph.D. candidate, Department of Sociology, and Research Associate, Centre for Anthropological Research, University of Hong Kong.

Kendall Johnson is an associate professor and director of the American Studies Programme at the University of Hong Kong. His recent books include *Henry James and the Visual* (Cambridge University Press 2007) and *A Critical Companion to Henry James: A Literary Reference to his Life and Work* (2009). He has also published essays on Native American law and literature. He is currently working on the literature of early United States trade and diplomacy in "Canton".

Yeewan Koon is an assistant professor of fine arts at the University of Hong Kong. She is currently working on a manuscript looking at art in Guangdong in the early nineteenth century as the region transitioned from a trading hub to a place of war, focusing in particular on the artist Su Renshan (c.1814–50).

Khun Eng Kuah-Pearce is an associate professor in the Department of Sociology at the University of Hong Kong.

Rogério Miguel Puga holds a Ph.D. on Anglo-Portuguese Studies (FCSH, New University of Lisbon), was a lecturer at Institute of Education and Sciences (ISEC, Lisbon, 2000–2005), assistant professor at the University of Macao (2007–2009) and is now a senior researcher at the Centre for English, Translation and Anglo-Portuguese Studies (CETAPS, New University of Lisbon), where he also teaches. He is a research collaborator at Centre for Overseas History (CHAM, New University) and the Centre for Comparative Studies (University of Lisbon), and an invited researcher at the University of Macao (History Department). He has published several studies on Anglo-Portuguese literary and historical relations, the Portuguese and British Empires, and on Lusophone and Anglophone Literatures, namely: *The Portuguese Historical Novel* (Lisbon, 2006), *A World of Euphemism: Representations of Macao in the*

Work of Austin Coates. City of Broken Promises as Historical Novel and Female Bildungsroman (Lisbon, 2009), *The English Presence and Anglo-Portuguese Relations in Macao* (1635–1794) (Lisbon, 2009), and *Chronology of Portuguese Literature, 1128–2000* (Cambridge Scholars Publishing, UK, 2011). He is the editor of the *European Journal of Macao Studies* (Portugal), and subject editor for the journal *Romance Studies* (United Kingdom).

Paul A. Van Dyke is a historian and the author of *The Canton Trade: Life and Enterprise on the China Coast, 1700–1845* (Hong Kong University Press, 2005). He has published many articles on different aspects of the trade in Canton and Macao, including Armenians, Muslims and the Chinese junk trade to Southeast Asia, and is presently writing new histories of the Chinese merchant families.

Introduction
Revising First Impressions

American Stereotypes of China and the National Romance of Free Trade

Kendall Johnson

> What China now is—that will it be as long as the Empire shall exist. Its arts, tastes, costume, manners, and government, are *stereotyped*; and the author who shall write its history, or visit its coasts and canals in order to describe them a hundred years hence, will have but little more to do than to copy the works that were published in the nineteenth century.
>
> It is in consequence of this permanent character—this tideless oozing of Chinese life—that we do not hesitate to write of the country from our personal recollections, albeit some twenty years have elapsed since we trod the "flowery land."
>
> —Brantz Mayer, "China and the Chinese"
> July 1847, *Southern Quarterly Review*, p. 8

In justifying Britain's tactics in the Opium War (1839–42), it might seem that the Baltimore-based lawyer and historian Brantz Mayer (1809–79) had a tough case to make. His article "China and the Chinese" (1847) acknowledges that England had disregarded China's rule of law by saturating its economy with opium, and he further notes the devastation visited on the local population in Guangdong by both the opium and the war. But Mayer sees a greater good beyond this disaster, averring that England's aggressions are "an assertion of the right of all civilized nations to *demand* the sanction and safeguard of treaties from people with whom they entertain a large and lucrative trade."[1] Citing former US President John Quincy Adams, Mayer declares that "the great result of the China War was that it brought the stubborn Empire within the pale of diplomatic negotiation, and placed it upon the common platform of the commercial world."[2] One assumes that the prescription of trade would open the "tideless oozing" of Chinese life to civilizing channels of global commerce. Given the dramatic nature of Mayer's characterizations, the question arises: What degree or kind of communication and diplomacy between China and the United States would have been possible in the first decades of the United States' relatively insecure existence?

At least since John Gallagher and Ronald Robinson highlighted the informal and indirect pressures of England's global economic influence, the British practice of flooding the Chinese market with opium harvested in India has vexed the casual usage of the phrase "free trade" in scholarship about China and England during the late eighteenth and nineteenth centuries.[3] In *The Rise of Free Trade Imperialism* (1970), Bernard Semmel extends the skepticism by arguing that the nineteenth-century era of so-called "free trade" was an extension, rather than a refutation, of the overtly political and constitutional terms by which England had administered its imperial "system of mercantilist colonialisms" in the eighteenth century.[4] Semmel points to articles in the *Westminster Review* on the Opium War by Liberals and Radicals who lamented England's endurance of Chinese insults and of the emperor's close-minded and putatively arbitrary interference with commerce. Amitav Ghosh picks up on the evangelical tone of these articles' indignation, weaving into the narrative of his recent novel *Sea of Poppies* (2008) a rather chilling quote attributed to John Bowring, a good friend of Jeremy Bentham and Lord Byron, as well as a co-editor of the *Westminster Review* and the British Consul at Canton for four years beginning in 1849, and fourth governor of Hong Kong (1854–59).[5] While campaigning in 1841 to be a member of parliament for Bolton, Bowring summed up his moral claim in the stunning chiasmus: "Jesus Christ is Free Trade, and Free Trade is Jesus Christ."[6]

President John Quincy Adams also dipped his hand into the fount of biblical adage to justify the British war on China. In an 1841 speech to the Massachusetts Historical Society, which Brantz Mayer later quoted from its republication in Elijah Bridgman's *The Chinese Repository*, Adams declared: "The moral obligation of commercial intercourse between nations is founded, exclusively, upon the Christian precept to love your neighbor as yourself."[7] Seeming deeply concerned with violations of the Christian law, Adams perceives China to be a diabolical adversary whose "enormous outrages upon the rights of human nature, and upon the first principle of the rights of nations," lead to the damning conclusion: "the fundamental principle of the Chinese empire is anti-commercial."[8] However, as Sibing He argues in his essay in this volume on the American firm Russell & Company, the phrase the "imperialism of free trade" more fittingly describes the political and economic mode to which China was reacting.[9]

Today, how should we react to these caricatures of China and the Christian nations of the United States and Great Britain? We might begin with the word *stereotype* itself, which developed from early nineteenth-century print technologies of image reproduction, whereby printers stamped out a metal plate from the plaster mould of an engraved wooden block. These metal plates were more durable than the wooden forme, but they also sacrificed the engraving's clarity. By mid-century, about the time that Mayer invited future historians to describe China by merely copying pictures of its "coasts and canals" (see this introduction's epigraph), the English term *stereotype* was beginning to connote the limiting effect of preconceptions on our abilities to perceive the world.[10] Generalizations may be necessary in coping with life's complexity, but they potentially settle into a deceptively solid foundation of prejudice.

Looking over the centuries of textual materials printed in Europe after Marco Polo's thirteenth-century travels and before the existence of the United States, China seems to promise fantastic but elusive wealth, the pursuit of which fueled the imaginations of Christopher Columbus and many other fifteenth-century imperial explorers who embarked under the flags of Catholic kings. In the first half the of the sixteenth century, Portugal was the first to establish a foothold in China, even as the Chinese relegated them to Macao, which was geographically positioned to be a key site from which to regulate the traffic up the Pearl River Delta; the Jesuit missionaries Michele Ruggieri and Matteo Ricci lived in Macao and composed the first Chinese-Portuguese dictionary. Ricci eventually traveled to Peking (Beijing), where he worked for decades before his death in 1610. In the seventeenth century, after the fall of the Ming Dynasty and rise of the Qing, and as various Jesuit priests continued to publish about China from Peking, European financiers and traders set their course for Canton. The royally chartered East India Companies of Austria, Denmark, England, Estonia, France, Portugal, Prussia, Scotland, and Sweden as well as the Dutch United East India Company (Vereenigde Oost-Indische Compagnie or VOC) established a global mercantilist system that swelled the coffers of banks and busied the workshops of Europe.[11]

By the eighteenth century, China still did not have much interest in Western goods although the extraordinary profitability of tea continued to draw many Western traders to China. In order to regulate the European expectation of trade, the Qing Dynasty instituted in the 1760s the "Canton System" that quarantined Europeans to a specific zone outside the walls of Guangdong Province's port city of Guangzhou.[12] In this zone, all trade was administered by thirteen Chinese merchant organizations called *Cohongs* to whom the emperor had granted exclusive privileges of transacting with foreigners.[13]

In the city of Canton and the quarantine zone, fires were frequent and feared occurrences. In 1822, the foreign factories burned nearly to the ground. Figure I.1 is a retrospective picture of what the factory buildings in Canton looked like before another devastating fire in 1856 consumed the entire factory area and prompted their relocation to Honam Island and eventually to an area on Shamian Island.[14] In the days of the Canton trading system, Cohongs rented the buildings to the countries of France, the United States, and Sweden, whose flags fly in front.

The rules governing Westerners' presence in this space were strict. All foreign women were banned, as was the teaching of Chinese to foreigners. The sale of opium was prohibited by law, making smuggling a very lucrative practice that was facilitated by an unofficial headquarters on Lintin Island and by trading companies quartered in the Portuguese-controlled city of Macao, about 120 miles (195 kilometers) down the Pearl River. Under this Canton arrangement, the market in tea worked greatly to Chinese advantage. Hong merchants such as the immensely wealthy Howqua leveraged European demand into massive transfers of silver specie, exacting a heavy toll on Western stores of the precious metal. Even when silver was in especially short supply, the Hong merchants managed to control the market for tea by extending credit in notes underwritten by promises to pay in silver.

Opium helped Britain to shift this commercial balance of power and lessen the dependence on silver. With their late eighteenth-century colonial control of India they established the "Country Trade" by which the East India Company and an increasing number of private traders shipped Indian products to China, generating a paper-based system of exchange in Canton that was facilitated by London banks. The most powerful of England's colonial products from India was opium, with which the British company began to saturate the Chinese market in the nineteenth century. Although in 1729 the Qing emperor had issued an imperial decree banning the trade of opium, by the early nineteenth century, there were highly developed networks in place to smuggle the drug and facilitate its lucrative traffic.[15] In this context, the idea of "free trade" had very little to do with mutual respect or mutual benefit among those participating in a shared market. Instead, those who claimed freedoms to trade demanded that no restriction be placed on them in their attempt to traffic whatever it was that they wanted to sell.

In the very year that the North American colonies declared their independence from England, insisting on their rights of direct trade unfettered by mercantilist restriction, Adam Smith offered in *The Wealth of Nations* (1776) what has become the classical description of liberal economic sentiment.[16] He theorized, in language that has endured, the aggregate benefit of individual participants' pursuits of economic self-interest. In describing China, Smith marvels at the wealth that agriculture has brought to the empire, which, he writes:

> has been long one of the richest, that is, one of the most fertile, best cultivated, most industrious, and most populous countries in the world. It seems, however, to have been long stationary. Marco Polo, who visited it more than five hundred years ago, describes its cultivation, industry, and populousness, almost in the same terms in which they are described by travelers in the present times. It had perhaps, even long before his time, acquired that full complement of riches which the nature of its laws and institutions permits it to acquire.[17]

In representing China as "stationary," Smith sets up an allegory of what happens without free trade. It goes something like this: China's despotic ruler artificially confines the country's prodigious wealth to circulating in a closed system of imperial tributaries that ought rather to flow into the economic channels forged and agitated by more enterprising nations of Christendom. Smith finds it "remarkable, that neither the ancient Egyptians, nor the Indians, nor the Chinese, encouraged foreign commerce, but seem all to have derived their great opulence from this inland navigation."[18] To Smith, China exemplifies a relatively primitive agrarian plan, framed by "several great rivers" that "form, by their different branches, a multitude of canals, and, by communicating with one another, afford an inland navigation much more extensive than that either of the Nile or the Ganges, or, perhaps of both of them put together."[19] It is difficult not to read into Smith's description an implicit encouragement for the private investors of the world's nations to open lines of commercial navigation and thus communicate their way through what Mayer calls in the epigraph the "tideless oozing of Chinese life."

As John Rogers Haddad argues in his contribution to this volume, the China Trade inspired the imagination of many Americans in the decades after the Revolutionary War; and yet, within the contemporary field of American Studies and literature, China's influence on the early United States seems underappreciated.[20] In the field of historical studies, scholars have had much to say about the fundamental and formative influences of the China Trade on the development of the United States.[21] Sydney Greenbie and Marjorie Barstow Greenbie averred in *Gold of Ophir; or, The Lure that Made America* (1925) that "the trade with the Orient [*sic*] is one of two great economic facts of the history of the United States between the Revolution and the Civil War, the other fact being the development and westward extension of negro [*sic*] slavery."[22] To these two economic facts, we might add a third, of the nation's systematic removal and quarantine of Native peoples in the development of a Far West beckoning in the wake of the Louisiana Purchase (1803) and the United States' war on Mexico (1846–48).

Whereas Mayer's notion of the stereotype borders on ridiculousness, it affords us an opportunity to consider the underappreciated role of China in the "imaginative geography" of American national development.[23] As a young man in 1827, Mayer had traveled to Canton to ply the China Trade and earn his "competency," enough capital with which to establish himself comfortably as a gentleman in Maryland.[24] He did not stay long, returning to study at the University of Maryland and to practice law in Baltimore. In 1841, he signed on as the secretary of the United States legation to Mexico, an experience that inspired him to write *Mexico as It Was and as it Is* (1844) and the *History of the War between Mexico and the United States, with a Preliminary of its Origin* (1848), tomes in which he argued that the war against Mexico was unfortunate but would, just like the tough love expressed by England in the Opium War, prove ultimately civilizing and beneficial.

Mayer's article "China and the Chinese" makes clear that the "economic facts" of the nineteenth-century China Trade are bound up with the belief that the United States was rising to international prominence in what we might call a national romance of free trade.[25] In Mayer's article, China appears as a third point of cultural reference in charting America's rise, thus turning the conventional formula of double-exceptional distinctiveness (whereby America realizes a cultural continuity by distinguishing itself from Europe and Native America), into a formula of triple-exceptionalism. Mayer's brand of triple-exceptionalism juxtaposes the related (but ultimately different) civilizing forces of England and the United States against two different styles of Chinese and Native American savagery. In marveling at the long duration of the Chinese Empire, Mayer quotes an article entitled "War with China, and the Opium Question" that had appeared in the British Tory magazine *Blackwood's* in March 1840, just before the Opium War. In the article, Alfred Mallalieu claims that China "alone, has stood firm, immovable, permanent, for thousands of years—scarcely ruffled by dynastic changes, giving the law even to its Mantchew [*sic*] emperors, who wisely merged the claims of conquest in those of adoption, and sank their own nationality in that of the vast country, pure, homogeneous, unmixed, and uncontaminated alone of all the earth, in its people and lineage."[26] Mayer goes on to recognize in China's "permanent character" a profound durability expressed in historical narrative (they have existed during all remembered time) and captured in literal textual representation by Western traders, travelers and missionaries (images of China will exist forever). Against China's incredible power of sustentative assimilation Mayer contrasts North America's "powerful red tribes" that have ostensibly vanished; he eulogizes the "red tribes" for whom we search "the modern atlas [...] in vain: while China alone remains the stereotyped impression of every map, and the enduring monument of every age. She alone substantially connects all the various and ever-varying phases of the past with the present, from all time unchanging, as still unchanged herself, amidst change and revolution all around her."

Put in the context of the impending United States aggression against Mexico (a country that wavers in Mayer's account between European degeneracy and American savagery), the stereotypic figures of the Chinese and tribes of red men are more similar than they might first appear. Both stereotypes are fixed points of reference for Mayer's national American reader, whom he asks to appreciate the Mexican War as righteous territorial expansion and virtuous cultural development of the United States. The red savages have fallen out of time and the Chinese barbarians have risen above it, but both are out of the bounds in which the contractual time of the free trading market advances a national romance. Whereas the barbaric and savage peoples are frozen in stereotype, the United States moves through time like a developing character in a sequential narrative that plots the rise of a nation whose dynamic borders cannot be fixed in any single stereotyped map. One assumes that only a continuous series of maps would approximate the nation's spatial extension of postcolonial (i.e. post-British) self-realization. In this context, it makes sense that Mayer freezes in a paradoxical sense of time both the Chinese and tribes of red men whose communal story is over, relegated to the past while remaining fully and eternally accessible to present American readers as they gauge a future course of national progress in reference to the manifested truth of Mayer's printed stereotypes.[27]

It could go without saying that the rhetorically eternal Chinese Empire and the evanescent red man have little to convey about any actual Chinese or Native people, and much to imply about Mayer's own tangle of professed confidence in, and underlying anxiety over, the instability of his own rapidly transforming country. Consider that his article appeared in the *Southern Quarterly Review* published in Charlestown, South Carolina, which in twelve years would be a treasonous state bound to others in the Southern Confederacy. Consider too that the seemingly confident narrative voice of Mayer's 1847 article depends on fusing citations from the Scottish Tory publication *Blackwood's* with quotes by President Quincy Adams from a speech delivered to the Massachusetts Historical Society and later reprinted in *The Chinese Repository*. The Civil War proves the precarious nature of Mayer's linkages across the contested geographies of putative free trade, suggesting his romance of American exceptionalism is more akin to a tangle of political compromise formations than the documentation of historical fact.

Nevertheless, even instances of stereotypical thinking as reductive as Mayer's are part of social contexts in which those peoples ostensibly frozen as stereotype were actually active agents in an unfolding relationship. In appreciative reconsideration of Edward Said's characterizations of Orientalism, Arif Dirlik emphasizes the relational nature of Western depictions of the Oriental Other in order to recover the ways in which Western fantasies were influenced and shaped by the experience of engagement. In proposing a key term for this style of relational thinking, Dirlik suggests Mary Louise Pratt's notion of "transculturation," whereby the "contact zone" is "not merely a zone of domination" but also a "zone of exchange, even if it is unequal exchange."[28] In this relational model, the interpretative concern is not simply to debunk stereotypes or to condemn their injustice. Instead, as the essays in this collection show, the goal becomes to think carefully about the relationships behind the stereotypes—relationships unfolding in contact zones too easily reduced in the romance of American expansion to the phrases the *Far East* and the *Far West*. If we pursue a more culturally dialogic sense of the past, we can continue to consider the perspective of Chinese merchants, government officials, and the wide variety of Chinese people participating in and affected by the Canton Trade. As our eyes continue to pass over many of the same literally stereotyped books and journals that were available to Mayer, it is safe to say that we are interested in the commercial networks and social relationships behind the nineteenth-century copies representing "China," the "United States," "Great Britain," and "free trade."

First Impressions

Where might we begin the story of Sino-American encounters? In the early days of the United States, China was a tangle of psychic energy in the American imagination, and it is difficult to designate a *first* American to record his or her impression of China during or after the American Revolutionary War. One can only muse over the moments when North American British colonists trading in Canton (Guangzhou) or serving on ships anchored off Macao might have relinquished their affection for a particular colony (i.e., Pennsylvania or New York or Massachusetts) and acknowledged, let alone embraced, the early federal affiliation offered by the Articles of Confederation (1781–88) and the Constitution (ratified 1788). As indicated by the title of James Fichter's recent *So Great a Proffit: How the East Indies Trade Transformed Anglo-American Capitalism* (2010), it makes little sense to consider the United States' involvement in the China Trade apart from the United States' relationship to England. Most of the Americans highlighted in this collection were rather anxious about their own financial and cultural standing. For those Americans who took pride in a culturally American distinctiveness, Britain seems an abiding point of reference, whether for the dominance of the British East India Company and the Royal Navy or for the influential precedence of Britain's diplomatic etiquette and putatively refined standards of social courtesy.

By emphasizing the roles and professions of the China Trade, the eminent twentieth-century historian John K. Fairbank provides a broad outline of how we might see these first Americans. He presents three kinds:

> First to arrive was the merchant, who tried out what he could do on the foreign shores, and then, particularly if the merchant got into trouble, the naval diplomat, a captain or a commodore with a warship who provided a little gunboat diplomacy to help out the merchant. The missionary followed along behind, seizing the opportunity to try to improve the local people's spiritual welfare.[29]

The bibliography to this volume is not comprehensive but does suggest the wealth of primary documents and the historical scholarship concerning Americans' impressions of China. The most sustained account of the United States' first decade comes from Samuel Shaw, the supercargo of the first successful round-trip voyage to Canton aboard the *Empress of China* in 1784. Although not recognized as an official diplomat by the Qing government in China, Shaw was appointed by the United States to be the nation's first consul at Canton. His impressions did not become widely available until the 1847 publication of his posthumously edited memoir, *The Journals of Major Samuel Shaw, the First American Consul at Canton, with a Life of the Author by Josiah Quincy* (1847), which the second essay in this collection considers.

In 1790, a ship owned by Shaw named the *Massachusetts* carried to China Amasa Delano, another early American who recorded his observations in *A Narrative of Voyages and Travels in the Northern and Southern Hemispheres: Comprising Three Voyages Round the World; Together with a Voyage of Survey and Discovery, in the Pacific Ocean and Oriental Islands* (1817). The earliest American accounts also include Connecticut-born John Ledyard, who embarked on Captain James Cook's third voyage in July of 1776; Ledyard landed in Macao in December 1779 after Cook's demise, and he returned to England in October 1780.[30] Ledyard subsequently advocated the fur trade and helped to inspire the Boston merchant John Barrell who, with five other investors, planned and financed two early voyages, one in the late 1780s and a second in the early 1790s.[31] In June 1787, Thomas Reid captained to Canton the *Alliance*, the ship of John Barry's Revolutionary War heroics.[32] In January 1788, Commodore John Barry, the "father of the American navy" himself, embarked for China as the "commander of the merchant ship *Asia*," and returned to Philadelphia in June 1789.[33] American voyages to China subsequently became more numerous.

As the nineteenth century began, private traders such as Samuel Snow, the more successful John Jacob Astor, Stephen Girard, Samuel Russell, and other many other financiers based in New England, New York, and Philadelphia amassed fortunes in the China Trade, particularly through direct opium dealing or indirect facilitation of its traffic.[34] In *The Golden Ghetto: The American Commercial Community at Canton and the Shaping of American China Policy, 1784–1844* (1997), Jacques Downs documents the rise of American trading companies such as Perkins & Company, J. P. Sturgis & Company, Russell &

Co., Olyphant & Co., Nathan Dunn & Co., Wetmore & Co., and others. As the essay by Paul A. Van Dyke considers, whereas the British East India Company was a monopoly operation that established a vast global network centered in its trade with China, the new breed of United States private traders worked on a smaller scale and on a different model, incorporating themselves under state jurisdiction as private companies or firms without either a monopoly advantage or any particular obligations to the federal government.[35] In these private company enterprises, a single person or small group of owners held the responsibilities of management, supervision of cargo, and the captaincy of the ships; this left little time for meticulous bookkeeping.

Some of the earliest ethnographic accounts of China penned by Americans emerge from those working with the private companies and firms in Canton and Macao. William Wood was an early influential American writer from Philadelphia who worked in Canton with Russell & Company. Not only did he publish the illustrated *Sketches of China: With Illustration from Original Drawings* (1830) but wrote for, edited, and published two early newspapers, the *Canton Register* in 1827 and, in 1831, the *Chinese Courier and Canton Gazette*.[36] Later in the century, Wood's more senior merchant contemporaries, such as Gideon Nye and William C. Hunter, published their accounts of life in Canton and Macao.

In the late 1820s, the American Christian missionaries David Abeel and Elijah C. Bridgman arrived. Sponsored by the American Board of Commissioners of Foreign Missions (ABCFM) and the Seamen's Friends Society, the two were also funded by the Philadelphia-based merchant W. D. C. Olyphant and, by their accounts, warmly greeted and supported by the British missionary and sinologist Dr Robert Morrison, who had arrived in 1807. In 1834, Abeel published his *Journal of a Residence in China, and the Neighboring Countries, from 1829 to 1833* (1834) with the stated objective being "to inform the Christian world of the state of these heathen countries."[37] Bridgman started the influential newspaper *The Chinese Repository* and worked to translate the Bible into Chinese. The missionary Samuel Wells Williams arrived in Canton in 1833. He worked in China for forty years, taking over the editorial duties of *The Chinese Repository* from Bridgman in the late 1840s, developing diplomatic relationships with China in the 1850s and 1860s, composing an English-Cantonese dictionary and other Chinese dictionaries; when Commodore Matthew C. Perry followed his naval victories in Mexico with his expedition to Japan, he enlisted Williams as his translator.[38] In 1877, Yale University appointed Williams the first professor of Chinese Language and Literature in the United States.

To Fairbanks's list, one should add American women who have left a treasure trove of written impressions. Because China banned all foreign women from Canton, the wives, daughters, and nieces of traders spent the majority of their time living in Macao. As Rogério Miguel Puga outlines in his contribution to this volume on the journals of Caroline Hyde Butler, these women's diaries and correspondence document social life at the international crossroads of Macao. The first American woman whose writings we have is Harriett Low (1809–77). She was born into a Unitarian family in Salem, Massachusetts, and at the age of twenty she took the four-month journey to China, where she lived for four years with her aunt and uncle in Macao in the early 1830s; she even sneaked into Canton for a short visit. From 1829 to 1834, as her uncle worked for Russell & Company, Low wrote nine volumes, sending them across oceans to her sister Mary Ann Law, who was living in the United States.[39] In addition to Low's volumes, there are writings by Lucy Cleveland, Rebecca Kinsman, Caroline Hyde Butler Laing, Mary Parry Sword, Eliza Bridgman and Henrietta Hall Shuck, the first woman from the United States to be a missionary to China.[40] Shuck died in Hong Kong in 1844, and her "Memoir," compiled by J. B. Jeter, was published posthumously in 1850.

As Brantz Mayer's article demonstrates, the abiding British influence helped shape the commercial and social life of Americans in Canton proper, and the Opium War marked a critical point of transformation in the United States China Trade. When Commissioner Lin Zexu (林則徐; 1785–1850) arrived with orders to enforce the emperor's long-standing prohibition on the opium trading in Guangdong, he shut down the factories at Canton, confiscating and destroying opium. England reacted to the confrontation with escalating rounds of aggression that resulted in the First Opium War (1839–42).[41] With their technologically superior naval ships powered by steam and their capacity to inflict destruction with virtually unrivalled artillery, they destroyed the system of checkpoints through which China had managed the Canton Trade. At the war's conclusion, England negotiated the Treaty of Nanjing (1842) that forced China to open officially four more trading ports (Xiamen, Shanghai, Ningpo, Fuzhou), to give up Victoria (Hong Kong) to British possession "in perpetuity," to pay a stinging reparation of $21 million, and to abide by the legal condition of extraterritoriality by which

English subjects would be judged under British law for any crimes committed on Chinese soil.

The Americans followed suit and dispatched their "envoy extraordinary and minister plenipotentiary" Caleb Cushing (1800–79), a Massachusetts congressman who chaired the US House Committee on Foreign Affairs. He was appointed by President John Tyler and negotiated with the imperial representative Qiying (耆英; 1787–1858) in a process that Yeewan Koon considers in this volume.[42] Although China had already extended the terms of the British treaty to the United States before Cushing's arrival, he went through with the negotiations in order to emphasize the sovereignty and demonstrate the military resolve of the United States. The result was the Treaty of Wangxia (1844). At the Temple of Kun Ian, outside the walls of Portuguese-controlled Macao, Cushing formally secured terms comparable to those of the British treaty. The Treaty of Wangxia echoed the Treaty of Nanjing in many respects, opening the four additional ports explicitly to the United States, although the treaty did not annex any land or demand an indemnity or a ransom. In its Article 22, the treaty secures peace, amity, and friendship in the guarantee that the United States will be able to "trade freely to and from the five ports of China open to foreign commerce."[43] This treaty also insisted on the condition of extraterritoriality, except in the case of Americans caught smuggling opium, the trade of which the treaty designated as illegal. However, with the premise of extraterritoriality in place, the Treaty of Wangxia's ostensible prohibition of the opium trade was purposefully and practically unenforceable. As Teemu Ruskola has argued, Cushing justified the condition of extraterritoriality by limiting the principles of international law to Christian nations, a group from which he disqualified China.[44] On his route back to the United States, Cushing continued his circumnavigation of the earth by traveling through Mexico, where he would return within two years as a brigadier general to fight in the Mexican–American War. China again registers as a crucial point of reference in the United States' supposed manifest destiny across North America.

For American China traders, as the historians Hosea Morse Ballou and W.E. Cheong have documented, the Cohongs in Canton were major power brokers before the Opium War. As intermediaries between the foreign traders and the imperial government, they managed a vast global network of commercial transactions that generated fabulous wealth. In this collection, May-bo Ching focuses on the styles of Cohong diplomacy that centered on food banquets. By asking straightforward questions such as "What kind of knowledge did the Chinese cooks and servants possess for entertaining foreign guests?" Ching derives deep insight into "What kind of impact might this material cultural exchange have left on Canton in the subsequent years?" It is important to realize how the geographical and cultural divides between China and the United States were simultaneously challenged and maintained across vast distances. For example, Howqua's collaboration with John Murray Forbes of Russell & Company continued after Forbes returned to the United States to pursue railroad development in 1836. Howqua "sent nearly half a million in surplus capital to invest in American enterprises" with Forbes.[45]

The final two essays in the collection consider the period after the United States Civil War. Paul Bové reconsiders the Open Door Policy through which Secretary of State John Hay was able to negotiate international agreement among the world's naval superpowers to not encroach on China's territory and to maintain the openness of China's treaty ports to all nations. In *The Education of Henry Adams* (1918), the eponymously entitled book by President John Quincy Adams's grandson, Henry Adams appreciates his good friend John Hay for understanding that the rising power of the United States depends on an agitating energy that is bound up with cycles of power that exceed the bounds of any individual nation-state. Looking to China as the eventual center of world order, Adams and Hay saw the interests of the United States served best by maintaining China as an open field through which to project the commercial influence of the United States. The historiography of free trade becomes much more complex as Adams and Hay see in China's rise to world prominence a way to sustain a romance of American trade that is not reducible to interests of the governing state.

In the collection's final essay, the focus pivots to suggest the cultural importance of Chinese immigration from Guangdong to the United States. Khun Eng Kuah-Pearce and Yedan Huang consider the cultural impact of the Chinese religious practices based in Tianhou (天后) or Mazu (Matsu, Ma-Tsu, Machor, 妈祖) in the United States. They take a long view that approaches the subject of American–Chinese encounters through the development of Tianhou in the early Northern Song Dynasty (ca.960–1127) and traces its expanding network throughout the world to its eventual impact on the formation of San Francisco. In consideration of this diasporic religious practice and the corresponding life experience of Chinese-Americans, the legacy of trade in China takes on dimensions that are fundamentally transnational in shaping the history and cultural identity of the United States. Kuah-Pearce and Huang suggest that the national terms (American and Chinese), through which this collection frames the theme of free trade, are themselves inadequate to sensing the force of religious practices that permeated the region of Guangdong in the centuries before and after Western presence. Their essay also suggests that the "United States" has been impressed fundamentally by a religious experience whose sense of commerce and kinship is not reducible to the axioms of Adam Smith.

There is an old saying that "you never get a second chance to make a first impression." But, in a sense, each generation of writers seems to receive and to revise its own version of a first impression in the process of selecting, assembling, and interpreting its archive of investigation. At the very least, this collaborative essay collection expresses hope that as scholars and human beings we will continue to cultivate ways of sharing senses of the past that build a better way into the future.

1
Bookkeeping as a Window into Efficiencies of Early Modern Trade

Europeans, Americans and Others in China Compared, 1700–1842

Paul A. Van Dyke

From the Italian Renaissance in the fifteenth century, international businesses have spread across Europe and the world, and with their expansion came a need for more sophisticated methods of organizing data. Businesses with multifaceted operations that were spread over several nations and continents had to be able to access information quickly, so that directors could monitor costs and calculate profits at each level of their operations. By the time Americans entered into global commerce, bookkeeping practices of the large East India companies had developed into massive operations, armies of scribes keeping multiple layers of records that were cross-referenced one to another. This high level of detail enabled directors to track products and services from their sources to end markets. As international trade advanced, it grew safer over time, so that by the late eighteenth century there was less need for the large companies that had formerly controlled commodities and markets. Freer trade was a possibility. As a partial sign of this transformation, when Americans entered the China Trade in 1784, they did not adopt any of the sophisticated accounting practices of the Europeans. And yet Americans, on the whole, were very successful in their trade, while at the same time the competitiveness of the East India companies declined. The bookkeeping practices of China traders provide a window into this world of global commerce and help to explain why the companies eventually lost out to private trade.

Among the most lucrative trade within the English East India Company (EIC) was that with China. Top captains and supercargoes were usually eager to participate in the China Trade. The Dutch East India Company's (VOC) trade with China was the most sophisticated of any in Asia. A separate committee in The Hague was assigned specifically to its management. The Danish Asiatic Company (DAC) apportioned part of the trade of each ship that went to China to the Danish crown, which is a reflection of its importance at the highest levels in the country. The Swedish East India Company (SOIC), General Ostend India Company (GIC), and French East India Company (CFI) assigned their top people to manage their trade with China, which is reflected in the sophistication of their account books. The records these companies produced are among the most detailed examples we have of the high level of sophistication that was attained by this time in international accounting practices. The China Trade was also highly prized by many Americans and other private traders from India and elsewhere. Portuguese and Spanish traders were, of course, also regularly involved in that commerce. Because all trade with China in the late eighteenth and early nineteenth centuries took place at Canton (or its subsidiary, Macao), the records produced in that port provide one of the best opportunities for a comparative analysis of early modern bookkeeping practices worldwide.

European bookkeeping practices had already reached a high level of sophistication by 1784, when Americans entered into trade with China. By this time, East India companies had evolved into the most sophisticated global enterprises of their time. Each one developed a systematic means of keeping track of assets and liabilities so that costs and profits could be easily analyzed. Whereas the ways in which profits were calculated differed significantly from modern accounting practices, there is no doubt that the companies' extensive bookkeeping provided a high level of transparency so that managers could make informed decisions. But if those records were really necessary for the companies to survive, then we must ask why private traders managed to outperform the companies without them.

I will briefly review the bookkeeping practices of the companies and point out some of the types of records they kept. Then I will point out some basic structural differences between companies and private traders, which will help to explain why certain records were created. With this information I can show more clearly why private traders in China, such as those from the United States, were able to flourish without comparably elaborate systems of record keeping.

The volume of goods and services that each of the European companies handled varied considerably in style and amount, which meant that each company developed a different method of accounting. All the East India companies kept multiple layers of records using double-entry accounting methods, whereby debits were balanced against credits. Imports that they brought to China (including silver coin) were balanced against exports they purchased, so that the overall profitability of each ship or fleet of ships could be assessed. Entries in the companies' books were cross-referenced to corresponding pages in other sets of books so that commodities could be traced each step of the way from the suppliers in China to the consumers in Europe. Supercargoes in China assembled annual reports and sent them to directors in their homelands. Directors, in turn, reported the companies' performances to stockholders.

Because the trade with China was prized by many foreigners as one of the most lucrative trades in the eighteenth and early nineteenth centuries, the record keeping and accounting of that commerce tended to be among the best available. And because Canton was one of the most cosmopolitan ports in the world at this time, Europeans, Asians, and Americans going there regularly to trade, it provides one of the best environments for a comparative analysis of early modern bookkeeping practices worldwide.

The China Trade records can be divided into four basic groups.[1]

1. *Personnel Records.* These records were produced before the start of the voyage and issued to the officers. They included oaths by which top employees swore allegiance to the companies; instructions to captains, supercargoes, and other officers detailing their responsibilities and duties during the voyage and their stay in China; and muster roles and wage books that listed the rank, salaries, and amount of private trade allowed to each crew member of each ship as well as to the factory personnel who remained in China (Figures 1.1 and 1.2).
2. *Ship Records.* These documents were kept aboard the ships, and include maps and charts laying out the course to be traveled; navigational journals of the voyage making hourly entries of wind, current, latitude, longitude (after 1765), depth of water, composition of seabed, shoals, storms, and sometimes drawings of land formations, islands, and coasts that had been encountered; receipts and expense books of the costs incurred during the voyage, such as piloting fees, equipage, and provisions purchased, repairs, etc.; bills of lading; stowage papers,

charts, and graphs detailing the loading and unloading of cargos and the placement of merchandise in the hulls of the ships; ship journals (or officers' logbooks) of all events that took place during the voyage, including ships and people encountered, problems with the crew such as illnesses and disciplinary violations requiring action, the receiving and departing of guests and officers aboard ships, craftsmen hired to make repairs, watering and provisional stops, repairs to the ship and equipage, and any other problems that concerned the ship or interested the writers (Figure 1.3).

3. *Trade Records.* These records were produced in China and include daily diaries of everything that transpired during their stay there; trade journals detailing every financial transaction; trade ledgers showing the purchases of each commodity and balancing accounts of each Chinese merchant; resolutions or consultations of all decisions made in the trade and reasons for the same; trade and loan contracts with merchants in Asia; the maintenance of the residences (called "factories") in China including factory expenses such as rent, repairs, service fees, etc.; manifests of each ship's cargo; balance sheets of each ship and of overall trade in general including the performance of each commodity as well as annual reports of the overall trade each year; and correspondence copybooks of every letter or document sent and received by the officers in China (Figures 1.4, 1.5, 1.6, 1.7 and 1.8).
4. *Central Management Records.* These records were produced and/or maintained for the benefit of company directors in Europe, and include copybooks of all correspondence and documents sent to, and received from, China; copybooks of all officers' instructions of their duties as well as how to maintain the companies' households in China, the high and low prices that residents were expected to pay and receive for commodities, Chinese merchants who were preferred in Canton, and instructions on how to interact with Chinese authorities; records detailing the purchases and sales of all company merchandise from China and profits realized from each commodity; annual reports of operations worldwide, with a breakdown of each colony and country; and topical indexes of everything connected to the trade with China (Figure 1.9).

East India companies generated and maintained records from all four groups, but they differed somewhat in how and what they recorded. Some of these documents were kept in duplicate or triplicate, a process that required many hours each week to copy them.[2] And while there were logical and practical reasons for generating all of the data described above, having that information did not necessarily mean greater efficiency. In fact, by the late eighteenth century, the inconvenience and great expense of keeping such massive volumes of documents was undoubtedly one of the factors that contributed to the companies' loss of competiveness to private traders.[3]

Table 1 shows some of the structural commonalities and differences between companies and private traders.

Table 1

Structural Commonalities and Differences of China Traders' Operations

	Private Traders			**Company Traders**					
Structural Characteristics	PT	USA	CJ	CFI	EIC	GIC	VOC	DAC	SOIC
1. Ships owned by company with monopoly rights	S			✓	Few	✓	✓	✓	✓
2. Ships leased from others					✓				
3. Ships have royal/crown charter/commission	✓*			✓	✓	✓	✓	✓	✓
4. Ships' officers allowed private trade	✓	✓	✓	✓	✓	✓	✓	✓	✓
5. Ships' crews paid monthly wages	✓	S	?	✓	✓	✓	✓	✓	✓
6. Voyages funded by outside investors	S	S	S	✓	✓	✓	✓	✓	✓
7. Ships could rent space on consignment	✓	✓	✓		SL		SL	SL	SL
8. Ships accepted passengers for a fee	✓	✓	✓		✓		SL	✓	?
9. Ships' crew received commission rather than wage	S	S	✓						
10. Ships were owned by ships' officers	S	S	S						

(continued on page 22)

Table 1 *(continued)*

Key	Name	Approx. years involved in direct trade with Canton
*	Some Portuguese and Spanish ships were royally commissioned and could represent, speak for, and fight for their nations. But by the eighteenth century, those crown ships did not usually include Macao- or Manila-based vessels, which simply defended themselves when attacked, like other private traders in Asia.	
✓	Yes	
S	Some ships	
SL	Sometimes, but limited and/or varied over time	
?	unknown	
PT	Private traders (non-American)	1517–(beginning year varies for each group. These private traders include: Portuguese, Spanish, Jews, Dutch, Danish, Swedish, Flemish, Italians, English, French, Parsees, Armenians, Muslims, and others)
CFI	French East India Company	1699–1807
EIC	English East India Company	1700–1833
GIC	Ostend General India Company	1715–33
VOC	Dutch East India Company	1729–94
DAC	Danish Asiatic Company	1731–1806, 1820–33
SOIC	Swedish East India Company	1732–1807
USA	American China Traders	1784–
CJ	Canton Junks (owned privately)	By the 1680s, there were several junks operating in Canton, and from about the 1740s to 1840s there were around 30 that were based there and sailed to Southeast Asia each year.

The shaded parts in Table 1 show areas where significant differences existed between companies and private traders. One of the differences was that companies either owned or leased their ships, whereas private vessels (including Chinese junks) were often partially owned by their officers (rows 1, 2, and 10). Because private traders were often owner-operators and therefore directly involved with the buying and selling of merchandise, there was no need to keep many of the records mentioned above. In contrast, because absentee directors in Europe managed the China Trade of the East India companies, these directors depended heavily on records for their understanding.

Row 3 in Table 1 shows that company ships usually doubled as "crown" ships (warships) if challenged at sea, which meant their crews had to be militarily equipped, trained, and prepared for any hostile encounters. In order to ensure that ships were properly staffed, extensive muster roles were kept listing everyone with the position and pay scale (Figure 1.1).

When East India companies' ships engaged in battle it was on behalf of their nations or kingdoms, so they sailed not simply as merchant vessels. This practice included Portuguese and Spanish ships commissioned from Europe (as pointed out in the note * in Table 1). This military factor is one of the reasons why companies' tons-per-man ratios tended to be less efficient than those private vessels. A company ship of 500 tons, for example, might be equipped with 20 cannons and would therefore need gunners and other sailors trained in their use, so that the crew would amount to around 100 or more men. In comparison, a private ship of equal size would normally have less than half the armaments (many private ships had only four or five cannons), and a crew of maybe seventy-five men.

The exception to this rule might be the Chinese junks, which were among the least efficient vessels operating in Asia, in labor, but were also the least equipped with armaments. The junks might only have a couple of cannons aboard. And as far as paperwork was concerned, few records with any detail have survived from the junks, making a comparison of their bookkeeping practices impossible. If we assume that the junks did not need accounting procedures, we can infer that they were unsurpassed in minimizing paperwork. But we do know that junks were losing trade to foreign ships when private traders (like the Americans) were entering the trade in the late eighteenth and early nineteenth centuries; so, having no paperwork (if that was indeed the case with the junks) was not necessarily a significant benefit in regard to competitiveness.[4]

Private traders needed to ensure that they had qualified men in their crews and a sufficient number to sail safely; and ship captains, who were often part-owners of the ships and/or cargos, could ensure that happened on the spot. Because they knew everyone on board, they had less, or even no, need for long lists of officers' names, skills, and ranks. Private traders had to keep track of wages, so we find lists of sailors included in many American logbooks, but they might just show a name and wage, no rank or skill mentioned. The American archives contain nothing like the sophisticated personnel account books of the East India companies. The lists of crews on American ships might also have been generated on the spot, when sailors were paid. They were not necessarily part of any bookkeeping protocols such as those that companies' officers were required to keep. In these cases, the downward shift of ownership, whereby owners were also operators, helped to reduce paperwork. But the smaller crews of private ships (some of which consisted of no more than a dozen men), left private trading ships vulnerable to pirate attacks. Thus, the greater risks of small vessels had to be weighed against the increased benefits from streamlined bookkeeping.[5]

All the companies issued instructions to their top officers before a voyage commenced (Figure 1.2), and owners of private ships did the same (if they were not themselves aboard). On some American ships, however, the owner and captain and supercargo were one and the same, so no instructions were needed.

The companies and private traders both kept detailed lists of equipage aboard their ships but did not necessarily record all of the expenses (Figure 1.3).

For tracking the costs incurred aboard ships, companies often kept expense books specifically for that purpose. Private traders might keep the receipts from all transactions but were likely to just throw them in a box without any organization and never to touch them again. For factory expenses in Canton (which both company and private traders incurred), most companies kept detailed records of everything purchased during the three or four months in Canton. The EIC operated a little differently from the others, in that it kept track of factory expenditures but only recorded overall expenses annually. The minute details regarding costs, which other companies kept, was not recorded in the EIC books. The American archives contain very little of this type of detail. Even the American consuls in Canton did not keep track of their daily maintenance costs while in China.[6] There was no need for Americans to have this information because most of those daily expenditures were at their own private expense.

Employees of the companies usually kept daily diaries of their trade and activities in Canton (Figure 1.4), whereas private traders usually did not.

The companies' documents detailed all of the important activities and happenings in Canton and Macao and are today among the best historical records available for the study of the eighteenth century. In addition to including major events and transactions, they usually recorded the comings and goings of all vessels, persons, and merchants, and any problems that arose in either China or adjacent regions that affected commerce. Some companies such as the VOC, EIC, and DAC kept these diaries in duplicate or triplicate and consist of anywhere from 50 to 300 pages or more of written text for each year. Writing, copying, and filing them was no small undertaking. Diaries were one of the primary sources of information for company directors. Private traders did not need these records because they did not have administrative bodies of directors overseeing their activities.[7]

Keeping track of financial exchanges was important for both companies and private individuals, so we do find trade journals (sometimes combined with diaries) in all of their archives (Figure 1.5).

Trade journals differ from diaries in that they only record financial transactions. Some of the Americans kept documents like this, but here again, even the best of them cannot compare with the sophistication of the companies' records in which everything is cross-referenced to other account books and documents.

Trade journals went hand in hand with trade ledgers. The latter separated the financial transactions into individual components. For example, all of the Bohea tea or raw silk that was purchased in a single year would be listed in the ledgers under a heading of the same. Some companies, such as the DAC and VOC, kept accounts of each individual Chinese merchant as well, showing every product that they had purchased from, and sold to, them each year (Figure 1.6).

The pages in the journals, ledgers, and daily diaries were numbered so they could be cross-referenced. Whereas ledgers were standard for most companies, few of the American traders kept such detail. Instead, Americans would simply throw their receipts from China into a folder or box and leave it at that. There was no need to spend many hours re-entering the figures into ledgers.[8]

American officers kept logbooks, but those documents are much different from the European companies' trade journals. The American logbook is more an amalgam of a European navigational journal and a ship's journal. Companies kept navigational journals that recorded all the sailing details such as latitude, longitude, current, wind speed, water depth, weather, sailing speed, storms, etc. Companies' ship journals, in contrast, recorded the problems encountered during the voyage, the ports that were visited, the ships with which they communicated en route, the repairs that were needed, the cannon salutes that were given to officers and ports of call, the unloading and loading of cargo, and any other information that might pertain to the ship and/or be of interest to the writers. These European ship and navigational journals contain very little, if any, data about trade. Americans combined all of this information into one logbook per voyage. Some American logbooks include trade transactions and other observations. On the whole, however, the details contained in American logbooks do not come close to matching the details contained in European trade journals, ledgers, and diaries. It was obviously more efficient to omit those records if they were not needed. But for the historian, this streamlining of bookkeeping by American traders means that an enormous amount of important historical data was omitted.[9]

Price lists and general reports of the trade were important for both private and company men, but the latter's records were much more sophisticated (Figure 1.7).

The companies required these documents to be created each year, whereas the collection of information by private traders happened in an ad hoc fashion. Private traders might give complete coverage of prices and trade in a given year but then not give that information in other years. In contrast, companies created price lists and trade reports annually without fail, and they entered their data in a very consistent manner from one year to the next. This detail was necessary for companies' directors to better manage the trade.

Consider, for example, Figure 1.8, which is a detailed stowage chart from 1760 for the VOC ship *Oosterbeek* in China.

The document shows how the ship was to be loaded, with specific-size chests in each layer, and instructions of what the chests were to contain. All the companies had strict regulations concerning the loading of their ships so they could ensure cargos were properly stowed and space maximized. Private traders did not need such sophisticated accounting of cargo details. Owner-operators themselves ensured that payloads were maximized, because it was in their personal interests to do so. Thus, they had no need for such details.

Letter copybooks and topical indexes of the trade (Figure 1.9) were very important to the companies. These types of documents, however, required much time and labor creating them, so most private traders did not bother with them.

The maintenance of these records was important for directors in Europe but expensive to keep, because someone had to be employed full-time just to create them. Price Currents of commodities throughout Asia were useful to everyone, but creating those lists also required much time and labor. Private traders might note the different prices that they encountered in each port, but they would not usually take the time to assemble lists such as shown in Figure 1.7. However, after printed Price Currents became more widespread in Asian ports during the early nineteenth century, Americans purchased and used them for reference.[10]

Table 1 shows other differences between company and private traders. Private crews sometimes received a commission on the profits earned from voyages or rented space to carry their own goods (row 7). And private ships (including junks) usually accepted passengers or freight, if they had room (rows 7 and 8). The one freedom that all ships had in common was that officers were allowed to conduct some private trade (row 4), but the amount and limitations placed on that trade by owners of the companies and ships varied widely between groups. One significant difference between company and private ships was that companies allowed officers to control an allotment of space aboard the ships they were in charge of. This was allowed because companies' officers did not own any of the companies' cargo. Officers aboard private ships, in contrast, were often part-owners of the ship's cargo and might also have space for their own private trade. In this way, the risks of the voyage, and whether or not a profit was made, was shifted downward to the owner-operators.

Companies allowed officers to engage in some private trade, but it was usually closely monitored and tightly restricted to very specific volumes (such as half a chest or one or two chests, according to the rank of the officers). And companies' officers were often restricted to trade in certain items that the companies did not handle. In order to ensure all of this was carried out correctly and according to company policies, many more records were needed to document what every officer brought aboard each ship. This involved close inspections of every chest—documenting their contents, sizes, and weights—so that directors could see all was done according to policies. The goods had to be inspected again when they were unloaded in Europe, which doubled the labor involved and paperwork generated. Private traders had no need for these documents.

All this company activity was carried out in order to ensure that employees conformed to company regulations. But the details were also used to ensure that Chinese merchants in Canton were held responsible. If improperly packed chests arrived in Europe with faulty or insufficient tea, then the paperwork provided a way to determine whether the chests had been received that way in China or had been tampered with during the voyage. In case of the former situation, the chest numbers would be tracked through the records to the respective Chinese merchants whom the company would then hold responsible.

The EIC managed to minimize the need for such minute detail by simply telling the Canton merchants that new contracts would not be issued to them unless they compensated the company for previous losses. This method proved very effective, and Chinese merchants usually honored the English officers' claims even though they were often not provided with proof of the asserted losses.[11] Other companies could have done the same but tended to rely more on their extensive and detailed paper trails to prove beyond a shadow of a doubt that the goods had been received in Canton in poor condition. This is an example of how practicality sometimes yielded to the bureaucracy of the companies, because the carrying out of the policy seems to have proved more important than the policy's utility.

Private traders usually did not have the leverage over Chinese merchants that large companies enjoyed. It is unlikely that extensive documentation would have changed this situation, because Canton merchants could simply tell smaller private traders to go somewhere else with their business. But Canton merchants would not usually want to risk losing the trade of large companies for the sake of benefits gained from a few mispacked chests.

Some company ships allowed passengers aboard, but they were often closely scrutinized. Companies generally permitted passengers who were citizens of their respective nations and rejected anyone who was from another company or nation. This was done to protect trade secrets from leaking out to the competition. Some companies in China, such as the VOC, generally refused all passengers but made exceptions in certain years. Private traders, in contrast, simply decided on the spot whether or not they wanted to admit persons aboard. By so doing, they were able to maximize the profits of the voyage, without all of the worries of the companies.

In the sixteenth and seventeenth centuries, the Catholic empires of Portugal (including Macao-based Portuguese subjects), and Spain (including Manila-based Spanish subjects), often forbade Protestant passengers or Protestant-owned cargos from their ships. But by the eighteenth century, many of those restrictions had disappeared, and the motive to maximize profits dictated who and what would be accepted aboard those vessels. By the eighteenth century, Chinese junks also generally accepted anyone aboard, and consigned space to any paying costumers.[12] Americans operated in the same manner, allowing the economic opportunities of the voyage to dictate who and what was to be taken aboard. This open attitude towards passengers and freight was largely the result of international trade becoming much safer than it had been in previous decades.

If we compare the records kept from one company voyage and one American voyage to China, the disparities between them become more obvious. A company voyage to China would likely produce a muster role with details of every officer and his wages, many pages of instructions to officers, dozens of resolutions and contracts, cargo manifests, stowage charts and papers, daily diaries of the four or five months spent in China, factory expense books, trade journals, a trade ledger, a ship journal, a ship expense book, navigational journals, trade reports, balance sheets, and numerous correspondences. An American voyage to China, in comparison (regardless of the size of the ship), would likely produce only a logbook, cargo manifests, a few correspondences, and a box full of receipts (which might include a contract or two).

In summary, the structural differences between companies and private traders resulted in the latter generating much less paperwork than the former. Below is a list of the records that are prevalent in company archives but rarely found in American archives.

1. factory and ship expense books (but there might be receipts for the same in American archives)
2. trade ledgers[13]
3. books balancing accounts of individual voyages as well as the China fleet (but there are a few exceptions)
4. daily diaries/consultations (with the exception of logbooks, some of which contain entries similar to those in company diaries)
5. annual reports for directors and stockholders
6. stowage graphs and charts
7. resolutions (documents that explain the rationale used by supercargoes in negotiating the trade each year, which private traders, on the whole, did not need)
8. indexes of all trade conducted with China

Most Americans did not need these types of records, but they were at the operational core of large companies. Directors needed this data to analyze the prospects of each year's trading opportunities and to produce long-term forecasts so stockholders could see that their investments were being used wisely. Moreover, without those records, directors could not monitor costs, protect against embezzlements by employees, establish market trends over time, or manage other issues. Even though there were differences in the way companies kept their records, they tended to include much of the same type of data for the benefit of their directors. The EIC's early eighteenth-century China diaries and consultations (the G/12 series), for example, were equivalent to information contained in the resolutions of other companies. In the latter half of the eighteenth century, the EIC separated the diaries and consultations into two documents. The EIC retained the navigational journals (the L/MAR series) but did not collect ship journals or ship expense books of any ship it did not own. Those latter documents belonged to the captains and ship owners and are therefore not in the EIC archive today.[14]

This comparison of company traders and private traders suggests that, if the companies could have privatized certain parts of their operations, they might have been able to reduce their operating costs to become more competitive. And if companies had adopted smaller and faster vessels, with reduced military capacity, they could have brought their tons-per-man ratios more in line with those of private traders' ships. This latter move, however, went contrary to the companies' monopolies and responsibilities for protecting colonies and national interests. Because of these concerns, privatization was often not considered a viable option.

Privatization also ran contrary to the era's concepts of trade, whereby monopolistic companies' and armed ships protected profits and controlled markets to their benefit. Considering that Europeans were involved in wars throughout the eighteenth and early nineteenth centuries, there were good reasons for company ships to be heavily armed. Moreover, privatization would result in profits being shared with owner-operators and ran contrary to stockholders' ideas of receiving dividends and just returns for their investments.

Other factors that favored company trade were the ways that China regulated commerce in Canton. Large ships paid much lower port fees than small ships did, which is one reason why many private traders smuggled opium and other commodities along the south China coast.[15] If parts of the EIC trade had been privatized, it would have likely led to smaller ships being sent to China, and probably more smuggling. Small ships that did not smuggle had to pay high port fees, which counteracted benefits that might be gained by greater efficiencies in operating them.

European colonies in Asia were also maintained and supported by the companies that supplied them with protection, personnel, equipage, provisions, and much more. If parts of the trade were opened to individuals, it would have likely led to a lesser degree of maintenance by the corporation of the outposts in the trading network. To some extent then, private traders depended on European ports in Asia to provide protection and security for their trade. If those company posts weakened or collapsed, it might also lead to the collapse of all private enterprises. One can infer that the trend toward privatization depended on the infrastructure that corporations maintained in networking trade routes that stretch across the globe.

There are many other factors that have not been addressed here, but the primary point is that European ships continued to rely on their heavily armed crews for political ends and maintained vast networks of scribes and bookkeepers to keep massive records so that everyone could be held accountable. All of this activity was enormously expensive, which canceled the advantages of sending larger ships through the Canton Trade System. Private traders capitalized on the companies' inefficiencies by carrying out a more economical trade, without all the costs, protections, and restrictions. These advantages are clearly evident when we look at American China traders' bookkeeping practices, which were very simple operations, requiring minimal costs.

It is worth emphasizing that the American tendency to rely on owner-operators in their China Trade was not commonly practiced by Europeans at the time. Although Adam Smith argued in *The Wealth of Nations* (1776) that the maintenance of monopolies was a competitive disadvantage, not everyone agreed with his ideas. Moreover, theorizing the inefficiency of corporate models was quite a different matter from putting new practices into place. Privatization would have required both the restructuring of enormous commercial and political operations that were spread around the globe and the pulling apart of centuries-old bureaucracies that were the lifeblood to hundreds of elite families.

The companies helped create a safer trading environment in Asia. By the late eighteenth century, the risks of international commerce had been managed by an expensive apparatus that required a constant flow of information from posts throughout Asia. In the end, however, the fruits of the companies' efforts were enjoyed not by the companies' stockholders and directors but rather by Americans and other individual operators, who managed to carry on very extensive commerce with China with minimal paperwork and armaments.

2
A Question of Character

The Romance of Early Sino-American Commerce in The Journals of Major Samuel Shaw, the First American Consul at Canton *(1847)*

Kendall Johnson

In the decades after the Revolutionary War, American ventures into the China Trade presented an opportunity for American authors to tell a story of their new nation, winning international respect in the networks of global trade after having thrown off the colonial shackles of Britain's mercantilist restrictions. Consider the figure of Samuel Shaw (1754–94), a Revolutionary War veteran who served in the Continental Army as the aide-de-camp to the high-ranking General Henry Knox. This frontispiece to his posthumously edited and published *The Journals of Major Samuel Shaw, the First American Consul at Canton: With a Life of the Author* (1847) greets the reader with his image and signature (Figure 2.1).

After the war, in 1784, the twenty-nine year old Shaw helped to organize the commercial voyage of the *Empress of China*, regarded as the first American ship to arrive in Canton. Signing on as the supercargo under the command of Captain John Green, he embarked for China from New York on February 22, 1784, crossed the Atlantic Ocean, rounded the tip of Africa at the Cape of Good Hope, continued across the Indian Ocean and anchored off Macao on August 28, after 128 days at sea.[1] The ship returned to New York's East River harbor in May 1785, with much fanfare that promoted the sale of its payload; the estimated profits of twenty-five percent were vexed by acrimonious litigation centering on the embezzlement of silver specie by one of the voyage's financiers, Daniel Parker.[2] A year later, in 1786, the pre-Constitutional United States Congress, operating under the clumsy Articles of Confederation, designated Shaw as the first American consul in Canton; over the next eight years he made three more voyages there.

What drew the British, Spanish, Dutch, Swedish, Danish, French, and other European countries to Canton was what Shaw calls the "extraordinary demand for tea"—a demand so strong that it had "obliged [England] to export [...] large quantities of bullion."[3] Upon arriving in Canton in 1784, the *Empress of China* had as much silver as the trading partners in New York and Philadelphia could muster, but this was not very much given the ambitious scope of their enterprise. In forecasting the future of American commerce, Shaw promotes the medicinal root of ginseng as the new nation's most precious indigenous commodity. Whereas Shaw never published his journals or letters in his lifetime, he did submit after his first voyage an encouraging report on the China Trade to John Jay, the secretary of the United States for Foreign Affairs; after his second voyage a brief account to President John Adams on Dutch interference with US trade; and several optimistic articles on China for the Philadelphia-based periodical, the *American Museum*. One of these articles, "Remarks on the Commerce of America with China" (1790), advertised the profitability of trading ginseng in China.[4] He did not shy away from hyperboles, as when he boasts in his journal during his second voyage that the commercial "advantages which [*sic*] America derives from her ginseng" would make it "as beneficial to her citizens as her mines of silver and gold have been to the rest of mankind."[5]

If ginseng had actually proven to lend the Midas touch, this would be a very different story. However, its market fluctuated dramatically, even when it was readily available. The first shipment entailed a massive collection campaign that netted over twenty-six imperial tons (twelve metric tons), but the root was soon overharvested. Pelts, furs, illegal Turkish opium, and the carrying of cargo became the most lucrative commodities and services for American companies and firms in the China Trade over the next few decades. Even if it had been more plentiful, ginseng might not have translated into American capital in Canton. More likely, it would have been absorbed into networks of transaction at ports in the Caribbean or greater Atlantic, as was the case with two contemporaneous voyages by the *Harriet* and *Grand Turk* that did not get beyond Cape Town.[6] The logistics of ginseng's commercial viability aside, the following essay is more concerned with Shaw's use of it to establish the creditability of personal and national American character in Canton and with the ways that Shaw's subsequent biographical editor, Josiah Quincy III, represented Shaw's commercial endeavor as an inspiring national romance for a reading audience in the late 1840s.

Fifty-seven years after Shaw's death, Quincy redeemed for purposes of national instruction Shaw's China voyage in *The Journals of Major Samuel Shaw, the First American Consul at Canton: With a Life of the Author* (1847). Quincy was well known as a politician, serving as a representative to Congress for Massachusetts and the second mayor of Boston before he became the sixteenth president of Harvard University from 1829 to 1845, during which time he authored the *History of Harvard* (1836). He begins Shaw's *Journals* with a short biographical memoir derived from Shaw's wartime letters to his younger brother, his father, and his friend the Reverend John Eliot. He presents Shaw as a nationally representative man, concluding the first major section of the book, entitled "Memoir," with the claim that: "It was [Shaw's] fortune and happiness during his residence in that city [of Canton], by his official influence, to give to its inhabitants the first impression of the character and resources of a new nation, of even whose existence the Chinese had previously no knowledge."[7] The very title of the book weds the Revolutionary War service of "Major Shaw" to Shaw's subsequent post as the "First American Consul at Canton." In the model of other popular early national biographies, such as those written by Jared Sparks (who succeeded Quincy as Harvard's president), Shaw's memoir reassures the reader that the nation would endure any setbacks and uncertainties, eventually rising to match Shaw's achievements in the China Trade. The influential Boston-based literary journal *The North American Review* emphasized the book's instructive connotation in its assessment: "The memoir of Mr. Shaw is written with excellent taste and judgment. It illustrates one of the most pleasing characters that adorned the times of our great national struggle."[8] The review continues by appreciating Shaw's letters for "not only display[ing] the most amiable qualities, but giv[ing] very interesting glimpses of the scenes and characters of the Revolution."

With historical hindsight, we might read Shaw's memoir very differently and focus on his anxiety about the consistency and constitution of national character in a long "national struggle" that neither ended with the Revolutionary War nor would be contained by the retrospective "life" narrative that Quincy rendered as the country moved toward Civil War.[9] A close reading indicates that Shaw remained deeply distrustful of the terms of national economic speculation and its instruments of exchange. Throughout his journal Shaw assesses the new nation's creditworthiness with dramatic ambivalence, vacillating between exuberant optimism over ginseng's profitability and virtual despondency over the absence of a fiduciary foundation.

For example, he uses the word *character* to register the fiscal standards by which the United States would be evaluated and judged as distinct among the peoples of the world; at the end of the Revolutionary War he declares in a letter to his friend the Reverend John Eliot that, with the victory against England, "America is now become an empire, and the eyes of the world are fastened upon her.[...] We have a character to establish among the great powers of the earth, who will for the most part form their opinion of us from the manner in which we set out."[10] With the word "empire," Shaw predicates the respectability of American character less on a democratic style of governance and more on the young nation's military success of which the "great powers of the earth" ought to take notice. But the question remained: How to transform the revolution's military achievement into international commercial viability?

In the midst of the world's current monetary crises and the ongoing realignment of global capital networks, it seems a good time to reconsider Shaw's representation of his American character and his perception of China. In doing this through Quincy's edition of Shaw's life, we also have the opportunity to see how a subsequent generation of Americans in the 1840s imagined a commercial relationship with China after Britain's victory in the Opium War. This essay continues by relating Shaw's commercial aspirations in China to his anxious reflections on American character. The China Trade will highlight the international context of Shaw's struggle to see in American character a consistency between individual and national identity. On a complementary but more abstract level, we can infer from Shaw's example of an American personal economy the international terms of trust that were necessary in correlating a person's outward appearance to his creditworthiness.

In the end, it seems that Shaw sustained his optimism about a national future neither through an unqualified belief in republican democracy nor through a jeremiad of redemptive frugality. Nor does he promote the nation by embracing the liberal tenants of market competition advocated by Adam Smith in that author's realignments of the virtue and self-interest.[11] Rather, Shaw took great pride in helping to establish the Society of Cincinnati, a fraternity of former officers of the Revolutionary War in whose mutual affections he felt a guarantee of national integrity. For Shaw, a deep distrust of the signifying practices of domestic and international speculation seems to underlie his advocacy of the Society in which he placed a faith that emboldened his China enterprise. However reasonable it is for Shaw to have held deep affection for his fellow Revolutionary War officers, the Society of Cincinnati, as we will see, was not a democratic organization but rather an oligarchy of military officers collaborating in pursuit of commercial opportunity and planning to perpetuate its membership through the logic of bloodline. From a political perspective, Shaw does not seem to offer us much hope that republic forms of representative democracy will best position the United States in a global market. To find that story, we would need to read elsewhere.

China and the Prospect of an American Market

It is difficult to think of a better premise on which to script the introduction of the newly formed republic of the United States to the ancient empire of China. In 1784, the *Empress of China* set out on the high seas under the flag of a nation whose self-declared existence merely a decade before had precipitated a hard-fought war against the naval superpower of Great Britain—a war that had ended with a victory sealed just a year before in the Peace of Paris of 1783. In the aftermath, the United States Navy was in shambles and could no longer rely on the British flag to protect it against privateers. As Quincy's version of the story goes, by voyaging to China, Shaw saw himself proving the virtue of his country's political sovereignty in the practice of global commerce. Considered politically, Shaw's voyage to Canton was indeed uncharted territory for the fledgling United States. England's Navigation Acts of the 1650s and 1660s had bolstered British manufacturing by requiring the passage of all foreign goods and raw materials through England, and the "commercial monopoly in Far Eastern trade, granted by the Crown to the British East India Company," further precluded direct trade between China and the colonies.[12] In 1784, when Shaw showed up in Canton, the question would not be *where* the American flag would fly but *if* it would at all.

In part to prevent the *Empress of China* from being mistaken for British, the Continental Congress provided Captain Green with a dramatic announcement, hoping to communicate across a global spectrum of languages and styles of governance. It reads:

> Most Serene, Serene, most puissant, puissant, high, illustrious, noble, honorable, venerable, wise and prudent Emperors, Kings Republicks [*sic*], Princes, Dukes, Earls, Barons, Lords, Burgomaster, Coucillors [*sic*], as also Judges, Officers, Justiciares [*sic*] of Regents of all good Cities and places whether ecclesiastical or secular who shall see these patents or

> hear them read, We the United States of America in Congress Assembled make known that John Green Captain of the Ship call'd [*sic*] the Empress of China is a Citizen of the United States of America and that the Ship which he commands belongs to the Citizens of the said United States and as we wish to see the said John Green prosper in his lawful affairs, our prayer is to all the beforementioned [*sic*], and to each of them separately, where the said John Green shall arrive with his Vessel of Cargo, that they may please to receive him with goodness and to treat him in a becoming manner, permitting him upon the usual tolls of expences [*sic*] in passing and repassing, to pass, navigate and frequent the ports, passes and territories to the end to transact his business where and in what manner he shall judge proper: whereof we shall be willingly indebted. In Testimony whereof we have caused the Seal of the United States to be hereunto affixed—Witness His Excellency Thomas Mifflin President this thirtieth day of January in the year of our Lord one thousand seven hundred eighty four in the eighth year of the Sovereignty and Independence of the United States of America.[13]

One imagines first encountering an American ship in Batavia, Java, or Macao, having this handed to you, and feeling that those who were on board were surely a curiosity. But were they to be treated on par with the naval powers of Europe and their associated East India trading companies? To be fair as we assess the document's earnest hyperboles, there was little precedent for announcing oneself as a new people. Certainly there had been revolutions, and a century prior to the American revolt the English had even executed their king. However, Captain Green and his supercargo Shaw not only evinced the successful severance of the United States from its mother country but also expressed a new logic of political organization. Accordingly, rather than signing the document, President Thomas Mifflin *witnesses* the affixing of the national seal; furthermore, both the ship and the rules of governance "belong to the Citizens." On the open sea and in the pursuit of trade in Canton, the pronoun "We" boldly asserts a national solidarity that anticipates the phrase "We the people" of the Constitution of the United States, ratified in 1789 to replace the Articles of Confederation and its guarantee of sovereignty to each individual state.

And yet, despite the eventual antagonism of state and federal authority, the language and logic of business in this decree seems to make the recognition of a singular "United States" a matter of common sense. Notice that in the congressional decree, Captain Green's "lawful affairs of business" (to paraphrase) embolden his address to a great variety of political economies;

whatever differences there are between "Emperors, Kings Republicks [*sic*], Princes, Dukes, Earls, Barons, Lords, Burgomaster, Coucillors [*sic*], as also Judges, Officers, Justiciares [*sic*] of Regents of all good Cities and places whether ecclesiastical or secular," these differences are bridgeable in the young nation's pursuit of business. Thus in this diplomatic rhetoric, the voyage's commercial activity promises to alleviate anxiety about national distinctiveness and divisiveness as reaching out to potential trading partners and attempting to establish positions in international markets consolidates a *United* States.

In a similar spirit, when Shaw first arrived in Canton, he presented the Chinese with a map of the United States. He then attempted to turn their curiosity about the new nation into an appreciation of its potential power to consume Chinese goods. In his journal Shaw wrote that the Chinese "style us the *New People*, and when, by the map, we conveyed to them an idea of the extent of our country, with its present and increasing population, they were not a little pleased at the prospect of so considerable a market for the productions of their own empire."[14] Beyond the pragmatic goal of transacting the payload aboard the *Empress of China*, Shaw's gesture implies many subtle but politically significant assumptions about the national development of the United States and its relationship to China in the late eighteenth-century global economy.

Shaw's map of the new American prospect reflects his practical and enabling fantasy that "a market" is universally understood. With twentieth century historical hindsight, it is easy to take him at his word and assume that the United States offered an ideal site for Chinese merchants to sell their wares. However, in reporting that the Chinese traders were "pleased at the prospect" represented by a map of the US market, Shaw makes no distinction between the Canton merchants, governing authorities of the Qing Empire, and the people of Guangdong. It may be true that the Canton traders would have relished the opportunity to sell their goods in North America or to trade for the ginseng offered by the *Empress of China*. However, the very existence of Canton was predicated on the Qing emperor's resistance to unregulated access to the Chinese market or to allowing Chinese merchants to sell tea outside of Canton [see introduction of this collection]. Rather than a universally understood sign, "the market" would prove over subsequent decades to be a zone of creative and competitive translation bearing out struggles for authority between various interests and groups in China, the United States, throughout Europe, and the rest of the world.

Furthermore, a presumption of a universal market does not help us to appreciate the precarious nature of the early United States, which was in the process of putting and holding itself together at the expense of Native peoples on whose lands the American market would putatively develop. For the United States to offer China a market "prospect" in 1784, the United States would need to figure out how to manage many so-called tribes, which, in the century to follow, various state and federal governments would uproot with formal programs of Indian Removal and informal policies of frontier usurpation.[15] Nevertheless, Shaw's act of showing a map to the traders in Canton suggests that he and the investors of the *Empress of China* hoped that commercial traffic between the Far East and the Far West was a foregone conclusion in the territorial development of the nation's interior. In summary, Shaw's national map provided a useful fiction of expanding national American solidarity against which would struggle both Native peoples (whose land had become a speculative commodity of frontier settlement) and individual states (whose discrete sovereignties had been assured under the Articles of Confederation). Perhaps by reaching across the globe to China, early Americans such as Shaw and Quincy established a commercial point of reference so far away, so seemingly exotic, and so charged with lucrative adventure as to make the differences between states, the impending crises of Indian Removal, and the compromises of maintaining slavery seem prosaic by comparison. In any case, the development of the "new people" of the United States would bear unsettling implications for "old" peoples of the Far East and West.

Ginseng and the Early American Dream

During his second voyage to China, Shaw declares that, like the British, "the inhabitants of America must have tea—the consumption of which will necessarily increase with the increasing population of the country"; but he reassures his reader that "it must be pleasing to an American to know that his country can have it on easier terms"—terms not involving sorely needed bullion but instead the "otherwise useless produce of her mountains and forest," which will "in considerable degree supply her with this elegant luxury."[16] This was not merely Shaw's bluster, and to the reported alarm of the Europeans the *Empress of China* (during Shaw's first voyage) was able to procure a full cargo of Chinese goods with "thirty tons of Appalachian ginseng collected in the deep woods of western Pennsylvania and Virginia" and "not one fifth part of whose funds consisted of ready money."[17]

The *Oxford English Dictionary* traces the word *ginseng* to the Chinese phrase *jên shên*; the Chinese characters are 人蔘 and the pronunciation varies throughout China. In Putonghua, its pronunciation would be better rendered as "rén shēn" for "man root," suggesting the root's anthropomorphism, the degree of which is said to add (along with the oldness of the root) to its effectiveness, potency, and thus its market value. Beginning in the eighteenth century, the Linnean term for ginseng was *Panax quinquefolius*, literally a five-leafed cure. Although writers in the eighteenth century believed that the ginseng of Asia and North America were the same plant (albeit with different properties), today the *Panax ginseng* of Asia (northeast China, the Korean peninsula, Japan, and the east coast of Russia) is classified in the same genus but as a separate species from the North American *Panax quinquefolius*.[18] In any case, the recognition, definition, and classification of what is today called "ginseng" unfolded over the centuries through processes of translation that crossed various claims to dominion based in dramatically different cultural logics of value and principles of exchange. As Lydia Liu writes, issues of translation are particularly vexed in moments when "competing universalisms," with different configurations of value and grammars of representation, vie for the control over the terms of exchange and commerce.[19] Approaching China as potential trading partners, early US investors defined ginseng to emphasize the mutual indigenousness of the root to North America with China. This was at least in part a strategic assumption, on the basis of which boosters of the China Trade would claim a seemingly unlimited demand for the root by the Chinese—an unlimited demand that would guarantee unchecked returns of tea.

Shaw was not the first to correlate ginseng with the putative absolute value of precious metals. A more complete history of the root is beyond the scope of this essay, but one of the earliest written descriptions by a European appears in John Nieuhoff's *An Embassy from the East Indian Company* (1669). As a steward for the Dutch East India Company (VOC), Nieuhoff went to China in 1655, moving from Canton to Peking, as the VOC attempted to set up trade relations with the new Qing emperor. The first visual image of ginseng by Europeans comes fifty years later from the French Jesuit priest Father Pierre Jartoux, who was stationed in Peking. His *Lettres édifiantes et curieuses* (1713), which was published in Paris, makes observations similar to those of Nieuhoff, supporting the claims that ginseng acted as a general panacea.[20] Jartoux then offers the hypothesis that "it may be presum'd that if it is to be found in any other Country in the World, *Canada* is the most likely Place; whose Forests and Mountains, according to the Report of those who have lived there, very much resemble these I am speaking of."[21] Beyond the longitudinal similarity and assertion of similar environment between Canada and Manchuria, it is unclear why Fr Jartoux surmised that ginseng might be found in North America. In some sense, his supposition might have as much to do with the network of French Jesuits who were sending reports back to Paris for editing, publication, and dissemination. In addition, the prevailing theories of natural history regarded the environment as the key and determining factor on natural form. In any case, the French Jesuit Father Joseph-Francois Lafitau, stationed at Kahnawá:ke Sault Saint Louis, near Montreal, read Jartoux's report, began looking for ginseng, and eventually found it in Canada. He reported the discovery to the *Académie royale des sciences* in 1714 and followed this up with his *Mémoire présenté à S. A. R. Mgr le duc d'Orléans [...] concernant la précieuse plante du Gin seng de Tartarie, découverte en Canada par le P. Joseph-François Lafitau [...]* (1717).[22] Noting that the Iroquois called the plant "Garent-oguen" (which translates coincidently as "human thighs") Lafitau proposed a new name of *Aureliana canadensis*—or "Canadian Gold."[23] His name never stuck.

Ginseng appears with regularity in the writings of eighteenth-century British colonists in North America. Benjamin Franklin, John and William Bartram, William Byrd, and Thomas Jefferson all wrote about the root. Franklin learned much about ginseng through the work of a third French Jesuit priest, Jean Baptiste Du Halde, who was a scholarly editor and compiler based in Paris. In the *Pennsylvania Gazette,* July 27, 1738, Franklin wrote:

> We have the Pleasure of acquainting the World, that the famous Chinese or Tartarian Plant, called Gin seng, is now discovered in this Province, near Sasquehannah: From whence several whole Plants with a Quantity of the Root, have been lately sent to Town, and it appears to agree most exactly with the Description given of it in Chamber's Dictionary, and Pere du Halde's Account of China. The Virtues ascrib'd to this Plant are wonderful.[24]

Franklin's claim that "Gin seng" has been found in "this Province" of Pennsylvania is more than an exercise of classifying specimens according to the scientific protocols of Linnaeus. His announcement also puts

Pennsylvania in potentially direct and lucrative touch with China, implying the resultant wealth of direct trade that avoids mercantile triangulation with mother England. Nearly fifty years later, as the plans for the *Empress of China* came together, Franklin held at least a minor interest in the campaign; his name appears with a credit of seven dollars in the receipt book of Captain John Green (Figure 2.2).[25]

Ginseng: a product coveted by the Chinese, found in the shades of the Pennsylvania forest, and promising all the silver and gold that Mexico could deliver to the Spanish empire—what better vehicle with which to promote a course of trade and commerce between the United States and China after the Revolutionary War? Such a fantasy of ginseng's nationally virtuous profitability recalls Adam Smith's *The Wealth of Nations* (1776), in which he theorizes the putatively natural, inward-to-outward development of a national economy. In Smith's terms, the ginseng plant, indigenous to North America, would promise Shaw and Franklin the logic of a progressive development in a natural economy that begins with demand for a homegrown commodity whose cultivation and harvest become more efficient through specialization of labor and technological innovation. In 1785, under the Articles of Confederation, however, there would have been no map of the United States that could have represented Adam Smith's standard definition of a nation. In the face of the ambiguity over what kind of association thirteen sovereign states would add up to, Shaw uses ginseng to claim a collective consistency for the ambiguous market of a "new people." Ginseng becomes a powerful concept that affords Shaw a market fantasy through which the United States can extract tea from China and secure positions for the United States within the globe's networks of commercial transaction.

A plant indigenous to North America enabled Shaw to reach from the American countryside to Canton in the barter for tea; however, the goal was not a one-to-one exchange of products but participation in networks of exchange involving layers of signification in which the United States worked to be credited by China and Europe as a worthy trading partner. Given the ambiguities of space and shape riddling the presentation of American political, territorial, and commercial character in the 1780s, it seems serendipitous that both the Chinese and Iroquoian names for ginseng call attention to its resemblance to human form.

Figuring the New American

As mentioned, Shaw reports that upon first arriving in Canton the Chinese "style[d] us the *New People*." This might have been a polite way of withholding judgment on what must have been a confusing explanation of national origin and composition. The fantastic value that Shaw imagined for ginseng arguably corresponds with deeper uncertainties regarding American identity—uncertainties that had to be addressed in practical ways as traders and company representatives took market positions as Americans, rather than Englishmen or Pennsylvanians or Georgians, in international networks of exchange.

The economic challenge of the nation's ambiguous character might be best appreciated in the natural historical implications of illustrating a "new people." As he made his way across the globe, Shaw appears to have been reading Henry Home, Lord Kames, and the Irish writer Oliver Goldsmith.[26] When noticing the curious animal of the swordfish, he references Goldsmith's very popular *A History of the Earth and Animated Nature*, a book heavily influenced by the work of Kames.[27] In explaining differences of phenotype between human beings, both Kames and Goldsmith look to the influence of the environment. As proponents of the prevailing theory of monogenesis, they adhered to the assumption that all humans were of a single species. The difference in how people looked was a result of migration across a globe with varying environmental and climatic conditions. The temperature, humidity, soil, composition of air, amounts of sunlight, and dietary options made their marks on the forms of human kind. However, the premise of humankind's unity was no guarantee that all men were created equal. In Goldsmith's chapter on human beings he outlines six separate categories and differentiates among them to assert the profound influences of the environment not only on their physical form but also on their mental faculties. The six types that Goldsmith outlines are: the "Laplanders," "Tartars" (including the Chinese and Japanese), "South Asiatics" (including those from the peninsula of India, Persians, and "sensualist" Arabians), "Negroes," "inhabitants of America" and, finally, the "sixth and last variety" of "the Europeans."[28]

In the decade after the Revolutionary War, the Chinese were not the only ones confused over what it meant to be "an American." Consider the depictions of the "The American" and "The Chinese" in a 1782 edition of Goldsmith's *A History of the Earth and Animated Nature*, Volume 2 (Figures 2.3 and 2.4).

Shaw would probably not have chosen this "American" to represent him, although the figure seems relatively friendly and confident in his posture. His bow is not loaded with an arrow, and he offers a wampum belt (in his left hand) as a sign of diplomatic and commercial intercourse. In contrast, the "Chinese" figure seems aloof. Although his sword remains in the sheath, his posture suggests that he might be guarding the entrance to a garden-like area where the two white-robed figures (in the background) seem to be headed toward a pagoda for worship.

"The American" was a specimen that attracted much curiosity among natural historians. The prefacing image to a subsequent 1823 edition of Goldsmith's Volume 2 evidences in historically significant ways the malleability of the era's types of human character.

Acting as a preface to Chapter One, the illustration (Figure 2.5) is titled "Varieties of the Human Race:—The Chinese, Laplander, Hottentot, Negro, American." The tableau assembles the five types that were illustrated separately in the 1774 and 1782 editions. This composition reorients the specimens to place the Chinese figure eastward, on the left. Shaw would probably not have found the new version of the "American" any more reassuring. Whereas the American of 1782 stands in a posture that implies the possibility of communication and diplomacy, the American of the 1823 version appears worried and frightened, on the verge of flight and nervously clutching a tomahawk. It looks to be an icon of Indian Removal during which time the sovereignty of Native peoples was strategically denied in a series of Supreme Court decisions and in federal legislation.

Whereas the "American, Negros, and Laplander" hold primitive implements of hunting, the Chinese figure stands in front of a crate of tea or merchandise of some sort. He seems to have in his hand either a fan or a stamp by which he can "chop" the receipts of foreign traders. Given the crate behind him, the pagoda in the background seems less of a spiritual sanctuary that requires a posted guard, and more of a commercial landmark of Canton, such as those pagodas often mentioned in the writing of foreign traders or rendered in sketches, paintings and, eventually, photographs. Unlike the frightened American, the Chinese figure meets the viewer's eye. And unlike the Chinese figure standing guard in the 1782 picture, this figure strikes a pose, gesturing toward the chest, which seems to initiate a transaction.

It is worth noting that these editions of Goldsmith's *History* only illustrate five of the six proposed types of the human race and there is no picture of

"The European." One assumes that the reader already knows that category; indeed, it is the supposed genius of the European scientific enterprise that orders the world's confusion into the knowledge of taxonomy. For Shaw, the new American would not be a picture but rather the reader who holds the book in his hands and looks at and contemplates these illustrations. On his voyage Shaw never claims to discover any new species of animal or plant, but he does recite the correspondence between what he sees and what he has read in Goldsmith. Shaw's tone suggests that he is proud of his ongoing collaboration in the project of natural history—a project in which he participates as an American who is similar to and yet distinct from the unillustrated European variety of humankind. In this sense, his written impressions serve as evidence proving him to be an American capable of participating in the gentlemanly project of science.

In his description of the Canton port, Shaw shows off his powers of natural historical observation and anticipates the commercial revision of the Chinese character that figured in the various different editions of Goldsmith's book. In his *Journals* Shaw remarks that he actually saw very little of the Chinese people. He seems to regard the administrative system that moved boats up and down the Pearl River from Macao to Whampoa to Canton as a vast administrative screen hiding the "real" Chinese people and inhibiting the flows of the world market. Nevertheless, rather than presenting a Chinese figure dressed for war, Shaw presents a wealthy landowning merchant, Chowqua, who is half-heartedly hospitable. Shaw's ensuing description is a bit of an aesthetic puzzle, encoding the commercial ambition of the American nation in the description of a stagnant Chinese garden. Shaw writes:

> The factories at Canton, occupying less than a quarter of a mile in front, are situated on the bank of the river. The quay is enclosed by a rail-fence, which has stairs and a gate opening from the water to each factory, where all merchandise is received and sent away. The limits of the Europeans are extremely confined; there being, besides the quay, only a few streets in the suburbs, occupied by the trading people, which they are allowed to frequent. Europeans, after a dozen years' residence, have not seen more than the first month presented to view. They are sometimes invited to dine with the Chinese merchants, who have houses and gardens on the opposite side of the river; but even then no new information is obtained. Every thing [*sic*] of a domestic concern is strictly concealed, and, though their wives, mistresses, and daughters are commonly there, none of them are ever visible. We dined with four of the co-hoang, at separate

> times, two of whom entertained the French gentlemen and us at their country-houses. On these occasions, the guests generally contribute largely to the bill of fare. Both at Chowqua's and Pankekoa's, the French supplied the table furniture, wine, and a large portion of the victuals. The gardens belonging to Chowqua are extensive; much art and labor are used to give them a rural appearance, and in some instances nature is not badly imitated. Forests, artificial rocks, mountains, and cascades, are judiciously executed, and have a pleasing effect in diversifying the scene. The Chinese, however, discover a vitiated taste in their fondness for water. Every garden must have abundance of this element, and where it does not flow naturally, large, stagnant ponds, the middle of which are summerhouses, supply the deficiency. Chowqua says that his house and gardens cost him upwards of one hundred thousand taels.[29]

There is not much ethnographic information in Shaw's aesthetic assessment of this landscape of "the Chinese." But his description does say a lot about the terms of his national romance of trade. In positioning himself vis-à-vis Canton, he represents his line of perspective on the Chinese landscape as being restricted by China's factory buildings, and he rues the fact that his gaze cannot extend unfettered, beyond the Canton quarantine, to get a full view. Shaw does more than tell us that he is unable to see beyond this confined view—he offers himself to the reader as a curious American who strives to broaden the horizon, to redevelop the landscape, and to know more about the life of China behind these bounds. Reading this as an allegory of Adam Smith's brand of nationally virtuous trade, the Chinese architects and gardeners of this "rural appearance" seem stuck in a mode of composition that is at its heart "stagnant." The scene's water, which should be flowing (and one assumes supporting the currents of commerce), have been artificially pooled, thus defying what may at first seem an impressive diversifying effect.

But, reading carefully, we can again sense national insecurity at the heart of Shaw's impressions of China. Do the terms of monetary signification by which he sums up Chowqua's achievement convert into an equivalent of United States currency? In an actual transaction that involved United States dollars, one would have to be willing to accept Shaw's signature on a rather incredible promissory note that converts 100,000 taels (the equivalent at the time of 72,000 Spanish dollars) into what would have been millions and millions of Continental bills headed for further depreciation. Furthermore, this inflationary crisis of conversation implies the larger difficulty of translating the terms and scope of Hong wealth into a comparable national currency in the republican democracy of the United States. Recall that, from the 1780s to the 1840s, the United States struggled to stabilize not only a unit of national dollar that could reliably hold value but also a federal government's authority to determine the terms of legal tender across states and regions that would be at war with one another. Even in Shaw's hopeful formulations of the market, ginseng would only go so far in establishing terms of commercial reciprocity. In the end, it was not a commodity that reassured his sense of American integrity, but rather the Society of Cincinnati.

America and the Question of Character

To fund for the Revolution, the Continental Congress printed money to circulate throughout the thirteen states. Its untrustworthiness provoked a severe crisis in confidence, highlighting a difficult question: Would the thirteen states add up to a single nation when the Articles of Confederation insured "sovereignty" to each state? At the time, each state printed its own paper currency, which it backed by references to the British pound (a pointed irony during the war) or to the Spanish milled dollar. Very little silver was on hand to back the currency, so its utility as a medium of exchange depended on precarious linkages within and between local contexts that extended to more general networks of exchange between the cooperating states. To maintain value, non-perishable commodities or precious metals were often the better bet. Given the scarcity of resources, war profiteers had merely to play the demands of the British Army off those of the Continental troops.

Figures 2.6 and 2.7 are the obverse and reverse of a $5 Continental bill, part of the $3,000,000 in notes authorized by the Continental Congress by resolution on May 10, 1775, and payable in "Spanish milled dollars." Benjamin Franklin explains the symbolism:

> ...we have a thorny bush, which a hand seems attempting to eradicate. The hand appears to bleed, as pricked by spines. The motto is, SUSTINE VEL ABSTINE; which may be rendered, Bear with me, or let me alone; or thus, Either support or leave me. The bush I suppose to mean America, the bleeding hand Britain. Would to God that bleeding were stopt [*sic*], the wounds of that hand healed, and its future operations directed by wisdom and equity; so shall the hawthorn flourish, and form an hedge around it, annoying with her thorns only its invading enemies.[30]

Put in relation to economic exchange, Franklin's bleeding colonial hand seems to embody the abusive effects of arbitrary and tyrannical powers; the image anticipates the invisible, benign superintending hand that Smith's *Wealth of Nations* (1776) would conjure the follow year to metaphorize the ineluctable forces of a free market's drift toward the equilibrium of resource distribution. On the bill's reverse are images made from actual betony and sage leaves that suggest a palliative to the wounded hand on the bill's front and whose unique design Franklin hoped would discourage counterfeiting.

It is amazing to consider how the printing of paper money was able to finance the war. After the May 1775 authorization of three million bills, supposedly backed by Spanish dollars, Congress authorized three million more in November, making the year's total six million. For the next four years, the amount of currency that was printed skyrocketed, so that by 1779, Congress authorized the printing of almost 100 million in US bills. In the spring of 1778, Continental script, when accepted at all, was exchanged at half its denominated value; by 1779, Continental money was circulating at less than one-seventh its statement value.[31]

As a Continental soldier during the United States Revolutionary War, Shaw not only risked his life but also endured this debasement of the federal Continental currency in which soldiers' salaries were irregularly paid. In the midst of the war's campaigns, Shaw repeatedly decries the reasons behind his fiscal binds. At one point he sheepishly asks to borrow money from his father because he is owed two months of back pay from the army.[32] Later on he complains of not having enough money to clothe himself properly, pleading, "My whole stock is reduced to one shirt and a borrowed one. Somehow or other, I must have shirts" and then lamenting the "Depreciation of virtue—of paper currency, which you know touches the poor soldier."[33] Near the end of the war, Shaw suggests the dramatic extent of the currency's devaluation when he excoriates the greed of those profiting from wartime sales in Philadelphia, charging that these opportunistic traders' virtue has depreciated "equal to that of the currency—*thirty to one*."[34] He concludes grimly to his younger brother Nathaniel, "In truth, it may be said *that our country neither pays, feeds, nor clothes its armies*."[35] In a letter from the same period, Shaw reacts to his personal financial distress with a more general lament about the young nation: "is America prepared for the reception of the long wished-for blessing [of independence]? What system has she adequate to the government and prosperity of her rising empire? No money, no funds, and what is worse, no disposition in the people to establish funds, the certain consequence of which must be the death of public credit."[36]

Despite Shaw's grim assessment, he dramatically rebounds to promote the nation's future. For example, he counsels Nathaniel to join the army, writing to their father:

> The army has been esteemed no inconsiderable school for the study of mankind; and Nat, poor lad, has had no opportunity for acquainting himself with this necessary branch of science. He is now at an age well calculated to receive the best impressions; and I am happy in having it in my power, not only to provide genteelly for him in the army, but also to introduce him to its first characters.[37]

It may seem odd for Shaw to describe the army as a school that affords the opportunity for the "study of mankind" and that trains students in this "branch of science." However, in Shaw's encouragement of his young brother he highlights the double nature of the word "character," which here suggests "types" or "kinds" of men. His advice to Nathaniel is that, by understanding these types and kinds, one is able to gauge a person's integrity and by extension a people's internal worth and integrity. Shaw often folds the internal and external connotations of "character" into one another; in a letter he advises Nat:

> You cannot be insensible, my dear Sir, of the stress which the world lays on *external appearances*, and that the opinion formed of a young man *at first sight* is commonly the strongest and most lasting. Therefore it will be absolutely essential that he come on completely equipped as an officer. For this purpose I have annexed an estimate of such articles as will be necessary, at the same time having as much regard to economy as possible.[38]

Shaw then lists the clothes necessary in signifying a "young campaigner"—boots, sword, coat, beaver hat, all of which add up to 200 silver dollars. In Shaw's formulation, understanding the power of how one *looks* to others is crucial to winning social respectability that enables one to *seem to be* a gentleman. The designation of "200 silver dollars" is significant—offering hard currency as the crucial point of reference in the project of coordinating one's personal appearance. Shaw would not, for example, add up the cost of these necessary clothes to "200 Continental dollars"—or, factoring in the depreciation of currency, 1,400 or 6,000 Continental dollars. For Shaw to imagine an

American with a respectable and trustworthy character he must refer to a Spanish standard of currency. His anxieties over how to best represent the economic character of the new nation would continue to haunt his subsequent economic ventures. During his four voyages to China, he often worries if an indebted United States will be able to negotiate and maintain access to the Chinese market in Canton alongside competing companies from Europe.

It is safe to say that today Samuel Shaw is not a popular figure and his name is not recognized by most Americans. Nevertheless, as a reader in the first decade of the twenty-first century, it is interesting to reconsider how and why a subsequent generation in the 1840s resurrected his story. To those reading in 1847, whose nation was at war with Mexico and who were still dealing with the reverberations of the economic Panic of 1837, as well as with violent sectional antagonisms over slavery, the continuity of biographical character that Josiah Quincy gave to Shaw's experiences must have been as reassuring as it was hypothetical. Consider again the frontispiece portrait of Shaw in Figure 2.1. With equanimity he meets the viewer's gaze directly, dressed as a gentleman with the flair of a French style. The engraving is a copy of a portrait by painter John Johnston (1752–1813), whose original depicts Shaw in the process of writing and with the *Empress of China* in the background. In this frontispiece, one can barely make out the shadow of a quill with which Johnston equipped Shaw in the original. It is unclear what exactly Shaw would be writing—maybe the reports in support of the ginseng trade that he later sent to Secretary of State John Jay and published as an article in the Philadelphia-based magazine the *American Museum*. Or, Shaw might be writing another document for which he was known: the constitution of an exclusive society of Continental Army veterans called the Order of Cincinnati, formed to provide for veterans and their families. Its membership included George Washington, the painter Johnston, and most of the financiers behind the *Empress of China* enterprise. Whatever we imagine Shaw's text to be, he would have used a similar quill to produce the bold signature that the frontispiece copies below his picture. To American readers in 1847, this version of Samuel Shaw must have offered an inspiring relief. Nevertheless, the heroic signature beneath his portrait in the frontispiece to the 1847 edition is very different from the anxious one he would have rendered to sign a promissory note in 1780.

Near the end of the initial "Memoir" section of Shaw's *Journals*, Quincy presents Shaw after the Revolutionary War: "Like other soldiers of the

Revolutionary army, Major Shaw was destined to enter upon civil life, in debt, without property, and with no other foundation of hope than the character he had attained, and the general confidence which his talents and integrity had inspired."[39] Quincy uses the word "character" here to suggest that Shaw had control over the process of creating his economic success through the honorable actions he performed. In effect, Quincy assumes that Shaw earned trustworthiness and respectability through his deeds and therefore encountered more opportunities to secure more capital. Thus Quincy is able to use Shaw's complaints about the unreliability of paper money as an exercise that further strengthens his American character.

However, we might ask, in an international context, what exactly distinguishes Shaw's character as American? In Quincy's account of Shaw rising from debt and economic disenfranchisement, Shaw's wartime commitments earn him friendship with other Revolutionary officers and the "attention and general interest" of an "association of capitalists who had united for the purpose of opening a commercial intercourse between the United States and China."[40] Quincy also notes that Shaw "took an active and efficient part in the formation of the Society of Cincinnati" and that he drafted the Society's constitution, which begins:

> It having pleased the Supreme Governor of the universe, in the disposition of human affairs, to cause the separation of the colonies of North America from the domination of Great Britain, and, after a bloody conflict of eight years, to establish them free, independent, and sovereign states, connected by alliances, founded on reciprocal advantages, with some of the greatest princes and powers of the earth:
>
> To perpetuate, therefore, as well the remembrance of this vast event, as the mutual friendships which have been formed under the pressure of common danger, and in many instances cemented by the blood of the parties, the officers of the American army do hereby, in the most solemn manner, associate, constitute, and combine themselves into one society of friends, to endure so long as they shall endure, or any of their eldest male posterity, and in failure thereof, the collateral branches, who may be judged worthy of becoming its supporters and members. [...][41]

In the shadow of currency depreciation, the Society shores up the national character by appealing to the "mutual friendships" of its war officers, whose victory God has insured. Notice that this "society of friends" pays tribute to "Cincinnati" but is not democratic in its organization—its constitution continues by dedicating the Society to cultivating between the states the "unison and national honor so essentially necessary to their happiness and future dignity of the American Empire." In the provision of extending membership to the oldest son of deceased members, there is an echo of bloodline inheritance against which the constitution guarded in Article 1, Section 9, and Section 10 (Clause 1), prohibiting state and federal governments from granting titles of nobility. Furthermore, in asserting individual states' sovereignties as a vital point of principle, the Society's constitution foreshadows the tensions between the states that would ultimately lead to the Civil War. Quincy's memoir of Shaw finally presents us with a character that is rife with contradictions that matter in how we understand the relationship between commerce and American citizenship. Shaw ostensibly fights for a republican order of representative democracy, grows disillusioned over the lack of a currency that is capable of representing value, and then rebounds by promoting the Society of Cincinnati, whose battle-tested affections seem to transcend the realm of representation.

Despite positing the "mutual friendship" of Revolutionary War experience as a sort of transcendent signifier of trustworthiness, Shaw and his fellow members went through a fair amount of trouble in trying to represent it. Figure 2.8 is the Society's insignia bearing homage to "high veneration for the character" of the Society's namesake. Lucius Quintius Cincinnatus was a Roman farmer and soldier living around 50 BCE about whom Livy writes in Book Three of the *History of Rome*. Drawing inspiration from his life, the Society's motto is: "He gave up everything to serve the republic." Cincinnatus was an attractive symbol in the early United States because he balanced military and political strength against relatively democratic principles and procedures of republican, anti-dictatorial governance. In moments of crises, Cincinnatus rose to absolute power in Rome, defending his country against external threats in war with the Aequians and against internal threats, by protecting the Roman aristocracy from the demands of the Plebians. After these crises had subsided, he relinquished his power and returned to his life as a citizen and farmer, thus preserving the republic. The scene depicted on the medal is of the Roman people pleading for his leadership.

As we re-encounter Quincy's version of Shaw's life in the twenty-first century, it is worth emphasizing the crucial role that China played not only logistically in the investment schemes of the early republic but also ideologically in two centuries of subsequent attempts to revise and re-represent a coherent historical romance of American commercial development. On his first trip to Canton, Shaw ordered porcelain tea sets with the Society's insignia painted on them, which he presented as gifts to fellow Society members upon his return. These tea sets would sit in the family homes as reminders of the voyages to China. Consider Shaw's instructions to a Canton painter whom Shaw enlisted to commemorate the Society of Cincinnati on the porcelain:

> There are many painters in Canton, but I was informed that not one of them possesses a genius for design. I wished to have something emblematic of the institution of the order of the Cincinnati executed upon a set of porcelain. My idea was to have the American Cincinnatus, under the conduct of Minerva, regarding Fame, who, having received from them the emblems of the order, was proclaiming it to the world. For this purpose I procured two separate engravings of the goddesses, an elegant figure of a military man, and furnished the painter with a copy of the emblems, which I had in my possession. He was allowed to be the most eminent of his profession, but, after repeated trials, was unable to combine the figures with the least propriety; though there was not one of them which singly he could not copy with the greatest exactness. I could therefore have my wishes gratified only in part. The best of his essays I preserved, as a specimen of Chinese excellence in design, and it is difficult to regard it without smiling. It is a general remark, that the Chinese, though they can imitate most of the fine arts, do not possess any large portion of original genius.[42]

In Shaw's desire to copy this insignia on Chinese porcelain while in Canton, we might read his attempt to establish a point of national reference beyond the uncertainty of the debased Continental script or the vagaries of the trade in ginseng—a point of reference grounded in his fraternity of veterans that reaches, through the China trade, back to the republican character of a Cincinnati, who salvaged the authority of the Roman Empire by resisting invitations to authoritarian rule and returning to his citizen's life of a farmer. Nevertheless, one imagines the reasonable confusion that must have arisen in this unnamed Chinese painter's mind as Shaw explained the emblems, weaving together the stories of Cincinnati, of Minerva, and of Fame to symbolize American distinctiveness in the terms of classical Roman republicanism.

Shaw's most serious criticism of the Chinese painter is his inability to "combine" the figures. So, while the painter can replicate with great exactness, he (and the Chinese for whom he is a synecdoche) is unable to exercise a higher degree of aesthetic creativity. With his tidy smile, Shaw claims a superior energy of mind and capacity for aesthetic judgment. But, Shaw seems to overlook the porcelain. He regards it as a mere canvas, on which he strives to inscribe American character, rather than as a socially situated craft that exceeded the capabilities of Americans who traveled the world in order to secure it or settled for cheaper imitations from Great Britain [cf. Haddad's essay in this volume].

Figure 2.9 is an example of a bowl that Shaw brought back with him. It was part of a serving set that presented tea on the tables of Society of Cincinnati members. To our contemporary eyes, it might seem a quaint but hopeful symbol of Shaw's adventure. Early American speculators never found the indigenous commodity that Shaw imagined ginseng to be. Instead, the United States followed in the footpaths of England, as American companies facilitated British trade in opium and capitalized on their access to opium harvested in Turkey. After the First Opium War (1839–42), Caleb Cushing arrived in Macao with a small but assertive battalion of gunboats to secure for the United States terms of commerce similar to those that China had conceded to England. Fourteen years after Josiah Quincy III published the *Journals* of Samuel Shaw, tensions between states overwhelmed the romance of Quincy's biography, as the bloody struggle of the Civil War again revolutionized the United States' terms of national composure. The crisis of constitution fractured the nation into confederated parts that no artist or financier could synthesize. Rather than resolve antagonisms between democracy and imperialism or state and federal authority, Shaw's advocacy of the Society evinces an ongoing process of national storytelling that continues to this day. Historical hindsight enables us to appreciate the layers of reinterpretation and reinvention by writers, editors, and publishers, who have themselves speculated on the economic, legal, and political potential of a "new people."

Given the precarious terms of national identity in the decades after the revolution and the fragility of life more generally, it is instructive to see how intensely people's self-awareness was caught up in these commercial circuits of character reference. If I have seemed to reduce Quincy's redemptive romance of Shaw's life to the mere hypocrisy of delivering a new imperial Caesar, dressed in the republican trappings of Cincinnati, let me conclude by appreciating the ways that these terms of character sustained for Shaw, his family, and Shaw's contemporaries what I feel to be sincere statements of "deep affection" and "mutual friendship." In March 1790, Samuel Shaw embarked on his third voyage to Canton with his younger brother Nathaniel on the ill-fated *Massachusetts*, a ship that Samuel co-owned and whose construction in Boston harbor he had financed. Serving on the voyage as the second officer was Amasa Delano, the adventuring sailor and an eventual ship captain on whom Herman Melville later based the account of a thwarted slave revolt in the chilling short story "Benito Cereno" (1855). When the *Massachusetts* arrived in Canton, it had disastrously rotted beyond Shaw's financial ability to afford its repair. He salvaged a fraction of the cargo, disbanded the crew, and sold the ship off. A few months later, in 1791, the brothers Samuel and Nathaniel embarked from Canton on a British ship bound for Bombay. During the voyage, Nathaniel succumbed to illness and died. Amasa Delano mentions Samuel and Nathaniel Shaw at the beginning of his *A Narrative of Voyages and Travels in Northern and Southern Hemispheres: Comprising Three Voyages Round the World; Together with a Voyage of Survey and Discovery, in the Pacific Ocean and Oriental Islands* (1817). He describes Nathaniel on the 1790 voyage of the *Massachusetts* as the "purser, and brother to the owner," noting that he later "died and was thrown overboard, on a voyage from Canton to Bombay in an English ship in 1791."[43] The next sentence may seem cold and unfeeling, unless one tunes to the frequency of commercial anxieties in the early national era. About Nathaniel, Delano concludes: "He was a good accountant, and of an excellent character."[44] In 1794, at age thirty-nine, returning to the United States on his fourth voyage to Canton, Samuel Shaw also died at sea.

Figure I.1

"Canton—Foreign Settlement. Before the Fire." Eliza J. Gillett Bridgman (ed.), *The Pioneer of American Missions in China: The Life and Labors of Elijah Coleman Bridgman* (New York: Anson D.F. Randolph, 1864), 39.

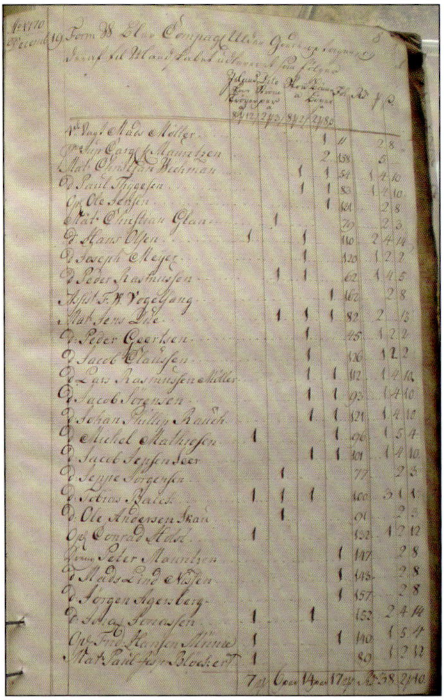

Figure 1.1

Muster role and wage sheet for crew aboard DAC Ship *Dronning Sophia Magdalena* bound for China in 1771. Wages were based on position and rank aboard the ship or factory, such as 1st, 2nd, or 3rd carpenter or sailmaker, etc. A new hire or promotion during the voyage would be noted in these documents. Top officers were allowed some private trade, and the items and/or amounts permitted were stipulated in the muster and wage books. Courtesy National Archives, Copenhagen: Ask 926 fo. 8.

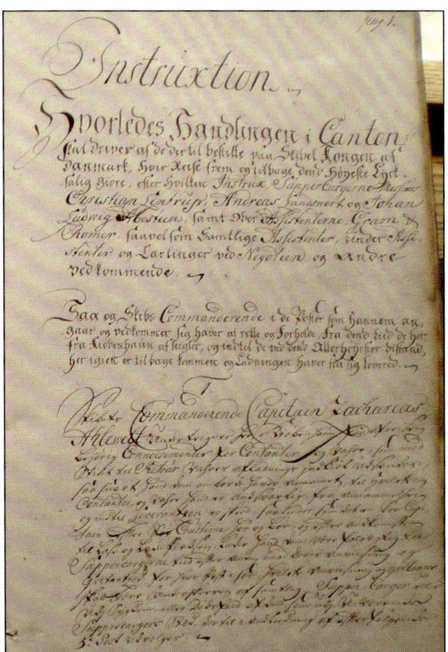

Figure 1.2

Instructions for DAC officers involved in the China trade in 1738. These were usually very extensive and included many pages describing such things as how much rent to pay, Chinese merchants that were preferred to deal with, the high and low prices for commodities, what route to take to China, how to pack and stow merchandise, and how to maintain the crew and company personnel during the voyage and while in China. Courtesy National Archives, Copenhagen: Ask 1118.

Figure 1.3

List of equipage aboard the GIC ship *Apollo* in 1731, including anchors, sails, cables, extra masts, etc. (multiple pages). Courtesy Stadsarchief, Antwerp: IC 5709.

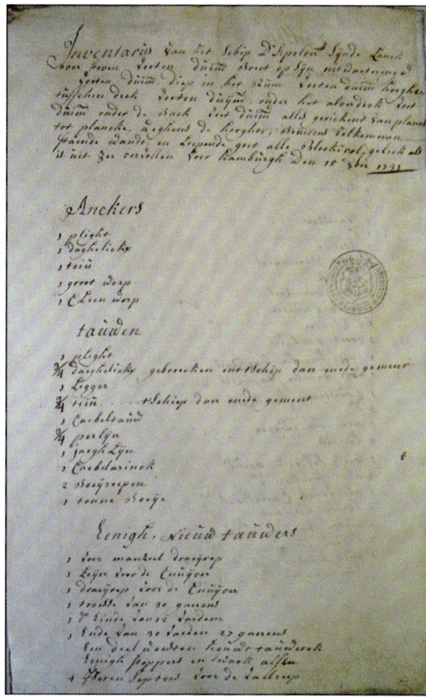

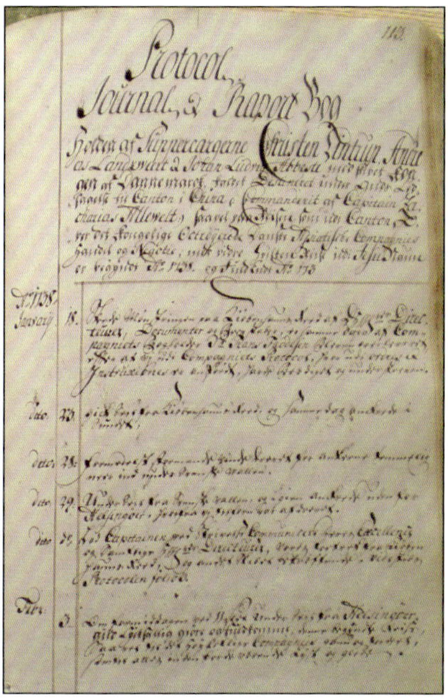

Figure 1.4

Daily Diary of the DAC's trade in China in 1738. Courtesy National Archives, Copenhagen: Ask 1118 fo. 113.

Figure 1.5

Journal from GIC China Trade in 1730 showing daily purchases and transactions with corresponding page numbers to the company's ledger book. Courtesy Stadsarchief, Antwerp: IC 5710 p. 11.

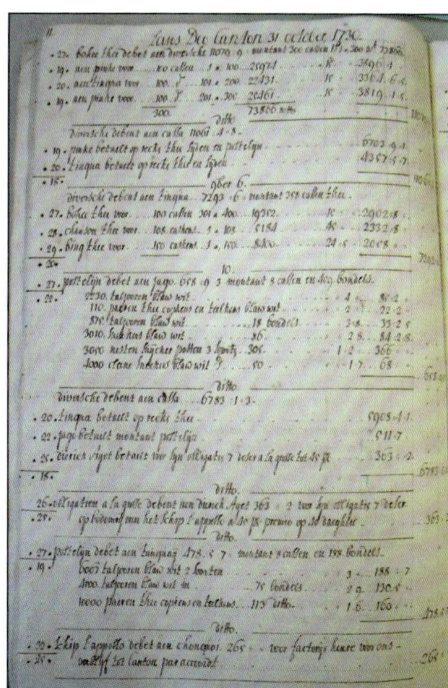

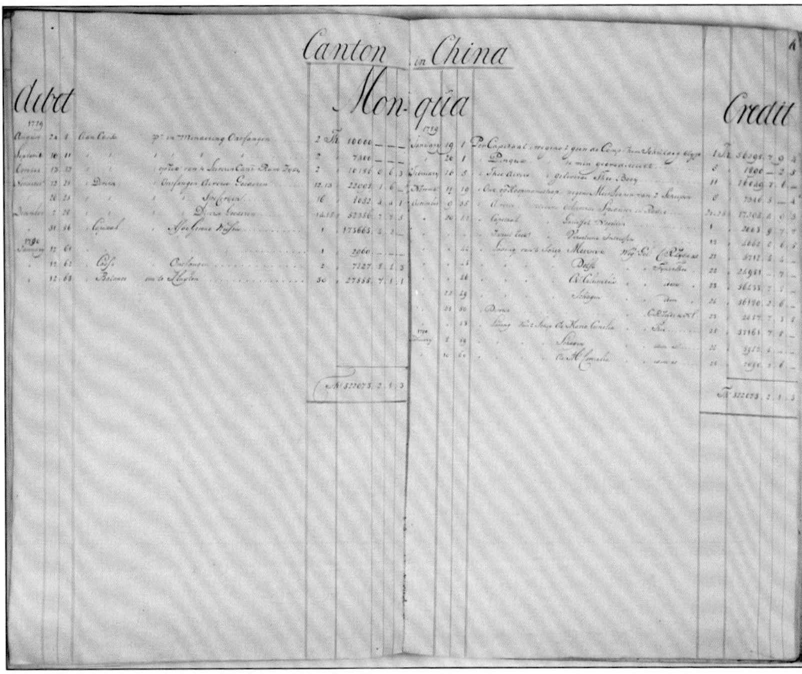

Figure 1.6

Ledger from VOC China Trade in 1789 showing Canton merchant Monqua's (Cai Shiwen) account balancing his debits and credits. Each entry is cross-referenced with the page number of where the transaction appears in the trade journal, and the trade journal page number was recorded in the ledger. All the companies kept balance sheets of each ship and/or each year's trade in China, but not all of them kept accounts of individual commodities and merchants as shown here. Courtesy National Archives, The Hague: VOC 4444 fo. 4.

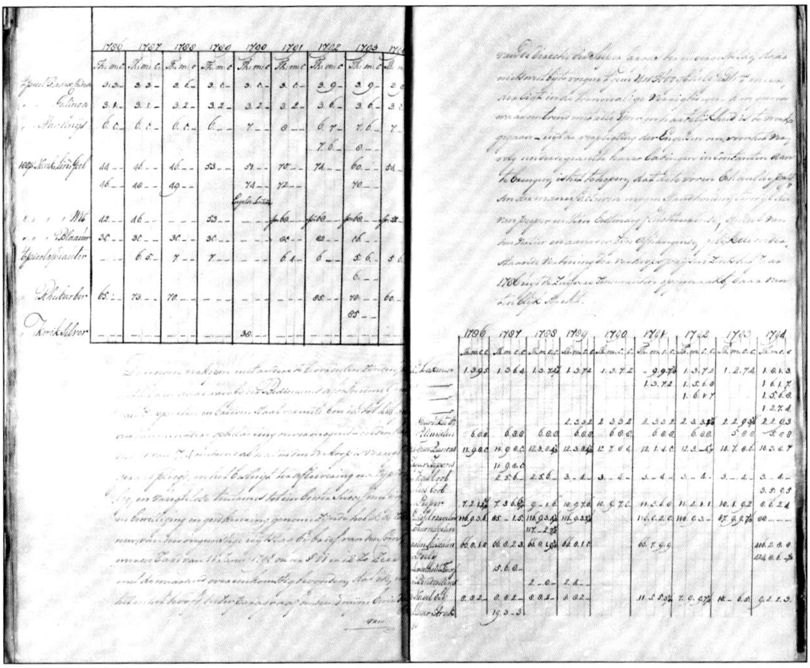

Figure 1.7

Extract from a VOC document showing the average prices of Chinese exports and imports from 1786 to 1794. This information was often included in the general reports sent to directors each year. Courtesy National Archives, The Hague: OIC 196.

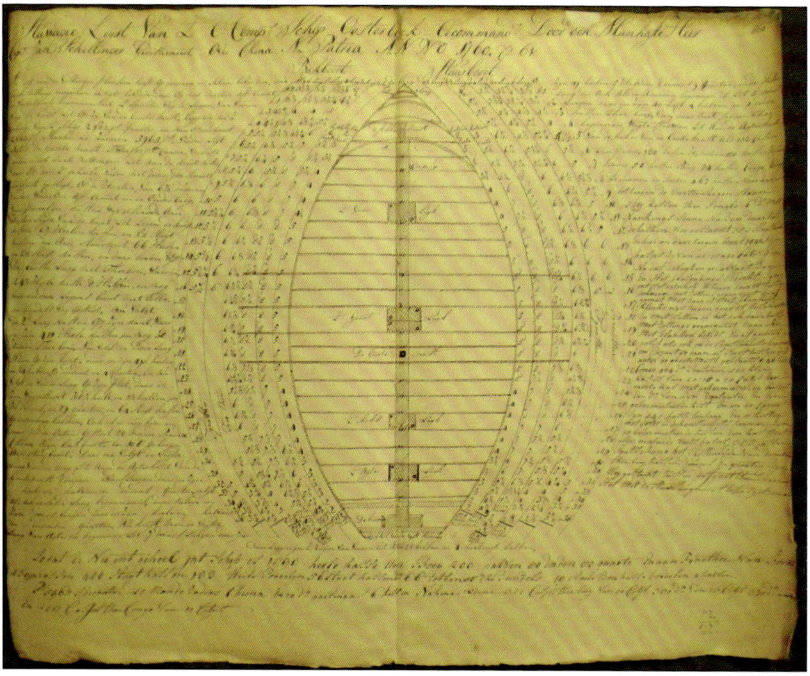

Figure 1.8

Stowage chart for VOC ship *Oosterbeek* in China in 1760. The chart shows the sizes of chests and how many were needed in each layer, as well as the products they were to contain. The companies had specific procedures for the loading of each different sized ship so the export cargo to Europe could be maximized. Each chest was given a number, and their locations in the hull were recorded, so if there was damage or theft it could be determined how it might have happened, who loaded and unloaded the product, and who was responsible for its care during the passage home. If it could be determined that foul play was involved, companies could charge the loss to the ships' officers who were responsible for that part of the cargo. Courtesy National Archives, The Hague: VOC 4387.

Figure 1.9

Three large handwritten topical indexes of the VOC's China Trade covering the years from 1756 to 1779. Courtesy National Archives, The Hague: VOC 4554-6.

3
China of the American Imagination

The Influence of Trade on US Portrayals of China, 1820 to 1850[1]

John R. Haddad

In the 1830s, a young girl named Caroline Howard King made numerous visits to the East India Marine Society in Salem, Massachusetts. Since Salem was a thriving center of maritime commerce, ships departed daily for destinations all over the world. When sea captains returned home bearing artifacts, they deposited these in the Society's museum—East India Marine Hall. The collection was especially strong in artifacts from China, India, the East Indies, and the Pacific Islands. The hall provided visitors with an intriguing way to experience Asia without venturing far from home.

King relished her encounters with Asia. In fact, in memoirs composed later in life, she reminisced about the magical attraction that these exhibits held:

> the Museum had a mysterious attraction for me and indeed it was an experience for an imaginative child to step from the prosaic streets... into that atmosphere redolent with the perfumes from the east, warm and fragrant and silent, with a touch of the dear old Arabian Nights [...] I [...] was greeted by the solemn group of Orientals [referring to several life-size statues] who, draped in eastern stuffs and camel's hair shawls, stood opposite the entrance...the hours were full of enchantment, and I think I came as near fairyland as one can in this workaday world [...] And in those days the Spice Islands seemed to lie very near our coast.[2]

King used the exhibits to compose a narrative of escapist pleasure. In her story, she escapes everyday life—the "prosaic streets" and the "workaday world" of Salem—and journeys to a strange and exotic land of "enchantment." In short, this "imaginative child" used this eclectic assortment of Asian objects to enjoy an excursion to "fairyland."

Caroline Howard King's behavior was far from unique. In considering American attitudes towards China, we often associate the nineteenth century with the ugly anti-Chinese sentiment that marred the Gilded Age. In doing so, we sometimes forget that, during the century's earlier decades, Americans were more likely to gaze upon China with a combination of curiosity, affection, and wonder. Interestingly, China's stock, so to speak, peaked during the years before the First Opium War (1839–42), a period in China's economic history in which Western traders did not possess open access to China's markets (Americans' affection for the Chinese would not reach a comparable level until the publication of Pearl Buck's *The Good Earth* in 1931). After Britain's military victory, China was forced to abandon the highly controlled and restricted Canton or Hong Trade System in favor of one that allowed trade at multiple ports (the "Treaty Port" System). It was at this moment that, in the United States, China's stock entered into swift and precipitous decline. The purpose of this chapter, then, is to explain why a largely closed-off China produced favorable American portrayals.

First of all, in the absence of hard facts, the American imagination enjoyed greater license to construct a China that did not require much grounding in reality. The highly restrictive nature of the Canton Trade System rendered it impossible to have first-hand observation of the vast territory beyond Canton—this at a time when scientific, diplomatic, and military expeditions were leaving very little of the globe untouched by Western influence, for good or for ill.[3] Yet amid this flurry of exploratory activity, the Canton Trade System ensured that the most colossal nation on earth would remain largely enshrouded in mystery. China is "the great unknown," wrote an American missionary in 1843, because "foreigners know but little more of it than they do of the moon."[4]

Into this vacuum of knowledge the imagination rushed to fill the void. In 1830, William Wood, an American merchant who had resided in Canton, remarked that a "romantic illusion" had enveloped American perceptions of China.[5] Similarly, in 1873, Gideon Nye, a retired American China trader, looked back wistfully upon the popular view of China earlier in the century: "The very name of China—the distant *Cathay*—was, at that day, pregnant of the Romance of History; and suggested imaginative dreams."[6] As readers are aware, Cathay was not exactly a synonym for China; it was, instead, the West's playful construction of a fantastical China that pleased the imagination while bearing little resemblance to the actual country. By invoking Cathay, Nye hinted at an unintended consequence of China's restrictive trade policy: Americans had, in the same manner as Caroline Howard King, invented fabulous stories about a Chinese fantasyland.

The second reason a largely closed-off China produced favorable American portrayals was that Americans' rare attempts at the scientific study of China, though severely hindered by this problem of access, actually supported the widespread view that China was an Oriental wonderland. This finding may at first seem counterintuitive, since scientific study should generate the body of facts necessary to puncture a myth such as Cathay. However, the dominant scientific paradigm of the day, which we shall call "Enlightenment science," operated under the basic assumption that the universe was static; therefore, knowledge was produced through the systematic naming, describing, and classification of the diverse elements of God's universe (in contrast, post-Darwin science focused not on simple documentation but rather on process or change over time). The few Americans who applied the theories and practices of Enlightenment science to China undertook vast collection efforts, during which tens of thousands of artifacts, images, and natural specimens were amassed. When these men installed their vast collections in museum settings, they inadvertently constructed marvelous Chinese worlds on American soil. Though some visitors understood the scientific underpinnings of these exhibition spaces, others luxuriated in this virtual tour of a three-dimensional fantasy world in which the ethereal Cathay of their dreams took on material form. We have Disneyland; they had Chinese museums. But if nearly all of China was off-limits to foreigners, how were these enormous collections assembled?

Third, the closed nature of China compelled American knowledge-seekers to expand the role of Chinese civilians in their grandiose projects. The Chinese were the ones collecting artifacts, gathering plant and animal specimens, generating visual images, and providing cultural information. In this way, the Chinese played an influential role in representing their country in the United States. And not surprisingly, the images that they created tended to be overwhelmingly positive, as it was simply not in their interests to portray China in a negative light. Interestingly, the most powerful self-image created by the Chinese appeared on the most ordinary of household articles—a ceramic plate.

Constructing Cathay: Chinese Ceramics

In the 1780s, the English traveler Claude C. Robin observed during his tour of America, "[t]here is not a single person to be found, who does not drink

[tea] out of China cups and saucers."[7] What Robin was witnessing was a sudden spread in Chinese blue and white ceramics that moved both horizontally across geographic regions and vertically through the social classes. Concerning the former, archeological digs, advertisements for auctions in newspapers, and manifests from vessels arriving in American ports all offer testimony to a tremendous proliferation of blue and white ceramics in domestic spaces across the eastern United States.[8]

Clearly, inexpensive Chinese ceramics found their way onto the cupboards of middle- and lower-income level families. And what these families saw delighted them. Typically, a piece of Chinese-manufactured porcelain carried a landscape design referred to as *shan shui* ("hills and streams") by the Chinese. Most such designs included a handful of basic elements: birds, fruit trees, a willow tree, a junk with a fisher, a bridge, an island, pagodas, and Chinese houses (Figure 3.1).[9] Though Americans may have purchased these ceramics because they were cheap and functional, they cherished them for their designs.

Why did American families find such simple pictures so alluring? For the individual with an active imagination, these images possessed more than just ornamental value; they offered a portal to a different world that many called "Cathay." While sipping tea, one could escape household chores, misbehaving children, debilitating illnesses, or the pressures of the workaday world and take a brief flight of fancy to a strange but wonderful realm. The land depicted was one of perpetual spring in which humanity lived in perfect harmony with the natural world. That nature was friendly, unthreatening, and, above all, giving: It bountifully provided fish from the river, gigantic fruit from trees, shade from the sun, and delightful pastoral vistas upon which to gaze. In short, for one with an imagination, a simple china plate seemed to present a portal to an Oriental Garden of Eden.

The Chinese were not alone in producing inexpensive ceramics for the American market. After many years and numerous mishaps, British potters in the 1780s finally produced porcelain with the same physical properties as the Chinese varieties. Having met Chinese standards, manufacturers next faced the challenge of crafting the appearance of their wares so that these could not only survive but also flourish in a marketplace that continued to embrace Canton china. Using the popular *shan shui* designs as models, English designers executed landscape scenes in the Chinese style and placed these patterns on bowls, plates, and cups through a mechanical process called transfer printing. The most famous and oft-repeated of these patterns acquired the name "willow" (Figure 3.2).[10]

The British-designed Willow Pattern pleased American consumers for mostly the same reasons that the Chinese *shan shui* patterns did. Still, because its production was in England, Willow Ware lacked one critical attribute that had contributed heavily to the success of its Chinese competitor: the origin in a distant Far Eastern country that could confer an aura of mystery and romance onto an object. Compensating for this shortcoming, a pseudo-Chinese tale evolved about the non-Chinese Willow Pattern. This willow legend, like the pattern that inspired it, emerged as a Western attempt to capture a Chinese essence. Whether the legend was the result of an ingenious marketing scheme by a British potter or whether it arose on its own out of the popular imagination, one cannot say for certain. Regardless, the story proved enormously popular in England and soon migrated across the Atlantic to the United States.

The most important feature of this legend, and what contributed to its contagious appeal, was that any piece of porcelain bearing the Willow Pattern provided the illustrations for the narrative. In an era in which pictured storybooks were both expensive and rare, the willow legend allowed mothers of modest means to tell a story to their children at bedtime or during meals and even show illustrations. Since the legend mutated as it moved from person to person and from one culture to the next, several versions of the legend eventually came into existence. However, all tell a romantic tale of two star-crossed Chinese lovers: a mandarin's daughter, Koong-se, and his lowly bookkeeper, Chang. Koong-se and Chang loved each other, but he was not of a suitable class to marry a mandarin's daughter. The mandarin had arranged for his daughter to wed a powerful duke. To protect their forbidden relationship, Chang and Koong-se had to escape and fled from the mandarin by running across a bridge. A fisher then ferried them across the water, and they sought temporary refuge on an island. After the mandarin and the duke discover their whereabouts, the romance seems fated to end in tragedy. However, the gods from on high took pity on the pair and turned them into lovebirds that flew away.[11] The story became such an integral part of American folklore that it even found its way into verse. In fact, along with the usual nursery rhymes, mothers commonly recited a poetical version of the story to their children: "So she tells me a legend centuries old / Of a Mandarin rich in lands of gold, / Of Koong-Shee fair and Chang the good, / Who loved each other as lovers should." Like any retelling of the willow legend, this poem was clearly designed to be repeated in the presence of a piece of willow ware, because it points out the various elements in the pattern that correspond to specific moments in the story: "Here is the orange tree where they talked, / Here they are running away, / And over all at the top you see / The birds making love always."[12]

Another folk poem suggests that many Americans actually believed that both Willow Ware and the romantic willow legend came from China, not England. And as the poem states, these mistaken origins played an integral role in transforming the dining experience of many nineteenth-century Americans:

> My Willow Ware plate has a story,
> Pictorial, painted in blue,
> From the land of the tea and the tea plant
> And the little brown man with a queue.
> Whatever the food you serve, daughter,
> Romance enters into the feast,
> If you only pay heed to the legend,
> Of the old chinaware plate from the East.[13]

Since the story sounded Chinese and the design looked Chinese, the Willow Pattern and the accompanying legend had the combined effect of masking the true origin of the ceramic wares.[14] Just as Caroline Howard King looked to the East India Marine Hall to alleviate her boredom, so too did ordinary Americans use Willow Ware and this spurious Chinese legend to imbue an ordinary meal with Far Eastern splendor: "Romance enters into the feast."

Marketing Tea

One can best understand the influence of ceramics—both *shan shui* and willow—by imagining that England, Canton, and the eastern United States form three points of a triangle. The idyllic vision of China conveyed by the *shan shui* patterns first traveled to England, where it was slightly modified for the inexpensive and mass-produced Willow Ware. That Willow Ware was then exported to the United States in large quantities, where it inspired the popular imagination and spurred a greater demand for Chinese goods other than ceramics that could only be purchased in Canton.

The tea trade in particular benefited from this triangular movement of goods and images. For along with the ceramic cups themselves, America's tea-drinking habit became suffused with an exotic romance, thanks largely to the shrewd marketing of tea merchants. Aware that China occupied a special place in the American imagination, tea merchants sought to increase sales of their product by portraying the daily tea-drinking ritual as a delightfully exotic Chinese experience. To achieve this end, the merchants used advertising to disseminate a carefully constructed image of China designed to accelerate sales. In newspapers, merchants purchased print ornaments; though simplistic and crude, these images attracted attention on a page dominated by small print (Figure 3.2). The advent of lithography at mid-century meant that merchants could create trade cards (Figure 3.3) and advertising posters (Figure 3.4) to further cement the link between tea and China. Often, the merchants did not generate their own images so much as they adapted watercolors by Canton-based Chinese painters (Figure 3.5). Lastly, tea retailers in America's eastern cities designed elaborate façades and interiors, all intended to infuse the tea-purchasing experience with colorful exoticism (Figures 3.6 & 3.7). Towards this end, the stores employed stacks of image-bearing crates (Figure 3.8) and statues of Chinese people that functioned like cigar-store Indians (Figure 3.9).

Due to these several forms of marketing, a timeless and picturesque vision of China emerged: In a sylvan setting of pagoda-topped hills and charming tea fields, silk-clad merchants sip tea and direct the armies of happy workers as the latter blithely go about their business of preparing tea for export. Instead of actual people, these workers come across more as tea elves, Cathay's colorful labor force living solely to cultivate this single crop and prepare it for export to the West. One assumes that, were the beverage to go out of style, these figures of laborers would have quickly vanished into the thin air of dispelled fantasy.

Nathan Dunn and the Chinese Museum

To this point, we have spoken exclusively about the construction of a fanciful or highly idealized China as Cathay that, while affording Americans and Europeans pleasure, provided almost no accurate information about the place or people of China. Thus, we could say that, during the early decades of the nineteenth century, the American imagination outpaced the rational mind in the race to describe China. It was not that those of a scientific mind lacked in curiosity. The interior of China stood as one of the most sought-after prizes in the exploration community. Instead, the dearth of reliable information resulted entirely from the strictly enforced Qing policy that forbid foreigners from straying beyond the confines of the foreign factories in Canton. Even the East India Company—with its army of agents, the backing of the British government, and deep monetary reserves—had tried to build a grand collection and failed.[15]

Remarkably, the Philadelphia merchant Nathan Dunn found a way to assemble the largest Chinese collection in the world, in spite of Qing restrictions. Though this achievement might be seen as a sort of victory of scientific discipline over the imagination, the resulting Chinese Museum presented China in such a favorable light that, for many museum visitors, the myth of Cathay was not dispelled. For despite the museum's scientific underpinnings, Dunn's splendid—almost magical—presentation of China's arts, customs, people, and animal life did not disabuse anyone of the preconceived belief that China was a land of wonder and enchantment. Rather, visitors felt as if the museum miraculously opened a door that had been locked tight, and granted them rare access to a forbidden land of Oriental mystery.

Nathan Dunn was born in 1782 to a farming family in New Jersey. His father died shortly after his birth, and his widowed mother moved with him to Philadelphia in 1802. In 1805, Dunn and a partner launched their own business; that same year, the Quaker Monthly Meeting of Friends received him as a member.[16] However, over the course of the next decade, Dunn slowly slid into a quagmire of debt so severe that, in 1816, the Quakers disowned him on the grounds that he was unable to pay his debts. Nathan Dunn had hit rock bottom by the age of 34.

Looking for both a fresh start and a way to pay off creditors, Dunn sailed to Canton in 1818 to enter the China trade.[17] His decision was far from uncommon, as many men mired in financial difficulty resorted to this risky yet potentially lucrative trade.[18] In a couple of respects, however, Dunn was different from the average China trader. First, few American traders at that time openly objected to the opium trade, and some confessed that they had derived one-half their income from it.[19] Nathan Dunn, however, was fervently against it and led the opposition to it in Canton.[20] Second, since it was possible to accumulate wealth in a short amount of time, merchants customarily entered the trade, made a quick fortune, and exited after two or three years.[21] Dunn, however, remained overseas for twelve years, staying away from home long after he had amassed enough money to pay off his debts, restore his good name, and live out his years in luxury.

As for the precise nature of Dunn's business, advertisements that he placed in Philadelphia newspapers indicate that his ships carried mostly the usual Chinese commodities: crates of tea, nankeens (a durable yellow cloth), and silken goods.[22] However, while the American side of the trade was fairly standard, on the Chinese side Dunn was able to make one key innovation that would eventually place him on a trajectory towards fabulous wealth. From the perspective of Europe and the United States, the problem with the China trade had always been that, while Western consumers demonstrated a strong demand for Chinese goods, the Chinese showed only tepid interest in Western products. Hoping to bring balance to the trade, merchants were always hunting for goods that appealed to Chinese tastes. During his first sojourn in Canton, Dunn identified a niche in the Chinese market that traders had yet to exploit. "I soon found when in Canton that there was an opening for the introduction of the different kinds of British goods," Dunn recalled, "and that by procuring them [...] better calculated for the Chinese wants, that a fair profit could be realized." In other words, if suppliers in England could tailor their manufactures and dry goods specifically to suit the Chinese taste, the Chinese would respond by increasing their demand. Dunn's next move was to sail for England, where he lined up several British manufacturers, including James Brown & Company of Leeds, who commenced filling his unique order.[23]

Writing to his brother and sister from Liverpool in November of 1821, Dunn informed them that he was heading back to China soon and that "I may be detained a little in Canton."[24] Unbeknown to him, that "little" stay in Canton beginning in May 1822 would swell to over eight years. In essence, Nathan Dunn was establishing what amounted to a triangular trade. American ships would convey American goods to England, where the cargoes would be promptly sold, the profits going towards the purchase of these specialized English manufactures, altered so as to appeal to Chinese consumers. The ships would then continue on to Canton, where Dunn had permanently stationed himself. When the ships docked in Canton, Dunn would sell these cargoes of British goods and then proceed to load their compartments with Chinese goods meant for the American market.[25] If the aforementioned triangle trade in Willow Ware worked mostly to the benefit of England as the producer of goods and trafficker in imagery, this second triangle was clearly designed to make an American firm very prosperous.

Dunn's uninterrupted residence in Canton was a key component of this strategy. From this post, he could watch the fluctuations of the Chinese market and, when prices dropped, buy up Chinese goods and warehouse them until his ships arrived. "I was to be found at my post through all the seasons," he wrote. "[T]his I thought I ought to do, both to take advantage of the market in selling the goods, and in purchasing silks, teas, &c., when no other persons were in the market."[26] The permanent residence also allowed him to forge alliances with the Hong merchants, a group of about a dozen men who owned the exclusive privilege of brokering the entire Western European and American commerce of the Chinese Empire. Though they paid Peking dearly for this right, they were often able to turn it into astounding profits.[27]

Dunn established especially strong ties with two Hong merchants, the more prominent of whom was Howqua. In a business rife with deception and bribery, Houqua secured the lion's share of the trade by maintaining a lofty reputation among foreigners as the most trustworthy and reliable of all the Hong merchants.[28] But Houqua's probity came at a cost, as he charged foreigners dearly for the right to trade through him. By 1834, Houqua had amassed such a vast fortune that his net worth was estimated at US$52 million—making him perhaps the wealthiest commoner alive in the world.[29] With seemingly limitless wealth and connections, Houqua was in a position to provide Dunn with invaluable assistance both in commerce and in his later attempt to collect artifacts.

Dunn also enjoyed strong relations with the lesser-known Hong merchant Tingqua, who handled Dunn's ships when they entered the harbor. Though Tingqua was relatively new to his position when Dunn arrived in China, on two occasions he acted to save Dunn's career. The more dramatic of these incidents took place in 1822, when a massive fire destroyed much of Canton. Late one evening in early November, a fire broke out in the Chinese city, just a short distance from the foreign factories. As gusty winds blew through the rows of houses, the fire spread easily and soon rose to the level of a full-scale conflagration. Soon pandemonium broke out as foreign and Chinese merchants made frantic attempts to transport their storehouses of goods onto ships anchored in the harbor. Adding to the mayhem, a torrential current of Cantonese citizens streamed out of the burning city to the water's edge, holding their belongings. Amid the hysteria, Nathan Dunn was unable to find any Chinese laborers willing to move the contents of his warehouse—holdings valued at the substantial sum of $150,000—to a safe location. And so as the fire began to encroach upon the foreign factories, Dunn stood helplessly in the street watching the brilliant red glow in the night sky. For the second time in his life, he faced the specter of utter financial ruin.

As the flames began to lick against the sides of structures close to Dunn's warehouse, Tingqua recognized his friend's dire situation and came to his aid by quickly dispatching about eighty of his own men along with a fleet of small boats. To Dunn's amazement, the men proceeded to load crate after crate of Dunn's goods onto the boats, rendering them safe from the fire. Remarkably, while Tingqua's men were busy saving Dunn's livelihood, the Hong merchant's own factory was severely damaged in the blaze. Yet Tingqua conducted business on a scale that dwarfed that of Nathan Dunn. And he knew that, whereas his deep monetary reserves allowed him to absorb the occasional pecuniary setback, the fire would have proved devastating for his friend. Tingqua had simply selected the only course that would permit both men to continue to seek prosperity. "All this is now gone by," Dunn wrote a decade later, "and I shall ever remember with gratitude to him."[30]

Tingqua's timely decision to send laborers over to Dunn's warehouse prevented Dunn from sustaining a huge financial loss that would have destroyed his nascent trading enterprise and sent him spiraling back into debt. And on another occasion, Tingqua risked his own economic future in order to protect Dunn from a colossal enemy intent upon sabotaging his trade. In fact, it was Dunn's triangular trading scheme that placed Tingqua's business in a precarious position. Though clearly an impressive display of Yankee ingenuity, Dunn's scheme depended heavily upon forays into England. Since Dunn was somewhat audaciously treading on the territory of the British East India Company, his activity soon drew the attention and provoked the ire of the economic colossus. "But here the East India Company's jealousy was awake," Dunn later wrote, as "they were not to be interfered with by an American coming to China direct from England with British Goods." Since Tingqua had been securing Dunn's ships, the East India Company employed a strategy of incentives followed by threats, to convince the Hong merchant to sever ties with the meddlesome American.

The company first called Tingqua into its offices to make him an offer. "Now you are a new house just beginning business," a company representative stated, and "we will aid you if you comply with our wishes." The company promised to channel $200,000 of its annual business to Tingqua if he would agree to cease handling "Mr. Dunn's ship," for "she has our kind of goods."

After Tingqua walked out of the office, refusing to make any kind of agreement, the company called on him later that day to issue an ultimatum: "If you secure this ship we will withdraw our business from you." Even in the face of such pressure, Tingqua remained obstinate: "I will secure Mr. Dunn's ship, and you may if you please take away your business." Thus, Tingqua remained loyal to Dunn despite the great risk to his own commercial enterprise, and Dunn never forgot his friend's sacrifice. He knew that, had it not been for this friendship, he would not have amassed the fortune that made his Chinese collection possible.[31]

An Idea Germinates

Along with trade, a second factor contributed to Dunn's prolonged term in Canton: his ever-expanding Chinese collection. Though the collection would grow to colossal proportions, the original plan was quite modest, it entailing only the formation of "a cabinet sufficient to fill a small apartment" meant both "for his own pleasure and that of his friends." So in the early stages, he was gathering items "not with any view to its general publicity." However, what began as a mere hobby quickly gathered momentum as Dunn proved unable to quench his ardor for collecting. As the Chinese collection grew, his "passion for accumulation" grew at a commensurate rate such that "every year his plan expanded wider and wider."[32]

Along with Dunn's obsessive nature, his collecting methodology helped produce a collection of mammoth size. Anyone looking to capture the essence of a culture through the collection of artifacts must make choices as to what to include and what to omit. To guide the decision-making, the conventional collector adopts a methodology through which he conveys a personal sense of what is important. For example, the naturalist hunts for specimens of plant and animal life; the ethnologist searches for artifacts that can explicate human cultures; and the art connoisseur seeks the finest works of painters and sculptors. Dunn, however, resisted the imposition of any such limits on the scope of his collecting. According to Benjamin Silliman, a professor of chemistry and natural history at Yale who would later visit and publish an article on the Chinese Museum, Dunn eventually "conceived the idea of transporting to his native shores *everything* that was characteristic or rare [...] no matter how costly that might be."[33] Instead of specializing in one particular area, the collection would encompass all things Chinese, taken from both the human and the natural realms.

This all-inclusive methodology, far from making Dunn an anomaly in his own time, was in fact consistent with the ideas that he frequently confronted in his young adulthood years in Philadelphia. In the first two decades of the nineteenth century, Philadelphia stood as the intellectual capital of America. Thanks to the city's people and institutions, Dunn's formative years were awash in the spirit of the Enlightenment. It was a period dominated by the ideas of the great Swedish botanist Linnaeus, whose system of classification imposed coherence and order on the confusion of the natural world. Having studied this work, amateur naturalists scoured the New World for plant and animal specimens that could be given a Latin name and assigned their proper place in the Great Chain of Being.[34] In Philadelphia, one could find Charles Willson Peale, who aspired to stuff, mount, and display in his museum all the links of the Great Chain, from the lowest plant forms to the highest form of *Homo sapiens*. Since no one epitomized the latter more than Benjamin Franklin, Peale hoped to apply his skills as a taxidermist to the great founding father, who apparently would have agreed to the arrangement. Franklin, however, died two years prior to the formation of the museum.[35] Also in Philadelphia, John Bartram tended an elaborate botanical garden composed of as many types of plants as he or anyone could find; it was a microcosm of North American botany. Alexander Wilson, a precursor to John James Audubon, sought to create a pictorial record of all the birds of North America. And George Catlin, who was a near contemporary of Nathan Dunn and who received his artistic training in Philadelphia, hoped to do the same for some Native American tribes.[36] In sum, these naturalists, ethnographers, museum proprietors, and painters all composed epic works suffused with the belief that humankind could catalogue the entire universe—or at least some corner of it.

Unfortunately for any collector in China, success depended upon more than just deep pockets and a desire to shop. The first step to collection was to circumvent the Qing edict that confined foreigners to the foreign factories. Like all foreign traders, Dunn lived, ate, slept, and conducted business in a space measuring just 400 yards in length and 300 in width—about one twenty-fifth of a square mile.[37] When Dunn's curious niece wrote to him asking for a description of China, Dunn could not oblige her request, stating that "the limits prescribed to foreigners are through the jealousies of the officers of the Government, very much confined."[38] The stringent nature of these conditions notwithstanding, Dunn enjoyed one advantage that other aspirants lacked: The Chinese supported his endeavor. Much of their support flowed out of his fervent opposition to the opium trade. Brantz Mayer, who met Dunn during a trip to Canton in 1827, observed the positive effect of Dunn's stance in the Chinese community. "Instead of dealing in OPIUM... and thus aiding (as too many Americans have done) in fixing on the Chinese all the curses which flow from the habitual use of that intoxicating drug," Mayer wrote, Dunn received "presents [...] of valuable curiosities [...] *from the natives*" who sought to show their "thankfulness for the virtue which induced him to abstain from assisting in the ruin of thousands of their countrymen."[39] Dunn, in short, cared about the health and well-being of the Chinese people, who reciprocated with gifts.

Dunn's stance on the pernicious drug eventually caught the attention not only of local officials but also of the Chinese government in Peking, and finally of the emperor himself.[40] As a result, Dunn was able to ingratiate himself with China's elite. According to Silliman, Dunn frequently entertained "the most distinguished officers of the Government" at his "house and table." After winning their "esteem and confidence," he "soon discovered that it was in his power to obtain favors not usually granted to strangers." Of course, the two Hong merchants, Tingqua and Houqua, who were already in Dunn's camp, also possessed the power and connections necessary to provide him with invaluable assistance.[41]

These powerful Chinese men transformed a seemingly impossible objective into a reality by providing Dunn with the means to circumnavigate the Qing restrictions on foreigners. In addition to presenting him with rare and valuable objects, they helped him hire Chinese agents who were willing to travel to other regions purely for collection purposes.[42] A guidebook to Philadelphia would later highlight this penetration of China's vast interior as Dunn's greatest triumph: "When it is considered, that most of the CURIOSITIES of the Chinese Empire, are entirely beyond the reach [...] the intelligent public will be able to appreciate the value" of the collection.[43] Likewise, the *Philadelphia Saturday Courier* credited Dunn's "Chinese friends and agents" for acquiring the artifacts "brought from the interior of China, where foreigners rarely if ever penetrate."[44]

Of course, to signify a total knowledge of China, one could not neglect the natural world. To bulk up this section of the collection, Dunn turned to another friend, William Wood of Philadelphia. Though a dismal failure as a merchant, the multitalented Wood possessed impressive training as a naturalist. Like all curious foreigners in Canton, he chaffed at the restrictions of the government. "The empire abounds with subjects of the greatest interest to naturalists," Wood wrote, "and it is to be regretted that the obstacles opposed to research by the Chinese government, render our knowledge of the subject so limited and imperfect." Making the best of the situation, Wood employed a scheme that depended heavily on the Chinese to supply specimens of natural history. Through "industry, money, flattery," "kindness," and "subterfuge," he was able to convince a team of Chinese agents to undertake fieldwork. Though these men were willing, Wood feared their work would not meet his standards. Convinced of the virtues of the Linnaean system, Wood judged the field of natural history in China to be both flawed and lacking in scientific rigor: The Chinese "possess no systematic arrangement of animated beings, and commit the most glaring errors in classification." To make sure that the agents followed correct procedures, Wood devoted considerable time and energy to training them in the proper handling of the specimens. After acquiring these skills, they fanned out, traveling "by land and water," in search of birds, fish, reptiles, insects, shells, animals, plants, and rocks. Upon returning to Canton, many were able to present "new and interesting animals" to a pleased William Wood, who summarily added them to Dunn's collection.[45]

The Chinese Museum in Philadelphia

In 1831, Dunn made preparations to depart Canton for good. That he was apprehensive about his return to the United States was evident in the following letter to a friend: "I am about [to return] to Philadelphia," he wrote, "so changed in appearance that none will remember me, and certainly I shall know but a few when I land."[46] Though heavily in debt when he had left Philadelphia twelve years earlier, Dunn was returning home one of the city's wealthier citizens.[47] He even invited all his creditors to a sumptuous banquet and placed under each plate a check for the amount of his debt with interest paid in full.[48]

But after only one year back home, Dunn became so nostalgic for China that he commissioned an architect to design for him a Chinese mansion outside the city. But even this did not content him, for he did not yearn for the detached life of the eccentric millionaire. On the contrary, he wanted to integrate himself into American life and sought civic responsibility commensurate with his newly acquired wealth and stature. For this reason, he joined the prestigious American Philosophical Society and the Academy of Natural Sciences. Most importantly, in 1836, the Philadelphia Museum Company, formerly known as the museum of Charles Willson Peale, appointed Dunn to its board of directors. In 1786, Peale had founded a museum on what he called the principle of "rational entertainment." When his son Rubens assumed managerial responsibility after 1810, competition from various other attractions such as panoramas, circuses, and theatrical troops forced the son to compromise some of the father's ideals in order to ensure the museum's survival. When Rubens Peale quietly removed the museum's more prosaic exhibits and replaced them with freakish curiosities, a museum founded upon "rationale entertainment" was beginning to veer away from the "rational" and toward pure "entertainment."[49]

In the 1830s, the museum was undergoing financial hard times as well. Escol Sellers, Charles Willson Peale's grandson, believed it could benefit from the invigorating influence of an entirely novel exhibit. Sellers conceived of a revamped Philadelphia Museum, to be housed in a brand new building, in which the Chinese collection of Nathan Dunn and Peale's exhibits would coexist. Dunn agreed to the proposition and immediately backed the project with the necessary capital. When construction of the new building was complete, Peale's exhibits moved into the upper floor, and on the spacious lower floor Dunn began to install his Chinese collection. The job proved to be difficult because Dunn's collection methodology had generated a collection of such enormous proportions that it exceeded the available exhibition space. Unable to display everything at once, Dunn resigned himself to the disappointing conclusion that he would have to keep many items in storage and introduce them into the exhibit on a rotating basis.[50] Dunn encountered the same problem in writing the *Descriptive Catalogue,* a booklet of 120 pages that would provide visitors with a guided tour. "A very large number [of exhibited items] have been omitted in the catalogue," he wrote, "as, if all had been introduced, it would have swelled the pamphlet to an unconventional size."[51] Despite these problems, Dunn worked at a feverish pace. "The Chinese collection requires all my time," he wrote to his sister in November of 1838. "I find without great exertions it cannot be opened by Christmas."[52]

On the evening of December 22, Dunn held a large reception for distinguished citizens of Philadelphia to introduce his exhibit, which now bore the title, "Ten Thousand Chinese Things." A group of well over 100 invited guests, composed of "artists, merchants, mechanics, editors, literati, military and naval officers, and a goodly representation from all the learned professions," sipped a beverage made by adding sugar and cream to a juice extracted from a Chinese plant. Dunn also served a variety of tea that was so rare and of such high quality that the Chinese refused to export it. Among those in attendance was E.C. Wines, a former principal in a Philadelphia school and a personal friend of Nathan Dunn. Wines described Dunn as glowing with gratification on this night as he beheld "his labours so happily terminated, and the long cherished object of his ambition crowned with so brilliant a success."[53] A journalist granted early access to the exhibit predicted that "the wonders of China" would "absorb the conversation of all, even of the busy politician and the solitary book worm." Though China had previously been a "sealed book," the museum revealed it to be "the most extraordinary nation on the earth."[54]

The next day, visitors paid twenty-five cents for admission (money that went to charity), and entered the spacious saloon that measured 163 feet in length, 70 in breadth, and 35 in height.[55] Twenty-two square pillars, each adorned with Chinese watercolor paintings, supported the ceiling. According to E.C. Wines, the initial sensory overload triggered a sense of wonder in the guests:

> Here, as if touched by the wand of an enchanter, we are compelled to pause.... The view is imposing in the highest degree. But it is so unlike anything we are accustomed to behold, that we are at a loss for descriptive epithets [...]. Brilliant, splendid, gorgeous, magnificent, superb—all these adjectives are liberally used by visitors.[56]

Guests were initially struck by the ten-foot, multicolored Chinese lanterns that hung from the ceiling, as well as the two enormous rectangular screens facing each other at each end of the hall. Each measured fifty feet in length and was divided into compartments that offered detailed depictions of Chinese flowers as well as panoramic views of landscapes, seascapes, and river scenes.[57] They also encountered three colossal gilded idols that presided majestically over the saloon, a representation of the Buddha in his past, present, and future manifestations (Figure 3.10). These were re-creations of originals that had caught Dunn's attention during a visit to a Buddhist shrine on Honam Island, across the Pearl River from the foreign factories.[58]

The senses of visitors that they had been magically transported to China was enhanced by the presence of fifty life-size clay statues representing all walks of Chinese life: mandarins, priests, mourners dressed in white, tragedians, itinerant barbers, shoemakers, smiths, shopkeepers and their customers, boat handlers, beggars, merchants, soldiers, and many others. J.S. Buckingham, a traveler from England, was impressed by how closely the statues and their settings approximated life:

> they are all actual figures, as large as life, moulded in clay, with a resemblance to life [...] greater than that of the finest wax-work figures. They are placed in the most natural and appropriate attitudes imaginable. They have all actual dresses of the exact kind worn by the several classes they represent and are surrounded by those several auxiliaries and accompaniments which belong to their respective dwellings or occupations, and have a reality about them, which comes the nearest to actual life of anything I have ever seen.[59]

The uniqueness of each statue augmented the realism of the museum. Unlike mannequins, which are only as interesting as the garments placed on them, the Chinese statues each bore the exact likeness of some actual Chinese personage. Dunn had spent three years supervising the production of these statues, employing sculptors who used a special technique to model the clay figures from the fifty "living subjects" whom Dunn had selected. And to add a final touch of realism, his sculptors embellished the statues with real human hair.[60]

The statues constituted only half of Dunn's strategy to teach visitors about Chinese life. By posing the figures, providing them with the appropriate props, and situating them before colorful backdrops, Dunn was able to create dioramas that showed the characteristic actions of the Chinese as well as the environments in which they lived and worked. In the case of the scholar and his student, viewers could observe not just their respective garments but also the deferential pose struck by the student. In another case, they could see three literati discuss intellectual matters while servants tended to their needs (Figure 3.11). And in Dunn's reproduction of a silk shop, visitors could watch the customer as he scrutinized the silk fabric while the shopkeeper made quick calculations on an abacus. In the most impressive of these dioramas, two sedan chair bearers carry a Chinese gentleman down a full-scale reproduction of a Cantonese street (Figure 3.12). Surrounded by statues, one guest felt he had traveled to China and found time mysteriously standing still: "The visitor must feel as if he were examining a country, where the breath of life and the noise of instruments had suddenly ceased, and every object animate and inanimate had been left unchanged."[61] Brantz Mayer called the combined effect of all these statues and backgrounds "a panoramic pageant of Oriental life," so eerily accurate that "we almost expect to hear them speak and see them move."[62]

The Descriptive Catalogue

Clearly, the Chinese Museum impressed visitors with the combined effect of its dioramas, paintings, screens, lanterns, and exhibit cases. But the overwhelmingly spectacular visual nature of the museum threatened to undermine its didactic mission. Indeed, there was the legitimate chance that the exhibits would overawe visitors—dazzle them without teaching them anything. For this reason, Dunn seems to have feared the aimless guest, that individual who would wander about in desultory manner, constantly amazed yet never really engaging the exhibits in serious study. Such a person was easily capable of spending hours in the museum without registering any detectable increase in knowledge. What's worse, instead of discarding the Willow Ware vision of China, this person might simply use the exhibits to inject color and detail into the bare blue and white outlines. In short, a visitor might continue to conflate China with Cathay even after visiting the museum.

Though many visitors doubtlessly did treat their tour of the museum as an excursion to Cathay, Dunn's purpose in writing and publishing the *Descriptive Catalogue* was to steer as many guests as he could towards knowledge acquisition. This booklet was designed to enrich the overall museum experience by covering the macro as well as the micro: It attempted to explain Chinese culture as a whole while also offering background information on many of the specific items on display. In this way, the catalogue represented Dunn's attempt to assert control over a guest's visit. Acting as a museum guide, it imposed structure onto the experience by directing the visitor's movement through the entire exhibit: "The visitor is requested to commence with the screen at the entrance, and then, turning to the left, to take the cases in the order in which they are numbered." Labeling cases with Roman numerals and individual items with Arabic numerals, Dunn established a specific sequence that visitors were encouraged to follow. And as they moved through the exhibits, they could glance down at the catalogue to gather quick information about any object they found striking:

> Case XIII...214. Splendid cameo, presented to Mr. Dunn by Houqua, the Hong merchant. This cameo is of extraordinary size. It represents an extended landscape, including earth and sky, and embracing various rural scenes.

And so that Chinese characters would not mystify visitors, the catalogue offered translations of anything in Chinese, such as the Chinese proverbs written vertically on the numerous wall hangings that adorned the salon. By equipping visitors with readily accessible information, Dunn hoped to forestall the usual vacuous utterances that could plague any exhibition of a foreign culture—that the objects were merely "strange," "bizarre," and "curious."

In its organizational structure, the catalogue followed the form of other works of Enlightenment science. Much like Thomas Jefferson's *Notes on the State of Virginia*, perhaps the quintessential document of the American Enlightenment that describes a region, the catalogue comprehended its subject by breaking it down into categories: government, the arts (literature, theater, music), religion (Daoism, Buddhism, and elements of Confucianism), education, natural history, military ("the army is little better than a rabble rout, mere men of straw"), population, women (it explains the practice of foot binding), marriage (a man could divorce a woman for her garrulity), funerals, costumes, festivals, sports and pastimes, vocations, diet, agriculture, manufactures, inventions (most notably, gunpowder, magnetic needles, and a printing press), transportation, architecture (the museum included models of dwellings, pagodas, bridges, and the Great Wall), trade, justice and the penal system (including *lingchy,* the punishment for treason, that involved cutting the offender into ten thousand pieces). An impressed Brantz Mayer couched Dunn's achievement in the terms of Enlightenment science: "*He has enclosed a whole people in glass cases,* and classified them."[63]

Excepting a few examples, Dunn used the catalogue to cast China in a positive light. Being a citizen of a republic that measured its age in mere decades, Dunn hoped to ascertain the secrets of civilization whose history spanned several millennia. After tapping the knowledge of his Chinese friends, Dunn was able to attribute China's longevity to two effective strategies. First, since "ambitious" men who are thwarted in their aspirations "generally overturn governments," the Chinese designed their civil service examination system to encourage these men to expend their energies constructively through official channels. No man in China "inherits office," regardless of his bloodline; instead, the examination system alone places men in positions of power and does so on the basis of merit only. In this way, the talented and ambitious assist in the governing of China, instead of "the dreadful alternative of revolutionizing the country."

Second, Dunn pointed to a complex set of duties and responsibilities that defined an individual's relationship with the family, with society, and with the government. This "doctrine of responsibility," as Dunn called Confucianism, enjoyed universal acceptance because it was effectively inculcated at an early age: "The sentiments held to be appropriate to man in society, are imbibed with the milk of infancy, and iterated and reiterated through the whole of subsequent life." In this regard, the Chinese "set us an example worthy of imitation" because whereas we speak only of "our rights," the Chinese focus on "*our duty*." Here, Dunn appears to show concern for a potential problem in American society that Alexis de Tocqueville had detected in 1830; that is, the need for a counterweight to offset rampant individualism.[64] Unlike the United States, China could count on state-sanctioned Confucianism to hold the destructive selfish impulses of individuals in check. The early and constant education on "personal and political duties" functioned as a kind of social glue, Dunn wrote, lending cohesion to the nation. The result was "a country enjoying [...] a perpetuity of national existence unequalled in the world's history."[65]

The catalogue also contains Dunn's appreciation of Chinese industry. "Whoever attentively examines the immense collection of Chinese curiosities," Dunn claimed, "will need no further proof of the ingenuity of the Chinese in arts and manufactures" and in the "several branches of labour, both agricultural and mechanical." As the United States was then in an early stage of industrialization, Dunn could appreciate the "various contrivances," many being "simple, ingenious, and efficient," through which the Chinese were able to "force nature to become their handmaid."[66] Dunn found an attentive audience in Yale's Benjamin Silliman, who saw the exhibits of "rakes, hoes, axes, shovels" and other implements to be particularly eye-opening. Whereas he had been taught to believe that an American tool offered the only way to accomplish a given task, the museum showed him that completely different tools of Chinese invention could accomplish the same jobs. A given "operation," he wrote, "is equally well executed by another of totally different figure." In addition, Silliman noted a "thousand things" that proved that many of our "common usages" were derived from devices in China, a country that "we are accustomed to believe" is "centuries behind us." Among these, he found especially amusing a Chinese mousetrap, of a design patented in America, "that has been used in China for ages." In short, the exhibit proved to him that his preconceptions regarding the innovation of the Chinese were wrong.[67]

In favorably describing Chinese civilization as accomplished, durable, complex, and even innovative, Dunn was merely conveying his own assessment to readers of the *Descriptive Catalogue*. Yet he also had a rhetorical strategy, as readers discovered when they met with his views on the opium trade at the end of booklet. For if a reader had agreed with Dunn's overall appraisal of the Chinese up until this point, outrage was the only suitable reaction to the opium trade. It was true, Dunn conceded, that through the sale of opium, the British had accomplished their objective in that a trade imbalance previously favoring China had reversed course (Dunn estimated that $20 million flowed annually out of China and into the English economy). But what were the moral ramifications of this apparently effective economic strategy? "Yet if the sum were ten times as great as it is," Dunn wrote, "it could not affect the question in its moral bearings. Opium is a poison, destructive alike of the health and morals of those who use it habitually, and, therefore, the traffic in it [...] is nothing less than making merchandise of the bodies and souls of men." In short, as silver bullion moved from the East to the West, filling English treasuries with wealth, morality flowed in the opposite direction, leaving England morally bankrupt.

Though much of the culpability deservedly rested on English shoulders, Dunn was quite familiar with the trading practices of his own compatriots after living for eight uninterrupted years with them in the foreign factories. "But it is not England alone that is to blame in this matter," he wrote "[M]ost of our own merchants in Canton are guilty in the same way, and to an equal extent." In mentioning American involvement, Dunn hoped that he could raise the ire of ordinary citizens. And to further augment their outrage, he explained the relationship between opium and the Protestant missions. As has been stated, Dunn was raised a Quaker; Quakers usually did not proselytize and certainly did not have any presence in China. Yet Dunn knew that America was then in the throes of a massive evangelical movement (now called the Second Great Awakening) and that the majority of the visitors to his museum were Protestants who supported the foreign missions. Acutely aware of this audience, Dunn explained exactly why missionaries were encountering so much resistance in China. The "grasping avarice" of opium traders, he wrote, undermines the moral and spiritual message of the missionaries and "sets at naught every Christian obligation before the very eyes of the people whom it sought to convert!" The Chinese would never choose to convert to Christianity as long as the most visible emissaries from a Christian nation, the merchants, continued to blight their society.[68] In this way, the generally uplifting *Descriptive Catalogue* ended on an ominous note.

Responses to the Exhibit

Did Dunn succeed in his didactic mission? If Brantz Mayer's shifting perceptions of the museum followed a sequence shared by others, then he did. Initially, Mayer expressed his impressions of the museum by employing a vocabulary of magic and fantasy: "The spectator seems placed in a world of enchantment—the scene is so unreal and fairylike." Yet though bewitched at first, he eventually shook off the trance and proceeded to use the exhibits to learn about China: "Never have I derived more instruction in the brief space of a few hours—never have I experienced more pleasure in the pursuit of knowledge—never has my imagination been more excited—never my mind more interested." Though initially entranced by the idea of escaping to a "world of enchantment" in the same manner as Caroline Howard King, Mayer eventually used the museum for its intended purpose: "the pursuit of knowledge."[69]

Mayer also went so far as to state that "a man may learn more of China... in a single visit to Mr. Dunn's Collection, then could be acquired in a month's reading, or even in a voyage to Canton."[70] A guidebook for Philadelphia echoed this sentiment, declaring "every one who takes pleasure in accurate knowledge, will here find, in a few hours, that which cannot be procured, from reading, views from engravings, or even an actual visit to China."[71] Similarly, J.S. Buckingham stated that one could learn more about China in the museum than by "a month's hard reading on the subject."[72] And in what was clearly a common refrain, Joseph Sturge, another traveler from England, agreed that "by spending a few hours in his museum, with the aid of the descriptive catalogue, one may learn more of the Chinese than by laborious perusal of all the works upon them that have ever been written."[73]

Indeed, Dunn's all-inclusive collection methodology had yielded an exhibit composed of realistic statues positioned in dioramas, a plethora of paintings, and a prodigious number of authentic Chinese objects. In the minds of visitors, all of these combined to simulate an actual tour of China, and they voiced the near unanimous opinion that a feeling of virtual travel made the museum experience remarkable. We will "long remember our last Saturday evening's excursion to Canton," wrote a reporter for the *Public Ledger*.[74] "Mr. Dunn's collection," agreed the *Saturday Courier*, "at once transports us to China."[75] Another journalist expressed awe of a quasi-religious nature at the illusion of travel: "You can hardly realize that you have not been transported by some superhuman power to the opposite side of the globe" because the many marvelous sights "combine to produce a most bewildering effect upon the startled gaze of the beholder as he enters, and it is long before he can realize that he is in the city of Penn."[76]

Brantz Mayer adopted this same theme in his description of the museum, claiming that Dunn had placed China "within the reach of the remotest inquiring inhabitant of our Union." "China re-existed in America," he wrote, "as by necromancy." Since Mayer had visited China in 1827, he felt qualified to vouch for the strong resemblance between Dunn's re-creation of China and the real place: "the verisimilitude is perfect and seems to be the prestige of magic."[77] As these references to "magic" and "necromancy" indicate, Mayer likened the experience of seeing China in the United States to the occult. For another visitor, the exhibit inspired a suspension of disbelief of the most powerful kind: "we find ourselves, as if by a whisk of Merlin's wand, or Aladdin's lamp, [...] transported to Canton, and this with such completeness of illusion that it is very difficult to believe one is anywhere else. Illusion, in fact, is no term for it. Here are realities—temples, idols, shops, artisans."[78]

From these responses, we can draw at least one conclusion. Though China had now been systematically explained and exhibited for the first time on American soil, the country had, in the process, forfeited little of Cathay's magic or charm in the minds of Americans. But change was in the offing.

Conclusion

When the American missionary Samuel Wells Williams returned to the United States in 1845 for his furlough, he noticed a change in the air. When Williams had first departed for China in 1833, he had left a country that was still enchanted by China.[79] Upon returning home, he was astonished to observe a precipitous decline in the public's opinion. A people who had been the object of admiration had, in the interim, become the target of cruel ridicule. China was now "the object of a laugh or the subject of a pun." In particular, Williams was bothered by a derogatory poem that, to his annoyance, people seemed fond of repeating in his presence:

> Mandarins with yellow buttons, handing you conserves of snails;
> Smart young men about Canton in Nankeen tights and peacocks' tails.
> With many rare and dreadful dainties, kitten cutlets, puppy pies;
> Birds nest soup which (so convenient!) every bush around supplies.[80]

The demeaning verses, Williams believed, epitomized this disturbing new attitude towards China. Americans now laughed at the Chinese for being comically foppish and adhering to a diet that was bizarre and grotesque. Upset by the change, Williams decided "to correct or enlarge the views" of the American populace and "to divest the Chinese people and civilization of that peculiar and almost undefinable impression of ridicule which is so generally given them." In 1848, he finished writing *The Middle Kingdom*, a massive two-volume work that endeavored to refurbish the image of China. In his introduction, he included the poem as a sort of challenge that he hoped his book would meet in disabusing the readers of negative impressions of China.[81]

Though Williams does not state how or when this tone of condescension first infected the public discourse on China, reaction to the Opium War certainly played a decisive role. For many Americans, China's humiliating defeat prompted them to cast the vanquished nation in a new light.[82] But since other nations had lost wars without becoming the objects of derision, why was China different? In 1842, Thomas Smyth, a Presbyterian minister in Charleston, South Carolina, explained why China suddenly elicited derisive laughter rather than warm respect. "We are very unwilling to believe that a whole people exist only to be laughed at," he wrote, "yet how is it, that the greatest nation upon earth, in point of numbers, is the only one which history exhibits in an aspect purely ludicrous?"[83]

In Smyth's view, China demonstrated an excessive affinity for highfalutin pomp, ridiculous ceremonies, and gratuitous formalities, all of which served only to provoke laughter, since they were conducted with an air of high seriousness. "Their most solemn acts of government, of legislation, of negotiation, and of war," he wrote "are comic, and, in many cases, farcical. It is impossible to read them without a smile." That the "Chinaman" proceeded with all of this "grave buffoonery" utterly "unconscious of his own absurdity" only added to the humor. In addition, Smyth faulted the Chinese for being haughty, supercilious, and self-superior in refusing to entertain the notion that the rest of the world could think or make anything of value. "In every national and individual act," Smyth observed, "they seem to say, We are the people and wisdom shall die with us." Considering themselves to be the "centre of the universe," the Chinese deigned to allow "the savage English and Americans" to leave their "howling wilderness" and "clamour at Canton for tea." This same cultural arrogance loomed behind the kowtow, a strictly enforced protocol that required foreign emissaries to fall to their knees and hands before the emperor.[84]

By themselves, this excessive pride and fondness for pageantry were not cause for ridicule. But to many, the ease with which British gunboats dispatched the Chinese Navy during the Opium War was eye-opening. The war delivered a revelation tantamount to Dorothy's as she appears before the Wizard inside the Emerald City of Oz. After the stentorian voice and pyrotechnical display of the Wizard have cowed Dorothy and her friends into prostrating themselves before his terrifying image, Toto pulls down a nearby curtain, and Dorothy finds herself staring not at an awe-inspiring power but an unprepossessing man operating a special effects mechanism. Similarly, in Smyth's view, the British victory tore down China's grandiose façade, exposing China's true military weakness for the world to see. Yet despite the overwhelming evidence of their own impotence and futility, the Chinese failed to adopt even a measure of humility and instead persisted in believing the illusion of their own power. "Every junk that puts out from the coast is to destroy the British fleet," Smyth wrote, "and when it fails, they are as confident as ever that the next will be successful."[85]

To illustrate the sudden and dramatic shift in public attitudes toward China, Smyth asked his readers to participate in a small experiment. Allow your "imagination" to "conjure up" before you "some familiar form from the Chinese Museum" of Nathan Dunn. Though the exhibits had once inspired respect for China, Smyth assured readers that, under the present circumstances, "they will find it much more difficult to keep their countenances"—that is, to hold back laughter. Americans still looked upon China as an object of fascination, but for many the majestic front had crumbled just like China's coastal forts when faced with barrages of British cannon fire.[86] In short, China was now open to a far less-limited trade. But the perception that arrogance and ineptitude had caused China's humiliating defeat dispersed forever the aura of mystery and wonder that had once enveloped the land in the American imagination.

4
Russell and Company and the Imperialism of Anglo-American Free Trade

Sibing He

During the eighteenth and nineteenth centuries, Asian-European maritime trade relations and the world political economy underwent fundamental transformations. The emerging strategy of free trade imperialism brought the age of partnership to an end, forging a new era of international trade based on unequal exchange. In their classic study on free trade imperialism, John Gallagher and Ronald Robinson observe that the most common political technique of British expansion in the mid-Victorian era was to impose a treaty of free trade and friendship on a weaker state. The "willingness to limit the use of paramount power to establishing security for trade," they note, "is the distinctive feature of the British imperialism of free trade in the nineteenth century, in contrast to the mercantilist use of power to obtain commercial supremacy and monopoly through political possession."[1] Within the context of recent scholarship on the origins of US China policy, this chapter discusses how the American merchants in Russell and Company worked with the private British traders to advocate an imperialist policy of so-called free trade in China; I then argue against the revisionist notion that the intense rivalry with Britain for the China market compelled the United States to adopt an "autonomous China policy" after the First Opium War (1839–42).

The era of "free trade" was sustained by the enormous expansion of European economic and military power. Several factors contributed to these far-reaching transformations, which included the triumph of the English East India Company (EIC) over its Dutch and French rivals, and the tremendous growth of the China trade, especially the trade in Bengali opium for Chinese tea.[2] The rapid expansion of American trade with Asia during this period accelerated these transformations. The coming of the Americans to Asia was marked by the historic voyage of the *Empress of China* to Macao in 1784, which not only initiated America's Canton trade but also marked the beginning of the age of American expansion into Asia.[3] As the maritime historian Leonard Blussé notes in his recent study of Batavia, Canton, and Nagasaki at the end of the eighteenth century, this development in American trade came at a time when Great Britain was rising in the East on the back of the opium trade and while Europe's continental powers were declining.[4] By the third quarter of the eighteenth century, the EIC had defeated its French rival and was steadily surpassing the Dutch East India Company (VOC). The Dutch were no longer the dominant European force in Asia that they had been during the seventeenth and early eighteenth centuries. The Napoleonic conquest of Holland created an opportunity for American traders to get involved in Dutch trade as US merchant ships carried cargos from Batavia in those years. Americans were even commissioned to ship Dutch cargos to Nagasaki, a route that had previously been exclusively in the hands of the Dutch. This situation allowed the Americans to develop their trade in Asia rapidly, and by the end of the eighteenth century trade with Canton had become a regular component of America's foreign commerce. By 1800, over 100 American trading ships had arrived in Canton via Macao, and in 1804, at least 74 American vessels visited Batavia.[5] American trading ships also began to call at Bangkok in 1821, and participate in the lucrative rice trade between Canton and the Spanish Philippines in the 1830s.[6]

Russell and Company was founded at a propitious moment in this development of early American trade. Its predecessor was Samuel Russell and Company, founded in 1818 by a group of merchants from Providence, Rhode Island.[7] Reorganized in 1824, this company was renamed Russell and Company and appeared in the Chinese records as 旗昌行 (Qichanghang).[8] In August 1829, Thomas T. Forbes, the resident manager of Perkins and Company in Canton, died in a typhoon, an accident that greatly affected the firm's subsequent development. Before his death, Forbes had left instructions delegating responsibility to Samuel Russell of Russell and Company for assigning the post of resident manager in case that position became vacant. Thus, in 1830, Russell and Company took over the business of Perkins and Company.[9] The firm subsequently emerged as the leading American commercial house in East Asia. Basing its operations upon family ties, the private company successfully established worldwide connections. Its interests reached beyond China to include India, the Philippines, Japan, England, and Continental Europe. From the old trade days of the early nineteenth century to the rise of multinational trading corporations in international commerce at the end of the nineteenth century, the firm occupied a dominant position in America's China Trade.[10]

Before the coming of the Americans to China in the late eighteenth century, the structure and pattern of trade between foreign traders and Chinese merchants in Canton had been strictly regulated by the Chinese government in an effort to contain Westerners within the Canton System. Under the regulations, foreigners were confined to their factory precincts and were not permitted to remain in Canton after the trading season. Foreign merchants were compelled to deal exclusively with the Cohong, a loose association of Chinese merchants licensed by the imperial government.[11] Before the mid-1820s, this carefully designed and managed system kept the Canton Trade balanced in China's favor, and Chinese sovereignty remained intact until the First Opium War. The Hong merchants enjoyed a reputation for honesty among their foreign patrons. "[A]s a body of merchants," William Hunter of Russell and Company asserted, "we found them honourable and reliable in all their dealings, faithful to their contracts, and large-minded." John Forbes, another Russell and Company partner, agreed: "I haven't seen such noble and fair business in any other countries."[12] By and large, American traders fitted comfortably into this special Canton System, although there were occasional conflicts.

The rationale for free trade in the nineteenth century developed during this dramatic expansion of the Asia trade. In the late 1820s and early 1830s, Manchester manufacturers and private British merchants persistently lobbied their government to end the monopoly of the China Trade by the EIC and to get rid of the restrictive Canton System imposed by the Qing government. The American China traders generally sided in principle with the private British traders on the question of free trade. Their views were reflected in the *Canton Register* and the *Chinese Courier,* edited by William W. Wood, an expatriate Philadelphian closely associated with Russell and Company.[13]

Wood was the son of the celebrated Philadelphia-based actors William Burke Wood and Juliana Wood. He arrived in Canton in 1825 and two years later established with a group of Canton traders the *Canton Register*, one of the first English-language newspapers published on the China coast. As editor of the press, he wrote most of the articles that appeared in the newspaper owned by British traders James Matheson and Alexander Matheson. In the second issue of the *Canton Register*, Wood began to criticize the EIC's censorial policies.[14] He also attacked the "despotic and corrupt" manner in which the Chinese conducted their relations with foreigners under the unequal Canton System, and expressed his strong opposition to the notion that Westerners in China should submit themselves to the "impositions" of the Chinese authorities.[15] The resident English community dominated by the powerful EIC would not tolerate these attacks on Britain's trade policy, and Wood was forced to leave the press after editing the sixth issue of the newspaper. When he later returned to Philadelphia, he continued his attack on the EIC's tyrannical administrative policy in Canton in his book entitled *Sketches of China* (1830).[16] Meanwhile in Britain, the free-trade lobby in Parliament, representing its constituents in the new industrial towns, successfully fought for the 1834 termination of the EIC's monopoly on the China Trade.[17] In Canton, both the British and American merchants were eager to capitalize on any relaxation of the restrictive trading system.

Wood returned to Canton in February 1831 on the American ship *Fanny*.[18] Soon after his arrival, he was employed by Russell and Company as the secretary to William Low, a partner in the firm. In this position he frequently visited Macao, where he met and fell in love with his boss's niece, Harriett Low.[19] In July, he left the company to launch his second newspaper, the *Chinese Courier and Canton Gazette*. In the first issue, published on July 28, 1831, he speculated on his audience, reasoning that, although there were only fifty-nine British and nineteen Americans in the resident foreign community, "some medium is necessary for the dissemination of those opinions which it is the policy of our contemporary to avoid [...]. Prudence and temperate discussion have been too often considered incompatible with a free Press." In an essay titled "Free Trade to China," Wood stated that the Chinese had no intention of expanding foreign trade in Canton. Instead, they would impose additional restrictions on foreign traders. "Treaties for the protection of the Foreign Trade," he predicted, "are to be dictated to the 'Son of Heaven' at the point of a bayonet [...]."[20] In another article, he wrote, "the Chinese must be taught by force, efficient and well-directed compulsion, to respect the rights of those they have so long trampled on with impunity."[21] Another anonymous writer asserted that the Canton System had to be abolished before free trade could prosper.[22] Wood echoed these sentiments: "Other ports in the Empire must be opened to foreign shipping," any tariffs must be arranged on more equitable terms, and the Cohong administration must be abolished.[23] He predicted that war between China and Britain would end with Britain's victory and would enable England to dictate terms that would establish free trade with China and result in great prosperity.[24]

In 1834, the EIC lost the monopoly on the British China Trade from which it had benefited since 1784. The British crown appointed a superintendent of trade to take over the administrative powers of the company's Canton Committee, which was responsible for taking care of British trade and for managing British merchants at the port.[25] Two British firms, Jardine, Matheson & Co. and Dent, Whiteman & Co., collaborated with Russell and Company to form a sort of coalition that virtually inherited the financial and commercial responsibilities of the EIC. This change made it easier for both private British traders and Americans to expand the drug trade in India. Russell and Company closely cooperated with the Scottish firm of Jardine, Matheson & Co., the largest opium dealer in China, and looked beyond Canton to cultivate the drug markets, extending its investments in the opium traffic to the north. The company's clipper *Rose* actively participated in selling opium on the northeastern coast of China during the mid-1830s.[26] Under Robert B. Forbes's energetic direction, before the outbreak of the First Opium War, Russell and Company had grown to be the third largest smuggler of Indian opium among the Western firms.[27]

However, the end of the EIC monopoly in 1834 did not bring about the desired benefits, and Manchester capitalists and British free traders continued to pressure the British government to open up the China market. The correspondence of Russell and Company's partner Robert B. Forbes makes it abundantly clear that he embraced the British view: The Chinese, like other "civilized" peoples, must join the community of nations; if the British had to intimidate the Chinese to bring this about, Forbes, like most other American traders, favored that course. On the eve of the Opium War, as Western traders in Canton were surrounded by Chinese troops, Forbes wrote to his wife in Boston, "I hope the day is not far distant when they will be drubbed into the list of civilized nations & were it not for you I would volunteer under *any flag* to help do it." At another point Forbes wrote to his wife that if he were in the place of the chief superintendent of British trade, Captain Charles Elliot, then he would not surrender a chest of opium to Imperial Commissioner Lin Zexu until the Western traders "should be guaranteed liberty."[28]

The pursuit of profit was the overwhelming motive for American interest in China during that period. Like the British, American merchants going to China were interested neither in saving souls nor in national aggrandizement. The China traders were merely pragmatic entrepreneurs; the partners of Samuel Russell and Company declared: "To make money is our first object."[29] Robert B. Forbes expressed it in a more straightforward manner: "I did not come here for my health, neither to effect a reform, moral or political, but to get the needful where-with-all to be useful and happy at home."[30] In order to pursue economic goals, the American China traders led by partners in Russell and Company consistently began to urge their government to adopt aggressive policies toward China.

As the largest American firm in East Asia, Russell and Company did not merely conduct business but also sought to orchestrate US foreign policy toward China. Because of its financial position, the Russell representatives exercised tacit leadership within the American communities in China. On May 25, 1839, as the situation in Canton deteriorated and war appeared inevitable, Robert Forbes and seven other Russell men sent a memorandum to the US Congress, petitioning their government not to stand idly by while Britain prepared to use force to secure what they feared might be exclusive commercial privileges and rights. The Russell men appealed that "The United States should take immediate measures" to "act in concert with the Governments of Great Britain, France, and Holland, or either of them, in their endeavors to establish commercial relations with this empire." Stressing their need for protection, they implored Congress to seek the appointment of a minister to the court of Beijing, and the deployment of "a sufficient naval force" to safeguard American lives and property in China. In addition, they recommended that the United States negotiate a commercial treaty with China. Through military and diplomatic coercion, they hoped that the United States would gain commercial as well as judicial privileges in China, including: a concession for foreign envoys to reside in Beijing; "a fixed tariff of duties on articles"; freedom to trade at ports other than Canton; "compensation for the losses caused by the stoppage of the whole legal trade"; and guarantees that the punishment for crimes committed by foreigners upon the Chinese "shall not be greater than is applicable to the like offence by the laws of the United States or England."[31]

On January 9, 1840, American traders in Canton sent to Congress another memorandum urging similar action. Three months later, the China traders in

Boston and Salem also pressured the government to send a fleet to Chinese waters in order to protect American interests. However, in their statement to Congress of April 9, 1840, they warned against any hasty action that might antagonize China and ruin the trade. P.W. Snow, the American consul in Canton, concurred with the merchants' requests. His reports were printed by Congress.[32]

In response to these petitions, Congress passed resolutions in January 1840 and December 1840 that sought information from the executive branch about the status of American merchants and commerce in China. Under the pressures of merchants both in the Canton-Macao area and Boston, President John Tyler ordered Commodore Lawrence Kearny, the commander of the US East India Squadron, to sail to China. Commanding his squadron of two vessels, Kearny arrived in Macao on March 22, 1842. He was instructed to protect American lives and property but to observe strict neutrality in the Opium War.

During the war, the attitude and actions of Russell and Company's men were also based on advancing economic self-interest. In fact, this remained a powerful drive throughout their stay in China. The selling of the British cargo ship the *Chesapeake* is a case in point. Only hours before the British naval blockade was to go into effect, a ship owned by the British entered Huangpu from Singapore. After it was unloaded, the captain realized that there was no way for him to get out of the war zone safely while flying a British flag. He sold it cheaply to Warren Delano of Russell and Company, who renamed the ship the *Chesapeake*. But before this vessel was employed to serve the Russell firm, Commissioner Lin requested that the Americans sell her to the Chinese government. Delano disliked what he regarded as the mandarins' arrogance and had no sympathy for the Chinese cause in the crisis. Early in the conflict, he wrote: "Great Britain owes it to herself and to the civilized world to knock a little reason into this besotted people and teach them to treat strangers with common decency."[33] Nevertheless, as a pragmatic merchant, he was in no position to refuse this business opportunity. The reasoning was simple: Economic interest should not be sacrificed to other considerations. The ship was sold to the Chinese at a lucrative price. Refitted and heavily armed, the vessel was then used as a battleship in the war. A year and a half later, the British sank China's first modern naval vessel.[34]

The formation of an American foreign policy toward China in the mid-nineteenth century can be explained primarily as a response to the First

Opium War and to the persistent petitions of the China traders and missionaries. The latter's voice was a significant addition to those of the merchants who pressured Washington to conclude a commercial treaty with China. As "soldiers of the Lord," the China missionaries had few qualms about advocating the use of force to open China for their spiritual enterprise. Their willingness to support militarism, explicitly expressed in missionary writings in the nineteenth century, seems to run contrary to their professed goal of saving souls in China.[35] For example, *The Chinese Repository* (1832–52) was an instrument used by both missionaries and the merchants who worked with them to express their aggressive intent to shape Western opinion in favor of war against China. Edited by American missionary Elijah C. Bridgman,[36] who worked closely with his British counterpart Robert Morrison, this newspaper covered issues from evangelicalism to trade and diplomacy. It also became a forceful organ of militant Protestant missionaries in Canton. Dismissing Chinese institutions, the *Repository* reinforced the views of Western business communities in Canton and their constituents in the West that China could only be "opened" by means of military coercion.

From the first year of its existence, the *Repository* advocated a dynamically aggressive policy toward China in order to establish the conditions for "free trade." In their first issue, the journal was adamant in calling for the abolition of China's policy of restricted contact.[37] For example, in a retrospective on British difficulties in Canton from the early trade days, a contributor presented his "contemporary view" of "free trade."[38] And in anticipation of Lord Napier's arrival in the summer of 1834 to take over as Britain's superintendent of trade, the *Repository* published a series of articles under the general title of "Free Intercourse with China"; these articles molded public opinion by presenting the relations between China and the West as a series of longstanding problems that the new trade representative would now face.[39] The missionary attitudes reflect in pleas for new trading policies that would advance the goal of saving Chinese souls; thus, pursuing profits and opening Chinese markets had spiritual benefits.[40] Having established coherent links between their missionary goals and those of the Western traders and diplomats,[41] the *Repository* covered Chinese–Western relations extensively, attacking the Chinese views of diplomacy,[42] and urging the Western powers to forge a new formal treaty with China. For negotiating such a treaty, various means were proposed.[43]

The 1842 Sino-British Treaty of Nanjing attempted to legitimate in law what the opium trade had already established in practice. The treaty required China to end its traditional tribute system and to accept the European conception of international relations. However, the extent to which the United States would share in the privileges obtained by the British was still uncertain, at least in the minds of those in the United States government. This ambiguity and a desire to display an autonomous American presence in the region motivated the sending of an American commissioner to China. On December 30, 1842, President Tyler sent a special message to Congress, stating that the United States ought to secure American access to the China market on terms as favorable as those gained by Britain. The major task of the China mission would be to determine whether American ships could operate under equal access to the trading ports that England had insured by their treaty.[44]

On May 8, 1843, Tyler nominated Caleb Cushing, a lawyer from Newburyport, Massachusetts, and a powerful member of the House Committee on Foreign Affairs, as the first minister to China. Raised in a family of seafaring tradition, Cushing had wide connections with the China traders. John Perkins Cushing, who merged his firm with Russell and Company in 1830, was his cousin. He was also associated with members of the Forbes family and other Russell men. Cushing's close association with the families of the China trade raised concerns among political insiders as well as merchants. In his letter to Secretary of State John C. Calhoun, New York merchant Charles Hall expressed his concern that because of the nurturing relationship among the Forbes, Perkins, and Cushing families, they would not only benefit from enhanced trade with China but also would profit handsomely from dealing in opium.[45] Despite his political opponent's criticisms, as a trusted confidant of the president, Cushing confidently charted his new career as diplomat.

Before this appointment, Cushing had been exerting his influence to pressure the Tyler administration to dispatch a mission to China. In December 1842, Cushing told Tyler that, while Britain did not seek privileges "for her own benefit only," other countries that desired "like advantages" would have to engage China to acquire them on their own account. He strongly endorsed the petitions of American traders in Canton and Macao, and those of Boston and Salem, all of which urged the sending of a "respectable national force" to China. Cushing proposed that the president should send "an Agent" not only to China, but also, assuming the successful conclusion of treaty negotiations, to Japan "for the same purpose."[46] In his message to Congress at the end of 1842, Tyler fully agreed with Cushing that the new situation after the Opium War required an American diplomatic presence in China.

On March 20, 1843, Secretary of State Daniel Webster issued a circular on behalf of the Department of State asking "intelligent persons" who were acquainted with China and who had been "concerned extensively in the trade between it and the United States" to provide the department with "opinions and suggestions" on how to cultivate "friendly relations" with that nation and on how to open and enlarge "commercial intercourse between the two countries."[47] The merchants who were associated with the China Trade quickly responded to Webster's circular. The carefully considered responses not only helped Webster in preparing the instructions for Cushing but also provide important sources of historical information about the China Trade under the Canton System and the attitudes of the American merchants toward the Chinese Empire. The most important response that Webster received was from John Forbes, a former partner in Russell and Company who was designated by the Boston merchants engaged in the China Trade to be their spokesperson.[48] Forbes expressed the primary concern of those who responded to the circular: American trade should be admitted to the China market "upon the same footing with the most favored nation." Tyler and Webster accepted much of Forbes's advice regarding the importance of diplomatic etiquette, the impressive potential of military technology, and the benefits of employing Peter Parker as interpreter. Stressing that negotiation must be backed with implicit threats of military might, Forbes reminded Webster, "All experience in Chinese affairs shows that no Foreign Nations ever yet gained any disputed point by peaceful negotiations." Forbes continued, "The Chinese want no political intercourse with Foreign Nations & they will only permit it either through fear of armed compulsion, or through a politic desire to offer to us voluntarily what has been forced upon them by others." Forbes concluded that the demonstration of US naval forces was necessary because the Chinese had "conceived the idea that we have but few ships of war, owing to their never having seen more than two at a time & always one of these a small vessel." Therefore, Forbes recommended "sending the Commissioner out accompanied by a respectable fleet, say not less than three or four square rigged vessels & a schooner of 100 to 150 tons, of light draft of water, to act as a tender or despatch vessel."

The outcome of the negotiations would have crucial effects on Chinese–American relations for decades to come, Forbes warned:

> It would be a great error to suppose that if we fail in our negotiations we shall be no worse off than if the attempt had never been made. [...] If they find that we recede from any position once taken they learn our weakness & will take advantage of it to the utmost.

Therefore, he claimed: "All we could ask would be, to admit our trade upon the same footing with the most favored nation & we think it would be impolitic to accept anything less."[49] Two other Russell partners, John Green and N. Alsop Griswold, also wrote to respond to the circular and insisted on the United States being granted the status of most favored nation. Like other merchants who replied to Webster, they expected the mission to gain commercial privileges, personal freedoms, and a degree of protection in the Chinese ports no less than that which other nations had obtained or would in the future.

Green and Griswold also advised their government not to take on the responsibility of prohibiting US citizens from engaging in the drug traffic even if China requested this of the US commissioner. Believing that any restriction on this trade would imply the failure of American policy, they advised that any regulation of opium should be avoided. Furthermore, American traders had long been involved in the business and would continue to engage in it. The emperor of China, they anticipated, would eventually legalize the traffic of drugs while imposing on it heavy taxes.[50]

Forbes's and Green's responses could be regarded as a reiteration of the 1839 petition by merchants of Russell and Company in Canton and Macao. These enterprising Russell men repeatedly proposed to send diplomats with warships to intimidate China. However, they understood that America was not ready to use military forces in China. Having carefully considered the British role in Sino-Western relations, they believed that the best US policy would be to follow other Western powers and to ride the coattails of England, sharing the privileges gained by them.

The opinions and suggestions of those who responded to the circular had a perceivable impact on the instructions of May 8, 1843, which Secretary of State Daniel Webster prepared with special care. Based on the information provided by the China traders, Webster specified three goals for the Cushing mission: The "leading object of the Mission" was "to secure the entry of

American ships and cargoes into these ports, on terms as favorable as those which are enjoyed by English merchants" and to try to see the emperor in person, although this was a secondary objective and used primarily as a threat with which to coerce Beijing to grant American commercial rights; Cushing was given the option of abandoning the trip to the Chinese capital if it endangered securing most-favored-nation status in China. Cushing's primary mission was to negotiate a treaty equaling or surpassing that containing the concessions granted to Britain.

These instructions of May 8, 1843, formed the first coherent US policy toward China and led to the establishment of formal relations between the two nations in 1844. Furthermore, these instructions to Cushing established the basis of American foreign policy for half a century. In this sense, the instructions could be viewed as the foundation of the Open Door Doctrine of 1899–1900; although Webster did not concern himself with China's sovereignty, he did insist that all countries maintain equal access to China's markets and not fall under the influence of a single Western power.[51]

The Cushing mission resulted in the first treaty between the United States and China and established official diplomatic relations between the two nations. In addition to assurance over the commercial concessions of the Treaty of Nanjing and a clause granting most-favored-nation status, it included four significant provisions: First, it validated and extended the doctrine of extraterritoriality; second, it laid out procedures for establishing formal diplomatic exchanges and relations; third, it gave Americans the right to build hospitals, churches, and cemeteries in the treaty ports; and fourth, it stipulated that at the end of twelve years either nation could renegotiate the treaty. This provision for treaty revision later provided aggressive Westerners with an opportunity to seek further concessions from China and resulted in the Second Opium War (1856–60).

Throughout modern Chinese history, the condition of extraterritoriality remained a contentious issue. Although an article in the treaty seemed to deem the dealing of opium an exception, stating that any Americans "who shall trade in opium or any other contraband" would be "dealt with" by the Chinese, the general condition of extraterritoriality made any prosecution impractical. Furthermore, under the treaty the United States did not assume any obligation of barring its citizens from the drug traffic. In practice, the provisions for extraterritoriality made any Chinese action against American opium smugglers almost impossible.

Over the past century, Cushing's mission to China has been a much-studied subject in the literature on early American–East Asian relations. Historians have presented various explanations of why US politicians and officials became interested in direct intervention in China in the mid-nineteenth century, and thus constructed the foundations of an American foreign policy toward China. Researchers often view this mission in the context of their own historical period, defining issues partially in ways that reflect present concerns. Interpretations of the origins of US China policy therefore have been subjected to constant challenge and modification. In the new century, there has been a revival of scholarly interest in the Cushing mission and the Treaty of Wangxia.[52]

In 2007, the Society for Historians of American Foreign Relations' journal *Diplomatic History* published independent historian Macabe Keliher's article on the origins of US China policy, which reinterprets the Cushing mission.[53] Keliher argues that "It was bitter rivalry with Britain for markets and influence in the Pacific that forced U.S. politicians and bureaucrats to assume a positive role in East Asia in the early 1840s." He notes that, before the Opium War, American traders in the Canton-Macao area had repeatedly appealed to Washington for governmental support of their commercial endeavors, but the US government remained inactive until Britain gained new trading privileges and territory at the conclusion of the First Opium War in 1842. This situation, Keliher argues, compelled Washington to dispatch a mission to China and to negotiate a treaty for securing rights that matched those that the British had gained. Otherwise, the United States would risk losing a huge market to Britain. Keliher concludes that "The mission to China and the treaty resulting from it was the reflection of a strong and autonomous China policy, a policy that found another voice in the Open Door notes half a century later." In his article, Keliher questions the conventional interpretations that the United States and Britain were predominantly cooperative in regard to China and that, prior to the Open Door policy, the United States did not have its own independent policy in China but merely followed Britain's lead. Instead, he emphasizes the rivalry and antagonism between the United States and Britain in China. He continues, "It was the threat of British monopoly of the Pacific markets that forced the U.S. government to move from a passive to an active role in Americans' interaction with China, and which led to the direct articulation of a China policy in the form of the Wangxia Treaty of 1844."[54]

While undoubtedly shifting the emphasis from the cooperation to the antagonism between the United States and England, Keliher's revisionist arguments neglect the extensive evidence in the China Trade archives about the lives of those conducting trade missions and shaping diplomatic policy. Correspondence between American firms and Jardine, Matheson & Co., for example, reveal that the American traders had good working relations with their British counterparts in the Canton-Macao area.[55] In Canton, American traders worked closely with the British, beginning with the arrival the *Empress of China*; and in Macao, residents of both nationalities socialized intimately with each other, sharing both a pride in their Anglo-Saxon heritage and similar racial prejudices.

During the pre-treaty days, an extensive Anglo-American social life developed within the European enclave.[56] Protestant missionaries from both countries often preached together. They co-founded benevolent organizations and cooperated to advance their spiritual enterprises in China.[57] There is little evidence to indicate that American diplomats regarded the British officers as their rivals. In fact, when Cushing's steam-powered flagship *Missouri* caught fire and sank off Gibraltar on the way to China, the American legation was transported to Bombay in a British ship. As the Cushing mission waited in Bombay to board the US navel frigate *Brandywine* and continue to China, it was well received by the British. Upon his arrival in Macao, Cushing, whom Keliher describes as anglophobic, immediately contacted Governor Henry Pottinger in Hong Kong to ask advice regarding how to negotiate with the Chinese. The British official cordially provided him with the supplementary Anglo-Chinese treaty signed in Humen (the Bogue).[58] The bitter rivalries and antagonisms between the United States and Britain in other parts of the world did not carry over into China, where private corporations from different nations collaborated in setting the conditions of "free trade." Along these lines, the Treaty of Nanjing did not deny American access to the China market, and all the privileges that the British had gained through war were automatically granted to other nations, including the United States. In many ways, Cushing's mission was more a matter of principle and for show than for securing concessions, most of which had already been granted.

To test the Chinese pledge of most-favored-nation treatment that had been made to the Americans, in July 1843, the US consular agent, Edward King of Russell and Company, requested that an American vessel's cargo be accepted under the new tariff in Canton. The imperial commissioner readily agreed to this, and he further confirmed that all foreign nations would be permitted to trade at the five ports that had been opened by the Anglo-Chinese treaty. By and large, American traders were well pleased with the commercial arrangements.[59] It is nevertheless true that American politicians such as Daniel Webster and President John Tyler firmly believed that the United States should secure respect and privileges by negotiating its own bilateral agreement with China rather than relying on a treaty obtained by the British. To Cushing it was a matter of national honor. But this was not a case of bitter rivalry with England.

Before the First Opium War, when the US government maintained a lax attitude toward China, American traders were compelled to improvise their strategies as they negotiated with Cohong merchants and pursued their commercial interests. The key elements in their improvised policies were maintaining the equal conditions of trade and insisting on a formal stance of neutrality in the conflicts between Great Britain and China. It is true that the American companies did not always follow the lead set by the British. During the opium crisis of 1839, for example, American traders in Canton did not join the British in retreating to Macao. They instead remained in Canton to carry on their lucrative business, taking advantage of the absence of their business competitors. Even this competitive advantage was not a sign of bitter rivalry, and the American trading presence in Canton during this period proved beneficial for both British and American traders. Russell and Company fared especially well from the commission business by taking advantage of British preoccupations. During this period, English ships were only able to discharge their cargoes through American agents. Because no other foreign merchants remained in Canton during the crisis, Russell's could charge rates of $30–40 per ton for British manufactures and $7 per bale for Indian cotton—a significant margin of increased profit.[60] All teas that went to English markets during the season 1839–40 came from Canton on American ships and were then transshipped either in Hong Kong or Singapore. English merchants, who once criticized the Americans for not following them to leave Canton in protest against Commissioner Lin's seizure of their opium, now appreciated their services and did not question their profits. An Englishman wrote to the chief of Russell and Company gratefully: "My dear Forbes, the Queen owes you many thanks for not taking my advice as to leaving Canton. We have got in all our goods, & got out a full supply of teas & silk."[61]

Before the Sino-British War, when the partners in Russell and Company repeatedly requested that Washington send diplomats with warships to protect their economic interests in Canton, they were well aware that their government was not ready to use military forces in China. They therefore suggested that the best US policy was to follow the lead of Britain as it orchestrated the other Western powers in securing commercial privileges. After the Treaty of Nanjing was signed in 1842, when the Chinese authorities had been severely weakened, the China traders seized this opportunity to call upon Washington to negotiate a treaty with China, demanding the official guarantee of privileges similar to those granted to the British. In the end, the Treaty of Wangxia reflected a China policy formulated by the Russell men and other American traders in Canton. The treaty shows that the private companies of the United States had refined both the rhetoric of free trade and the British techniques of political intimidation in forging their own informal empire in East Asia during the nineteenth century.

5
Chopsticks or Cutlery?

How Canton Hong Merchants Entertained Foreign Guests in the Eighteenth and Nineteenth Centuries[1]

May-bo Ching

Like what is happening in the conduct of Sino-foreign trade today, in the eighteenth and nineteenth centuries much business and social exchange between Hong merchants at Canton and their foreign counterparts happened at dining tables. Yet unlike the contemporary entrepreneurs who usually hold banquets in an impressive restaurant, old Hong merchants entertained their guests in their own luxurious residences, which were well staffed with experienced family cooks, decorated with stylish furniture and fine chinaware and, needless to say, sure to provide tasty food. To play host to their guests, Hong merchants offered dishes, wine, and dinner service in both Chinese and Western styles; and the result was a mixture of tastes and etiquettes served at the same table. In this paper, I ask some very straightforward questions: What food was served at the banquets hosted by Hong merchants, and how was the food presented? What kind of knowledge did the Chinese cooks and servants possess for entertaining foreign guests? What kind of impact might this material cultural exchange have had on Canton over the subsequent years? In answering these questions, this chapter uses firsthand accounts given by foreign residents from England and the United States in their diaries, letters, and travel journals.

Early Accounts

Engaged in a global trading network that tied the European, Southeast Asian, and Chinese worlds together, Hong merchants at Canton had long been good at entertaining their foreign patrons. Banquets given by Hong merchants in the eighteenth and nineteenth centuries were chiefly for their English-speaking patrons. This "English experience," as I will argue, had a long-term impact on Cantonese cuisine, and should be understood against the wider context of the Canton Trade era (1759–1839), in which the British and Canton merchants were the major actors. The historical sequence is well known: Compared to the Portuguese and Spaniards, the British and the French were latecomers in the Asian waters; even later were the Swedish and the Americans.[2] But it was the British who dominated China Trade from the early eighteenth century to the mid-nineteenth century. Excluded from Japan and insular Southeast Asia, the English East India Company (EIC, founded in 1600) concentrated more on Europe-China trade. The prohibition of junk trade and the Open Door Policy towards foreigners launched by the Qing government between 1684 and 1757 gave exclusive privileges of trade in China to these latecomers, notably the chartered companies, to trade at Canton and a few other ports.[3] In 1759, the imperial court explicitly decreed that Canton was the only port to be open to foreign commerce, and thereafter commenced the Canton Trade era, which came to a halt in 1842 with the rise of other treaty ports after China was defeated in the First Opium War.

During this period, the British and other Westerners were confined to a restricted area in Canton and resided in the factories (large warehouses with offices and accommodation attached) rented out to them by Hong merchants for the duration of the trading season, i.e., from August to March each year. To these Westerners, who spoke very little Chinese and whose activities in the city were highly restricted, life in Canton could be extremely dull. Outdoor activities were welcome diversions, including an occasional visit to the temple located in Honam (Henan Island) on the southern bank of the Pearl River, and to the *fa-tee* nurseries, flower markets that were located three miles upstream from the foreign factories. Thanks to Hong merchants, Western sojourners were also able to get some fresh air by visiting the merchants' country villas and private gardens.

It is thus no wonder that the British provide early accounts about how Hong merchants received their foreign guests. William Hickey, who traveled to the East as an EIC cadet in 1769, recorded in his memoirs descriptions of the banquets given by Pankeequa. This Pankeequa refers to Puankhequa I (Pan Qiguan 潘啟官), the principal Hong merchant at the time, whose Chinese name was Pan Wenyan 潘文巖 (alias Zhencheng 振承, 1714–88)[4]. When William Hickey went from Whampoa to Canton in September 1769, he was invited to two occasions at the country house of Puankhequa I. Hickey recalled that:

> These fêtes were given on the 1st and 2nd October, the first of them being a dinner, dressed and served *à la mode Anglaise* [*sic*], the Chinamen on that occasion using, and awkwardly enough, knives and forks, and in every respect conforming to the European fashion. The best wines of all sorts were amply supplied [...].
>
> The second day, on the contrary every thing was Chinese, all the European guests eating, or endeavouring to eat, with chopsticks, no knives or forks being at table. The entertainment was splendid, the victuals supremely good, the Chinese loving high dishes and keeping the best of cooks.[5]

Hickey's account is one of the earliest I have come across that describes how a Hong merchant would have offered both knives and forks as well as chopsticks to his foreign guests. Behind these spectacular receptions was no doubt the wealth of Hong merchants. On the first day, Puankhequa I even tried to amuse his guests by showing them a Chinese drama in which an English character was introduced. However, like the pastry *à l'Anglaise,* this English character was not appreciated by a true Englishman:

> In the evening a play was performed, the subject warlike, where most capital fighting was exhibited, with better dancing and music than I could have expected. In one of the scenes an English naval officer, in full uniform and fierce cocked hat, was introduced, who strutted across the stage, saying "Maskee can do! God damn!" whereon a loud and universal laugh ensued, the Chinese quite in an ecstasy, crying out "Truly have muchee like Englishman."[6]

The banquets were a place where the Chinese and English could communicate by observing each others' cultural manners and even poke a bit of fun at each other while maintaining a sense of respect, as this "universal laugh" implies.

In eighteenth- and nineteenth-century China, the only comparable individual who could afford similar functions was probably the emperor or high-ranking officials. The banquet given by Soo-ta-jin (Su Leng'e 蘇楞額, the minister of works) in Tianjin in the name of Emperor Jiaqing for receiving Lord Amherst's embassy on August 13, 1816, serves as a case for comparison. George Thomas Staunton, the second commissioner of the embassy, was perhaps preoccupied by whether to kowtow; during the earlier British Embassy of George Macartney in 1793, the refusal to kowtow had hurt its diplomatic effect. In 1816, the British refused again. About the banquet, Staunton observed roughly that "the dinner was served up in courses, brought in upon neat wooden trays, exactly covering the tables, and repeated four or five times." Clarke Abel, the chief medical officer, described the banquet in greater detail as follows:

> A crowd of servants immediately entered, bringing trays containing part of the feast, which they placed on the tables. Four courses were served: the first consisting of soup, said to be composed of mares' milk and blood; the second, of sixteen dishes of fruits and dried meats; the third, of eight basins of stewed sharks' fins, birds' nests, harts' sinews, and other viands used by the Chinese for their supposed aphrodisiac virtues; and the fourth, of twelve bowls of different kinds of meat cut into small pieces, and floating in gravy.

As Abel describes it, the menu comes very close to the Manchu Han Chinese feast that became popular among high-ranking officials by the 1830s. For example, we know of a Manchu Han-Chinese feast served in Chengdu, Sichuan Province, in 1838. It consisted of sixteen dishes of fruits and dried meats, eight big dishes of pricey items including sharks' fins and birds' nest, eight hot dishes, two head dishes (one of these being a roasted pig), and two dim sum dishes. Altogether, the banquet included thirty-six dishes, and was comparable to Su's banquet in the number and choice of major dishes.[7]

Regarding eating utensils, Staunton claimed that they "were enabled to use the chopsticks in the absence of the knife and fork." However, Abel offered a different account of the same dinner. He recorded that "in addition to the usual Chinese table apparatus of chop-sticks and porcelain spoons," they "were supplied with four pronged silver forks, curved like a scymetar [scimitar]."[8] Staunton's account also gives us the impression that different courses came one after another. However, unlike Hong merchants' receptions, dinner dressed *à la mode Anglaise* did not seem to be what the Chinese cooks working in north China would have supplied.

Very little about this particular banquet can be extracted from Chinese official sources except that it was considered "a repast conferred" from the Qing government's point of view, as also noted by Staunton. Chinese records expressed chiefly the Qing emperor's anger against the "barbarian tributary" for the reluctance to comply with the prostrations.[9] The British mission ended up a failure, but exchanges between Hong merchants and their foreign trading partners over the banquet table went on.

Courses and Table Etiquette

In the nineteenth century, there was a boom in the writing and publication of travel journals by European and American writers, who offer further details regarding banquets given by Hong merchants. Added to the list of Britons were the American merchants and captains who took part in China Trade since the 1780s.[10] Hitherto unpublished, the journal of Bryant Parrot Tilden, the son of Captain Joseph Tilden of Boston, contains a marvelous account of the "chopstick dinner" offered by Hong merchants at Canton. Between 1815 and 1819, Bryant Parrott Tilden traveled to Canton a number of times and made his fortune there. In December 1818, Tilden was invited to a chopstick dinner by Puankhequa II (Pan Youdu 潘有度, alias Zhixiang 致祥, 1755–1820),[11] who succeeded his father, Puankhequa I, as the principal Hong merchant. Puankhequa II resided in Honam. Tilden recorded in his journal the circumstances leading to the reception:

> I have had much pleasant intercourse with the venerated Paunkequa and this time have had considerable business with him, making purchases of silks, and teas. He lately did me a signal honor by giving a genuine Chinese *chopstick* dinner at his Honam residence leaving to me the choosing of any *seven* or *nine* or American guests for him to invite. The custom here the same as I believe it to be in some other countries, is to have on such occasions, always an odd number of persons at table. I accordingly named such gentlemen as I knew would make a pleasant party from among my friends who were not residents at Canton, which was according to (with) his particular request.
>
> The persons invited were my friend Captain Haskell, Mr. Dorr, Mr. Welsh, Captain Townsend, and his young son and Mr. Jenks (all three from Providence, RI). Also, having first explained to Puankhequa, an accomplished Italian translator and gentlemen, Signor Martucci, who is a commercial agent of the great Mr. Paiha of Egypt, and who, merchant like, employs agents with large amounts of friends both here and in various parts of India.
>
> The good old gentleman wrote the names of each guest in Chinese characters, and then *particularly* inquired who they were and counted their number to be sure that it was an *odd* one.
>
> I shall minutely record the whole order and circumstances as they occurred concerning this sort of dinner entertainment, it being quite different from any other heretofore described—more so (also) because such chop stick dinners are but seldom given by the Hong merchants to foreigners.[12]

Deeply impressed by such an occasion, Tilden first noted down the preparation work done by Puankhequa II:

> Early in the forenoon of the appointed day previous to which I had apprised my friends of the coming ceremony, Puankhequa called in style at my rooms attended by a few servants. Knowing who were to be the guests, he had brought red paper chops or billets of invitation for each individual, signed with his Chinese and English chop, or stamped name for me to direct them. These were then dispatched by the servants with chin' chin' compliments to be delivered from their masters particularly and separately to each of the invited gentlemen, at same time giving notice that boats would be in readiness to convey them from his Hong over to Honam at one o'clock.[13]

Then came the day when the grand dinner was finally served. Tilden carefully noted many details, as follows:

> [Some time after three o'clock] Dinner having been announced, our host led the way for us to a cool hall, and pointed out our respective seats at a round table.
>
> I was honored by being placed on his right, and Signor Martucci on his left hand, and William opposite.
>
> At first, there was only elegant cut English glass-gilt and silver cups and goblets, wine decanters, ivory and ebony and slender chop sticks—substitutes for forks and no knives, also queer shaped Chinese silver spoons.
>
> The customary ceremony of a chin' chin' glass of wine all round, in respectful serious manner having been observed, each guest showing the bottom of his emptied glass or goblet by requisition of Paunkeiqua: on came a splendid service of china ware fancy color painted, and gilt tureens, and large bowls filled with soups and stewed messes, together with the same style of smaller bowls—but no plates. Paunkeiqua discussed the merits and qualities of each dish or mess—and then politely requested us to follow his example and help ourselves, and now began the fun by exposing our awkwardness—we barbarians—having only chop sticks and the spout-like spoons to do it with.
>
> We tried a while under the teaching of our amused host but without success. Captain Haskell excepted, who had learned to eat with chop sticks among the chinamen [*sic*] at Whampoa.
>
> In attempting to bait out soup with the unfounded spoons, some of us filled the sleeves of our jackets which fortunately had been substituted for our dress cloth coats.

But Puankhequa II would not allow his guest to be embarrassed, and cutlery was always ready for their convenience. Tilden continued to note in his journal: "Finally, seeing our distress, the old gentleman ordered plates and English knives, forks, and spoons. These treacherous chop sticks are round at one end, and square at the others and we untutored barbarians ignorantly made use of either."[14] Having struggled with the dinner service, the foreign guests finally got to enjoy the meal. The journal continues:

> Twenty separate courses were served during three hours in as many different services of all sorts of elegant china ware.
>
> The messes consisted of the celebrated Bird nest soups, gelatinous food, a variety of stewed hashes, made of chopped meats small birds—cock's combs, etc, etc. some fish, and all sorts of vegetables, and pickles, of which latter the Chinese are very fond. Ginger and pepper are plentifully used, in most of their cooking.
>
> Not a joint of solid meat, or a whole bird of any kind, were seen on table.
>
> We conversed freely between each change of courses, trimmed with all sorts of fancy cut vegetable and fruit pick nicks, and partook of a chin chin glass of the choicest Madeira wine, or tea all round.[15]

Madeira wine refers to a wine produced on the Madeira Islands, an archipelago claimed by Portugal and located in the Atlantic Ocean about 310 miles (500 km) off the coast of Africa. The wine was famous for its robust taste that matured during long voyages across the sea. Madeira was a standard port of call for ships heading to the New World or East Indies since its discovery in the fifteenth century. It is said that by the sixteenth century a well-established wine industry already existed on Madeira. Into the eighteenth century, Madeira wine's popularity extended from the American colonies and Brazil in the New World to Great Britain, Russia, and northern Africa.[16] It must have been one of the favorite gift items presented by European and American traders to the Canton Hong merchants in the eighteenth and the first half of the nineteenth centuries. Likewise, other Western spirits such as beer (卑酒, 大卑, 啤酒), brandy (罷囒地酒), claret (紅酒), and port wine (砵酒) must have been known to the Hong merchants and those Chinese who were involved in the Sino-foreign trade. Cantonese transliterations of these terms appear in the *Vocabulary of the Canton Dialect* compiled by Robert Morrison as early as 1828.[17]

Tilden continues by recording his observations about the table service of the occasion. The journal continues:

> Natural and ornamental artificial flowers in small jars and vases were on the table placed to suit the taste of the servants at each change of courses.
>
> Our noble host discovered and amplified in true epicurean style at each change, of messes, and then desired us to keep ourselves without further ceremony.
>
> Between the courses the large table being entirely cleared.[18]

Much exchange was conducted over the dinner table. Puankhequa II asked his guests about the various countries that they had visited and the routes that they had taken as servants brought to the table more courses and wine of both Chinese and Western types. Tilden noted:

> To finish off our sumptuous chop stick dinner, two courses more consisting of delicate pastry, cakes, and delicious fruits and sweetmeats, were brought on by way of dessert, with the choicest of red and white European wines.
>
> Also a peculiar Chinese wine brought in silver vessels, and drunk warm, same as tea. Its name is Su-hing, and the flavour is not unlike that of toasted cheese. This luxury is in use only among the higher classes of mandarins, but we barbarians preferred the more cool French and Madeira wines.[19]

The dinner was so elaborate that it lasted for almost seven hours. Tilden did not miss the last bit of the courses and recorded that: "The ample round table being cleared for the last time at about eight and nine o' clock, sweet scented jasmine, orange, and other flowers were profusely strewed over it to admire, and play with...."[20]

Tilden's account indicates that it was common practice at a Hong merchant's dinner party to have courses served one after another, which is still common practice at formal Cantonese banquets today.[21] What is worth noting is that the order of these courses followed apparently that of a Western dinner. In a similar manner, Henry Charles Sirr, a barrister-at-law of Lincoln's Inn who visited Hong Kong, Canton, and Fujian in the late 1840s, noted that at a feast of an upper-class Chinese, different courses of dishes placed in porcelain of different types and shapes came one after another. Like Tilden, Sirr listed in detail the dishes of the banquet that he had attended. It is again tempting for us to classify the dishes he listed according to a three-course menu: (1) Entrée: "salted and highly seasoned meats, of various descriptions, pounded shrimps, and other fish, moulded into the shapes of various animals, a stew of sharks' fins, a kind of soup made from fresh water tortoise"; (2) Main course: "variously dressed poultry of every description, cut into small pieces, in the forms of animals and birds; birds' nest soup" and "water-fowl, salted, dried and smoked fattened mandarin duck, rice bird"; and (3) Desert: "pastry and sweetmeats, all being placed in bowls; the contents of these basins were formed into the shapes of animals, birds, beasts, fishes, and flowers, colored to represent nature in a very correct manner."[22]

Similar descriptions are found in William Hunter's *The Fan Kwae at Canton* and Water William Mundy's *Canton and the Bogue*. Staying in Canton for a long time before the treaty days, William Hunter was a frequent guest of Canton Hong merchants. Invited by "Pwankeiqua" (probably Puankhequa III, i.e., Pan Zhengwei 潘正煒, the nephew of Puankhequa II), Hunter enjoyed "the chopstick dinner prepared by his choice cooks." Hunter recorded in his published journal that the dinner was "served with such delicacies as birds' nest soup, with plover's eggs and Beche-de-Mar, curiously prepared sharks' fins and roasted snails"; and stated that "these forming but a very small proportion of the number of courses, which ended with pastry of different sorts."[23]

At a Chinese dinner in 1874, Walter William Mundy noted that "as soon as one course was finished, a fresh one immediately took its place"; "the dinner commenced with birds' nest soup, which is a white soup, and very glutinous; then came sharks' fins, which you dip first of all in various sauces on the table; then plovers' eggs; then chickens done up in different ways; claws of crayfish, and every sort of vegetable done up in as many kinds of sauces; pastry *a l'Anglaise*, which I found very difficult to get down; other kinds of sweets, and stewed pears; the whole winding up with a dessert, consisting chiefly of crystallized fruits."[24]

Changes in courses not only showed the affluence of Hong merchants but also offered them a chance to show off their collection of first-rate porcelain. The above-mentioned Henry Charles Sirr noticed that food was placed "in bowls, instead of dishes, but these bowls are arranged on the dinner-table with due attention to order and effect, the largest being placed in the centre; the surrounding bowls corresponding with each other accurately in size, pattern, and shape." While the chinaware for serving the first course was antique white porcelain (a small bowl containing boiled rice and an empty bowl being placed before each guest to eat his food from), colored porcelain and white porcelain with a four-clawed dragon design on its the milky background were used in the second and third courses respectively.[25] John Reeves (1774–1856), a tea inspector of the British East India Company, also noticed that "the Squire" (said to be Puankhequa's brother) was "famed for his plants and his China ware." "He had as large a collection of China ware, which he has an opportunity of displaying to great effect at a Chop-stick dinner, [...]"[26]

High-quality chinaware was not the only dinner service the Canton Hong merchants could provide. English cutlery was also easily available in their residences. At these dinner parties, ivory and ebony chopsticks, sometimes tipped with silver, were placed for each foreign guest, probably not for convenience but for making a bit of fun of them. As Charles T. Downing remembered, "At each unsuccessful attempt, the hearty laugh goes round, and the worthy host usually joins in the merriment caused by jokes which he cannot understand."[27] However, as Walter William Mundy noted, "But in case [the foreigners] fail to manage these satisfactorily, a sort of small pitchfork was also provided to help [them] out of the difficulty."[28] As mentioned, when Puankhequa II saw Bryant Parrott Tilden's distress about using chopsticks, he "ordered plates and English knives, forks, and spoons." In addition to Chinese chopsticks and English cutlery, Tilden noted that "elegant cut English glasses, gilt and silver cups or goblets, wine in decanters" were also placed on the dining table at Puankhequa's residence. In another case that Henry Charles Sirr describes, foreign guests were supplied with a knife in addition to chopsticks, and the handles of the knives "were richly carved, and composed either of jade-stone, ivory, sandal wood, or chased silver."[29] The easy availability of English knives, forks, and spoons at Hong merchants' residences was not surprising, as Canton was one of the best manufacturers of silver for export at that time.[30]

What is also worth noting is the practice of cleaning tables entirely between courses. In addition to Tilden's account, Walter William Mundy's journal draws our attention to another sanitary routine that he noticed at the Hong merchants' dinner table: "Beside each of us was placed a damp cloth to wipe away the perspiration from our faces; and this was changed once or twice during the evening."[31] In addition, in many other parts of China, the placing of a large number of dishes on the table at once and the presence of leftovers is a sign of the generosity of the hosts. This holds true today. After a formal dinner served in a high-quality Cantonese restaurant today, all tables are cleared and cleaned after the last course is finished. A pot of flowers is then placed on the table to indicate the completion of the feast. It is not unreasonable to relate this modern Cantonese routine with the practices of Hong merchants' residences conducted in the eighteenth and nineteenth centuries.

À la mode Anglaise

It is interesting to note that the phrase *à la mode Anglaise* or *à l'Anglaise*—meaning "in the English fashion"—appears twice in the passages cited above. The message is still revealing: The chefs of the Canton Hong merchants were trying to make a kind of pastry in accordance with an English style as they perceived or imagined it to be. It was not impossible for these chefs in Canton to secure knowledge of cooking Western cuisine. Some Chinese did have experience of taking part in Western feasts. When, in 1836, the new Hoppo (customs superintendent) informed the British merchants that he proposed to call on them, he was entertained by the British with a "true English breakfast" in the state dining room. But the Hoppo obviously found the "barbarous feast" unattractive. Charles T. Downing witnessed the episode and must have found it hilarious. He noted that:

> Along the centre of the spacious apartment a table was placed, spread with a snow-white cloth, and covered with dishes of the greatest delicacies in season. Blancmanges, jellies, and fruits, were abundantly supplied, in addition to the more substantial viands; and, in fact, every thing necessary to form a first-rate breakfast after the English fashion.
>
> The old man eyed the good things upon the table, and, as he had the whole of them to himself, no one presuming to take a seat, he whispered to his attendants to fetch them for him. As each dish was brought successively, and held up to his eye, he examined it very carefully all around as an object of great curiosity, and then languishingly shook his head, as a sign for it to be taken away. Thus he proceeded for a considerable time, until he had looked at every thing on the table, without finding a single article suitable to his delicate stomach.
>
> ....[The Hoppo] quietly proceeded with his examination of the exotic dainties, and when the table had been entirely ransacked, he shook his head once more in sign of disapproval, and then called for a cup of tea. The Fan-quis could not bear this; but the greater number left the room, leaving the prejudiced old Tartar to drink his national beverage by himself.[32]

William Hunter's record of a letter by a Chinese speaking of a "Fankwae" dinner also hints that some ordinary Chinese people did experience Western meals in Canton in the nineteenth century. According to Hunter's lampoon of the Chinese cooks, those dishes "in the English style" failed to entice his palate:

> Judge now what tastes people possess who sit at table and swallow bowls of a fluid, in their outlandish tongue called Soo-pe [soup], and next devour the flesh of fish, served in a manner as near as may be to resemble the living fish itself. Dishes of half-raw meat are then placed at various angles of the table; these float in gravy, while from them pieces are cut with sword-like instruments and placed before the guests [...]. There followed a dish that set fire to our throats, called in the barbarous language of one by my side Ka-Le [curry], accompanied with rice which of itself was alone grateful to my taste. Then a green and white substance, the smell of which was overpowering. This I was informed was a compound of sour buffalo milk, baked in the sun, under whose influence it is allowed to remain until it becomes filled with insects, yet, the greener and more lively it is, with the more relish is it eaten. This is called Che-Sze [cheese], and is accompanied by the drinking of a muddy red fluid which foams up over the tops of the drinking cups, soils one's clothes, and is named Pe-Urh [beer]—think of that![33]

Other records also suggest that Chinese chefs not only possessed the knowledge of cooking Western food but also became probably very good cooks of Western fare. European and American sojourners in Canton usually hired Chinese cooks and servants to take care of their daily lives. Ida Preiffer was an Austrian woman who traveled to the East in the late 1840s and spent considerable time at Canton. Her observations are revealing:

> The following is a tolerably correct account of the mode of life pursued by the Europeans settled here. As soon as they are up, and have drunk a cup of tea in their bed room, they take a cold bath. A little after 9 o'clock, they breakfast upon fried fish or cutlets, cold roast meat, boiled eggs, tea, and bread and butter. Every one then proceeds to his business until dinner-time, which is generally 4 o'clock.

It is worth noting that dinner in late eighteenth-century England was eaten somewhere between 3:00 and 5:00 p.m. By the 1820s and 1830s, the timing of dinner was changing to match the new daily routine. The business day in the 1850s was fixed to run from 9:00 am to 5:30 p.m, so the time for dinner fell between 7:00 and 8:00 p.m. The English expatriates in mid-nineteenth century Canton must have had the leisure to stick to the old practice, just as Puankhequa II's chopstick dinner that started as early as 3:00.[34]

Preiffer then turned to a detailed description of the content of the dinner:

> The dinner is composed turtle-soup, curry, roast meat, hashes, and pastry. *All the dishes, with the exception of the curry, are prepared after the English fashion, although the cooks are Chinese* [my italics]. For dessert there is cheese, with fruit; such as pine-apples, long-yen, mangoes and lytchi. The Chinese affirm that the latter is the finest fruit in the whole world. It is about the size of a nut, and the kernel black. Long-yen is somewhat smaller, but is also white and tender, though the taste is rather watery. Neither of these fruits struck me as very good. I do not think the pine-apples are so sweet, or possessed of that aromatic fragrance which distinguishes those raised in our European greenhouses, although they are much larger.
>
> Portuguese wines and English beer are the usual drinks—ice, broken into small pieces, and covered up with a cloth, is offered with each. The ice is rather a costly article, as it has to be brought from North America. In the evening, tea is served.[35]

Furthermore, given the dependence of foreigners on their Chinese servants, it is no wonder that the English-speaking employers had to learn some Cantonese in order to communicate with their Cantonese chefs and compradors. Consider the following account from Samuel Wells Williams's *Easy Lessons in Chinese*, published in Macao in 1842:

> Ask the comprador what he is going to get for dinner to-day; there are four guests coming here to dine.
>
> He says he has provided crab soup, boiled groupa, shell-fish, a roast pig, cutlet chicken, mutton chop, baked potatoes, greens and eggs, hashed turnips, onions with beefsteak, sweet potatoes, orange tarts, suet pudding, custards, cheese, biscuit, fruit of two or three kinds, wines and beer.
>
> Tell him these will be enough.[36]

For the purpose of instructing about the native tongue, Williams translates this passage into Chinese, and each Chinese character is transliterated according to Cantonese pronunciation. This allows us to identify a few peculiar Cantonese terms specifically invented for translating English food or cooking terminology. They are: "*kat lit*" (吉烈) for "cutlet"; "*tát*" (撻) for "tart," and "*pò'tin*" (布顛) for "pudding". Among these terms the character 撻 is obviously an invented Cantonese character by adding the radical 口 (*kou* in *Hanyu Pinyin*, meaning "mouth") to a proper Han-Chinese character to denote a novelty. It is important to note that these terms are still being used today, and the food or dishes they stand for are still Cantonese versions of food presented *à la mode Anglaise*.

Beyond Canton

The practice of entertaining foreign guests with a grand dinner party seemed to decline a few years prior to the outbreak of the First Opium War and on the subsequent collapse of the Canton Trade System. Bryant Parrott Tilden was sensitive enough to feel the change in the air. He noted in a journal that he kept during his fifth voyage to China (1833–34):

> As partly before remarked, strangers do not now receive such friendly invitations from the Hong merchants, as they did some fifteen years ago. The old social conversation, and intercourse, with occasional invitations to their interesting dinner entertainments have nearly ceased, and they but seldom see us except on business; all which unfortunate state of affairs, is altogether in consequence of the frequent misunderstandings between the British and the Chinese authorities, and whenever troubles are abroad, we poor fanquis suffer all alike. Even we quiet trading Americans—though estimated as No. 1 first chop fanquis customers, are nevertheless treated "all same same" as Englishmen.[37]

Nonetheless, if we follow the tracks of the Cantonese Hong merchants and their successors, we may realize that the uniquely Cantonese-style banquet, by then a blending of Western and Chinese tastes, appeared in newly emerged Cantonese dominated cities or ports such as Hong Kong and in San Francisco's Chinatown.

A typical banquet held in San Francisco's Chinatown took place in January 1868, when a new Chinese theatre, funded by Chinese capital and for Chinese dramatic companies, was inaugurated on Jackson Street.[38] According to the *Daily Alta California*, "as a prelude to the opening of the theatre, a grand banquet was served to one hundred invited guests at the Hang Heong Low Restaurant, No. 808 Dupont Street." "The list of guests are [*sic*] made up from attachés of each of the different papers of San Francisco, the entire bench, prominent members of the bar, the army, navy, Legislature, Board of Supervisors, foreign consuls, merchants and others." Because of the presence of American guests, the menu of the banquet seemed to be a combination of Chinese and Western services. The *Daily Alta California* reports:

> The dinner was served in the same rooms in which the "Colfax Dinner" and the "Burlingame and Van Valkenburg Dinner" took place, and the bill of fare was so near a duplicate of the last that it will hardly be necessary to repeat it. Suffice it then to say that it comprised, as was intended

> to comprise, seven courses each, consisting of about 20 dishes, or say 130 to 140 dishes in all, exclusive of tables at the outset, and fruits of all kinds now obtainable in the markets. Claret, Champagne and brandy of the costliest brands, cigars, cigarettes and Chinese liquors were served in profusion with every course, and the lavish hospitality of the Trustees manifested in every detail of the feast was remarkable.

From this description, then, we can infer that in San Francisco the host of a Cantonese banquet dinner provided both Chinese and Western spirits, echoing the practices in the pre-treaty era of Canton. The following description of the San Francisco feast might further remind us of those hosted by Puankhequa II:

> We could not, if we had space, describe a tenth part of the various dishes set before the guests. From bird-nest soup to water chestnuts and chicken tit-bits fried in batter, nothing whatever usually set before guests at such an entertainment was omitted, and everything appeared to be of the finest quality. Chopsticks of ivory were provided for the guests, but knives and forks were also set on for those who could not swing the food with the sticks.[39]

By the late nineteenth century, Cantonese merchants all over the world must have been accustomed to offering standard and elaborate banquets to entertain foreign guests. When the Duke and Duchess of Connaught visited Hong Kong in 1890, the Chinese community of the colony was "desirous of testifying their good wishes towards the Royal Visitors" with an entertainment that consisted of a Chinese dinner and a dramatic performance. What is particularly worth citing is the full menu included in a current account of the event. It runs:

Menu

1. Birds' Nest soup
2. Stewed Shell-fish
3. Cassia Mushrooms
4. Crab & Sharks' Fins
5. Roast Beef (*À L'Anglaise*)
6. Roast Chicken and Hams
7. Pigeons' Eggs
8. "Promotions" (Boiled Quail, & c.)
9. Fried Marine Delicacies
10. Roast Turkey & Ham (*À L'Anglaise*)
11. Fish Gills
12. Larded Quail
13. Sliced Teal
14. Peking Mushrooms
15. Roast Pheasant (*À L'Anglaise*)
16. Winter Mushrooms
17. Roast Fowl & Ham
18. Bêche-de-mer
19. Sliced Pigeon
20. Snipe (*À L'Anglaise*)
21. Macaroni ((*À La Peking*)

Table Dishes
Cold Sausages, Prawns, Preserved Eggs
Liver, &c., &c., &c.

Fruits
Preserved Apples, Citrons, Tietsin Pears, Pomegranates,
Carambolas, Greengages, Pine-apples
&c., &c., &c.

Pastry
Sweet Lotus Soup, Almond Rice Custard
&c., &c., &c.

Champagne (Krug), Claret, Orange wine, Rice Wine,
Rose Dew, "Optimus" Wine, Pear Wine[40]

Doesn't this menu astonish us in its suggestion of the extent to which the banquets given by the Canton Hong merchants more than a century ago influenced the subsequent practice?

Concluding Remarks

More research has to be done before more solid conclusions can be drawn about the possible connection between the table etiquette promoted by Hong merchants and the later Cantonese cuisine tradition. We are certain that until very recently many standard dining practices that are central to Cantonese lives were unknown in most parts of China. These practices include serving dishes course by course, completely clearing the table between courses, changing dinner services (such as plates and dishes) between courses, and distributing food to individuals' plates.[41] Furthermore, food terms such as 噠 (tart), 戟 (cake) and 批 (pie) have become so much a part of the Cantonese vernacular that people have almost forgotten their probable English origins. If it is true that the Hong merchants were the pioneers in blending Cantonese and European cuisines and dining etiquette, the next question we have to address is how these practices were popularized and became part of the Cantonese food culture. One of the keys to this question will be the knowledge and activities of the region's cooks and servants. All in all, the stories of the Canton Hong merchants remind us that "fusion" cuisine is not a new invention, and that their homemade global recipes should be considered a crucial part of the "pre-history" of twentieth-century Cantonese cuisine.

Figure 2.1

Frontispiece to Samuel Shaw and Josiah Quincy, *The Journals of Major Samuel Shaw, The First American Consul at Canton: With a Life of the Author* (Boston: Wm. Crosby and H. P. Nichols, 1847). Courtesy of the Rare Book and Manuscript Library, Van Pelt-Dietrich Library Center, University of Pennsylvania.

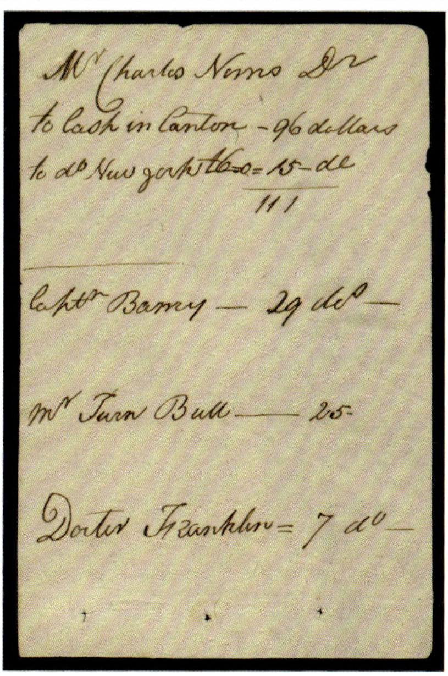

Mr Charles Norris Dr
to Cash in Canton - 96 dollars
to do New york 16=0= 15 - do
111

Captn Barry — 29 do —

Mr Turn Bull —— 25-

Doctor Franklin= 7 do —

Figure 2.2

"Doctor Franklin= 7 do." The other names recorded here seem to be Mr Charles Norris, the naval Captain John Barry, and Lieutenant Colonel George Turnbull, who fought in the Third American Regiment in the Revolutionary War. See final page of John Green's "Receipts, Canton in China, 1784–1786," Archival Materials in the Rare Book and Ms Library Manuscripts of the Van Pelt Library, University of Pennsylvania (Ms. Coll. 499).

Figures 2.3 and 2.4

"The American" and "The Chinese," from Oliver Goldsmith, *A History of the Earth and Animated Nature* (Dublin: Printed by James Williams, No. 21, Skinner-row, 1782), Vol. 2, opposite 229; opposite 221.

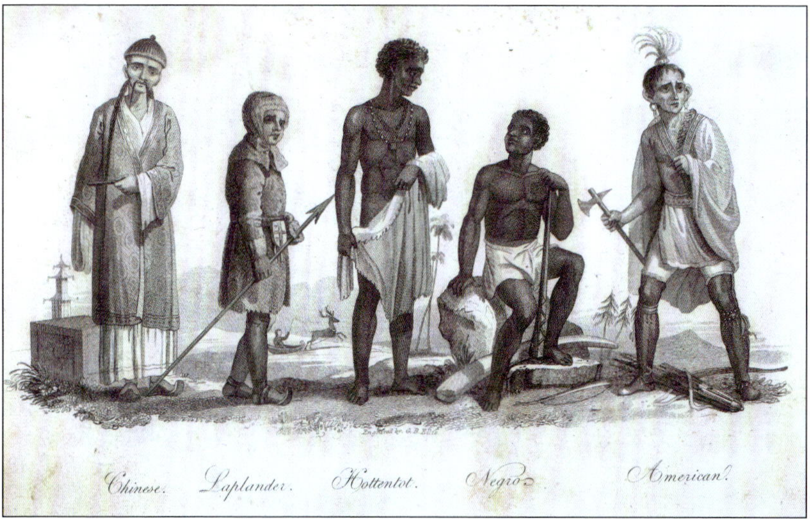

Figure 2.5

Plate II: "Varieties of the Human Race:—The Chinese, Laplander, Hottentot, Negro, American," from Oliver Goldsmith, *A History of the Earth and Animated Nature*. 5 vols. (Philadelphia, PA: Published by Thomas T. Ash, 1823). Vol. 2, p. 1.

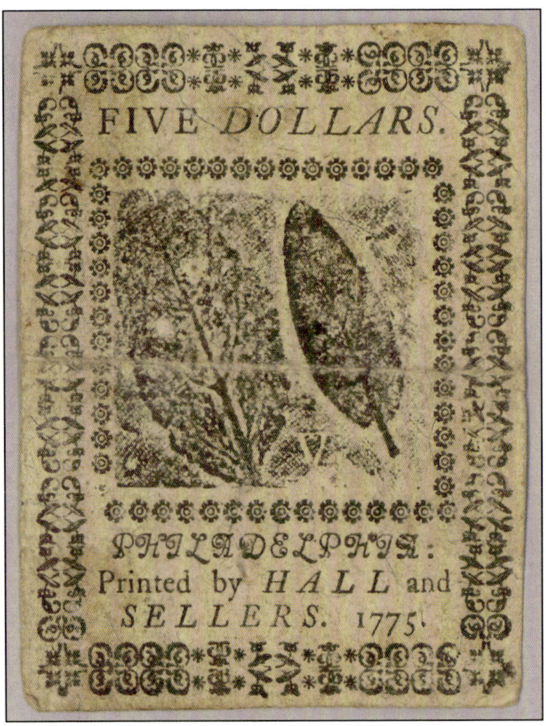

Figures 2.6 and 2.7

Continental Currency, 5 Dollar bill, May 10, 1775 (obverse and reverse). Reproduced from the original, courtesy of the Department of Special Collections of the Hesburgh Libraries of the University of Notre Dame.

Figure 2.8

Order of Cincinnati and detail from Benson J. Lossing, *The Pictorial Field-book of the Revolution or, Illustrations, by Pen and Pencil, of the History, Biography, Scenery, Relics, and Traditions of the War for Independence*. 2 vols. (1853; New York: Harper & Brothers, 1859), Vol. 1, p. 697.

Figure 2.9

Porcelain bowl with the insignia of the Society of Cincinnati, from the tea service ordered in China by Samuel Shaw, 1788. New York Historical Society.

Figure 3.1

Example of Willow Ware. The author's personal collection.

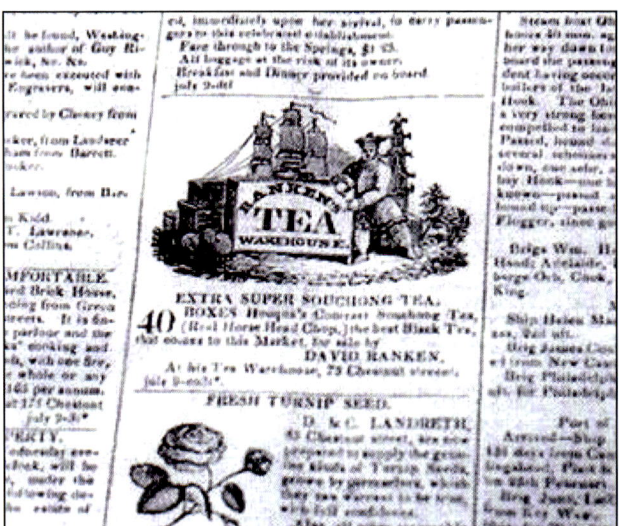

Fare through to the Springs, $1 25.
All baggage at the risk of its owners.
Breakfast and Dinner provided on board.

EXTRA SUPER SOUCHONG TEA.

40 BOXES Houqua's Concoct Souchong Tea, (Red Horse Head Chop,) the best Black Tea, that comes to this Market, for sale by

DAVID RANKEN,

At his Tea Warehouse, 75 Chestnut street.

FRESH TURNIP SEED.

D. & C. LANDRETH,

Figure 3.2

Advertisement for Ranken's Tea Warehouse, *Poulson's Daily Advertiser* (March 22, 1839).

Figure 3.3

Joseph Stiner & Company, Trade Card (undated). Warshaw Collection of Business Americana, National Museum of American History.

Figure 3.4

Great American Tea Company at 51 Vesey Street. Poster from the Bella C. Landauer Collection. Collection of the New York Historical Society.

Figure 3.5

"Packing of Tea," by Tingqua. Hong Kong Museum of Art Collection.

Figure 3.6

J.C. Jenkins & Company, Lithographic Print. Library Company of Philadelphia.

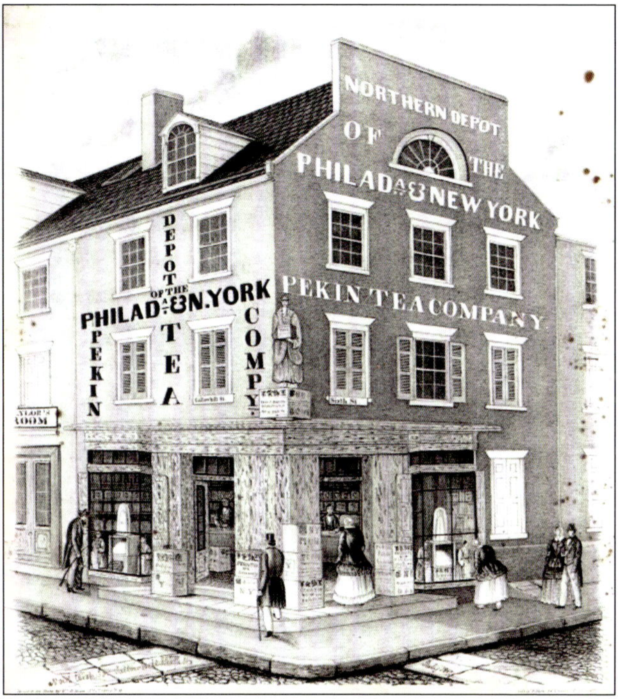

Figure 3.7

The Pekin Tea Company, Lithographic Print. Library Company of Philadelphia.

Figure 3.8

Tea Crate. Chester County Historical Society, West Chester, Pennsylvania.

Figure 3.9

Redding & Company, Trade Card. Warshaw Collection of Business Americana, National Museum of American History.

CHINESE TEMPLE AND IDOLS.

Figure 3.10

Chinese Temples and Idols. William Langdon, *Descriptive Catalogue of the Chinese Collection* (London, 1842), 13.

Figure 3.11

Literati. William Langdon, *Descriptive Catalogue of the Chinese Collection* (London, 1842), 22.

Figure 3.12

Palanquin on Street of Canton. William Langdon, *Descriptive Catalogue of the Chinese Collection* (London, 1842), 42.

Figure 7.1

George Chinnery, *Portrait of Howqua*, Courtesy of The Hongkong and Shanghai Banking Corporation Limited (HSBC Asia Pacific Archives) 2010.

Figure 7.2

Anon. Portrait of Qiying, 1844. Courtesy of the Museum of Fine Arts, Boston. Gift of the heirs of Caleb Cushing.

Figure 7.3

Anon. Broadside Advertisement announcing "The Great Chinese Museum, Largest Collection of the Kind in the Nation," Courtesy of Boston Athenæum.

Figure 7.4

Jules Itier, Daguerreotype of Pan Shicheng (whereabouts unknown).

Figure 7.5

Luo Ping, Ghost Amusement Scroll (detail). Handscroll, ink and color on paper, Private Collection.

Figure 9.1

Tianhou (also called Mazu) at Thian Hock Keng, Singapore. Photo by Khun Eng Kuah-Pearce.

6
Representing Macao in 1837

The Unpublished Peripatetic Diary of Caroline Hyde Butler (Laing)

Rogério Miguel Puga

> Can you judge of our delight, three Salem ladies meeting in Macao. Only think of it. [...] It must be a dream that we are so far from home and together.
>
> Harriett Low, Journal to her sister, 1829[1]

Since its Portuguese establishment around 1557, the enclave of Macao was the only western gateway into China until the foundation of Hong Kong in 1841. In the nineteenth century before the Opium War, the female relatives and children of China traders from North America and Britain resided in Macao while their husbands and fathers were up in the Canton factories during the trading seasons. This essay deals with the unpublished diary of one of these ladies, Caroline Hyde Butler (1804–92) who, like Harriett Low (1809–77) and Rebecca Kinsman (1810–82), described the many dimensions and spheres of Macao's everyday life. As we shall see, these China diaries and Canton female narratives form a network of Old China Trade texts that demonstrates an interesting process of intertextuality or intertextual travel.

Caroline Hyde Butler, daughter of Thomas Butler (1769–1822) and Sarah Denison Butler (1774–1839), is mostly known for her several novels, including *Child's History of Rome* (1872–75), and children's stories published in periodicals such as *Sartain's*, *New Mirror Magazine of Literature and Instruction* (1843–44), *Graham's* (1844–51), *Magazine of Literature and Art* (1848–51), and *Godey's Lady's Book*.[2] Like many early American women writers, aspects of her life remain a mystery.[3] Her unpublished "China Diary," held at the New York Historical Society, is a fundamental historical source for the study of everyday life in nineteenth-century Macao, where most Anglophone traders resided between the Canton trading seasons and where their female relatives and children, forbidden to enter mainland China, lived all year long.[4]

Born in Oxford (New York), in 1822, Caroline Hyde married her distant cousin, Edward Butler (1797–1849), who was involved in the China Trade. The couple married in Plainfield, Connecticut, settled in Northampton, Massachusetts, and had five children between 1824 and 1834. In 1836, Caroline was advised to travel to China with her husband due to her poor health, and she stayed in Macao. The writer's stay in the City of the Holy Name of God of Macao lasted around two months, and during that time she kept a personal diary, in which she recorded the daily life of the English-speaking residents in the south of China, as well as the (lack of) interaction between the enclave's different communities. On October 11, 1836, the couple left New York on the *Roman*, a ship belonging to the firm Oliphant and Co., and reached Macao in early February of the following year.

During the voyage Caroline mentions reading of the "Cruise of the Potomac," a reference to the narrative *Voyage of the United States Frigate Potomac*, by Jeromiah N. Reynolds (1799–1858), published two years before she left the United States of America. This shows that travelling authors read previous works about the countries they were to visit, thus creating an intricate web of intertexts that quoted and echoed each other. After mentioning the adventures of the *Potomac*'s crew, the diarist characterises herself as a (female) pioneer:

> Now that I am a voyager myself I think I take more interest in such Works than I did when all my navigation was on Long Island [...], to and from New York. Perhaps this cruise [of the Potomac] has interested me the more as the author visited Canton and Macoa [*sic.*]. If it is possible I am determined I will go up to Canton from Macoa, yet I hardly dare flatter myself, as there are so many obstacles existing to prevent us poor females from showing ourselves at the Celestial Empire—nous verrons.[5]

Reynolds's narrative of trade shares a lot of themes and observations with her own text. *The Voyage* describes the *Potomac* crew's stay in Macao during an expedition to protect the American trade in Asia. The text's Introduction contains the expression used by Caroline to refer to this same travel book: "the cruise of the Potomac."[6] The *Potomac* arrives at Macao in May 1832, and the description of the enclave and the Pearl River Delta shows great thematic similarities to Caroline's autobiographical text:

> the whole bay, or estuary, is thickly studded with rugged and barren islands. Macao is on the west side of the entrance; built on a peninsula, which is almost an island, being joined to the main by a very narrow isthmus, across which is erected a barrier or wall, about two miles north of the town, being the limit prescribed to the ceded territory, to prevent any intercourse between the Portuguese and the liege subjects and citizens of the Celestial Empire. [...] The approach to Macao, from the sea, is very beautiful in the daytime, and is not without its charms by a brilliant moonlight. [...] The land around seemed broken into a thousand hills, covered with stinted verdure. Macao, though distant, looked beautiful and highly picturesque. Every thing was new to the beholder, and strikingly characteristic of a foreign land. [...] Each stranger who visits this country is previously determined to be astonished at every thing he sees and hears; nor will strange things be wanting! [...] These people worship an idol, which they call *Jos*, supposed to be a corrupt pronunciation of the Portuguese *Dios*, God. [...] Those [foreigners] who have wives are obliged to keep them at Macao, and visit them as their business will permit.[7]

Many of these images and even words are repeated in Caroline Butler's diary in which, like Harriett Low and Rebecca Kinsman, she registers the whole new "splendid" world(s) she discovers once she gets off the boat.[8] These private narratives are valuable sources of information regarding the social and cultural history of Macao during the Old China Trade period before the First Opium War. These women, alone in a strange territory while their husbands are in Canton, have plenty of time to write about the daily life in the city administrated by the Portuguese and to record even the smallest details, which entrepreneurs would not have commented on. Many of these women left children at home, and their state of mind influences the way they feel in Macao and how they perceive and filter the city in their subjective and intimate narrative monologues.

The diarist's first contact with China is through the maritime population of the Pearl River Delta. Caroline describes the Chinese men aboard the two Chinese boats that approach the *Roman* as:

> all hallowing and jabbering together—their heads bald to the crown, from which they let their hair grow long and braid it into a queue, which dangles nearly to their heels—this with their wide blue trousers and long loose jackets, complete the very reality of all the figures we see on their blue china ware—and it would seem as if some of these images had really stepped forth in life from a large china dish, instead of a boat.[9]

A cultural *ekphrasis* gradually takes shape to reveal that stereotypes transmitted by the images on chinaware imported by eighteenth- and nineteenth-century American traders influenced the way that travelers filtered their first contact with the cultural Other. It is as if the chinaware images that Caroline had admired back home later gained a life of their own.

The initial contact is also marked by other characteristic reactions to the cultural encounter of East and West in Macao. Butler describes the natural landscape and the use of China Pidgin English both by the Chinese and the Western traders to communicate with each other.[10] The crew of the *Roman*, just like Samuel Shaw and the rest of the crew of the *Empress of China* years before, sees and hears China through the "singular jargon, half English–half I know not what" used by the captain.[11] The female diarist already masters some of the trade jargon and uses it when describing the decorated Chinese boats: "These are all for chin-chining Josh—or in plain English to offer to their god, to propitiate his favor for winds and weather."[12]

Upon arriving at Macao, the traveler observes the city using binoculars and describes it from the general to the particular:

> I cannot say its appearance is very prepossessing—it is situated at the base of a high hill or rather mountain, which has the same barren rock appearance of all the others [islands] which I have seen on the China coast. We are lying near the nine islands [...]—on our right [...] the barren peak of Lantau—before us is Macoa, and the Ladrone islands behind us—indeed we are perfectly encircled by islands.[13]

The ship arrives during the Chinese New Year. The festivities and local traditions are filtered by the author and mark the passage of symbolical and cyclical time: During "the only holiday [that] the Chinese have [...], they commenced their worship of Josh [...] by beating gongs and firing bunches of crackers, accompanied by the tossing of yellow and gilt paper in the air."[14] Before the crew and passengers land, while all the recently arrived Western ships try to gather as much trade information as possible before their rivals, the captain of the *Roman* visits Macao (hiding himself on a Chinese boat) and Lintin Island, where most of the opium smuggling was done after 1820. Upon arrival, the diarist compares herself to Columbus and confesses that she feels like kneeling down and kissing the (safe) land where she now stands after such a long voyage.

In the Anglophone community, Caroline Butler met several famous Macao residents, namely the missionaries Peter Parker (1804–88), Samuel Wells

Williams (1812–84), and Karl (Charles) Gützlaff (1803–51). The female members of the English-speaking community in Macao generally spent their time sewing, looking after their homes, writing home, praying, walking around Macao, visiting each other, and helping their husbands when necessary. In 1844, another American female resident described her lonely stay in Macao while her husband was in Canton. Rebecca Kinsman sent letters to Canton almost every week and confessed that she was the only representative of the American firm Wetmore & Co. in Macao.[15] When all the traders had moved to the Canton factories, she was forced to deal with both her domestic issues and the company's:

> I sometimes think it never could have been intended that such a variety of occupations should devolve upon one person—nursing a baby, mantua making, reading, writing letters [...], entertaining visitors, opening the treasury, (the key of which is confided to my charge, as I am now virtually "Wetmore & Co." in Macao) receiving & paying out money, with other & divers matters too numerous to particularize.[16]

The division of labour based on gender in the Anglophone community of Macao is therefore not as traditional as one might assume it to be.[17]

Since its founding by the Portuguese, Macao has served as a decompression chamber where missionaries, traders, and travellers like Caroline acquainted themselves with different aspects of the Chinese cultures.[18] The diarist visits the Protestant Chapel and Cemetery, comparing the former to the Catholic ones in the Luso-Chinese city, indeed strange for the North American visitor, who was forced to redefine herself as a cultural and religious Other in China. Just like other Anglophone visitors and residents, Caroline describes the Penha Hill, or the Ridge, and chooses one of the most used adjectives by English-speaking authors when characterizing Macao as "romantic." The Penha Hill "is situated at the south west extremity of the town, and on the summit is a church and convent—the ascent is very rugged—in which however, one is aided, at intervals by flights of stone steps—the whole distance commands a fine view of the town, and harbour, with its numerous islands. I never saw a more romantick [*sic*] view."[19] On page 127, another stroll up the same hill demands another description and the use of the same adjective:

> the view was beautiful—turn our eyes in any direction we would, they could not be arrested by the most romantick [*sic*] scenery. The town

> itself has a noble appearance—it has too, such an ancient look—for the Typhoons, and long rains, have the effect of giving an old look, to buildings in reality quite new—scattered over the town, are the dwellings of the foreigners—and the little Chinese villages—which are entirely separated from the near neighbourhood with "Barbarians." The lofty hills, rising in rugged beauty, crowned with Forts and Convents, the noble walls of the churches, here and there a small grove of trees, with the various groupes, passing and repassing the streets, which were mostly open to our view, and now and then, a party of Chinese descending the hills, in their singular dress, combined to rend the scene truly enlivening—and then to look from the town, upon the beautiful sea-view—especially the inner harbour [...]. It is a beautiful basin on whose surface were many large Portuguese vessels, and smaller craft—the majestick Lappa [island], rose proudly on the left—at its base a thickly settled Chinese village—further on was the Monkey Isle[20]—and then rose Heang-shan to which Macoa is joined by a narrow neck of land.[21]

The geography of the "city of the hills" is also presented to the reader, as well as the city's main military and administrative buildings:

> Macoa, is situated on a peninsula—connected by a narrow neck of land with the island of Heang-shan—across the centre of which runs the boundary wall—beyond which, no Barbarian must pass (by Barbarians are meant any one but a Chinese). Macoa might truly be called the city of Hills for they rise in every direction—presenting a most wild, and romantick [*sic*] aspect, which is heightened by the Forts and Convents which crown their summits. To the East is the lofty Mount Charil [Guia Hill]—on which is the Fort Guia, enclosing a hermitage—at the foot of this mount, on a point extending into the sea—is the Fort of St. Francis, with the church, also of the same name. On another high mount, in the centre of town, stands the lofty Fort of St. Pauls, called the Montefort. Besides these, there is the Bombarto Fort—which is on the west side of the Panha—and the Bar Fort—which is situated on a point, making into the Inner Harbour on the west side of Macao, the Fort of St. Peters, is on the Praya Grande, in front of the governor's house—but looks so little like a fort—that it needs inscription to designate it as such.[22]

Caroline describes gardens, forts, and other prestigious buildings throughout the document, which I classify as a peripatetic diary, as it gains shape by describing the wanderings and walks of the author along the narrow and cobbled streets of Macao, a city presented as being controlled by Catholic priests. Its old and picturesque ruins please the Romantic taste, and the local architecture reminds Caroline of imaginary and real places represented in

European novels. The exotic gardens and aviary kept by the famous trader Thomas Beale (1775–1841) are described through the use of comparison and enumeration. Beale had spent the last thirty years collecting exotic fauna and flora from all over the world, and would later lose his fortune during an opium crisis.[23] These two attractions were also visited and described by other nineteenth-century travelers and were a notable part of the cultural and natural landscape of Macao, as Caroline herself suggests:[24]

> the Garden is laid out in terraces and gravel walks—not a blade of grass is to be seen, or any thing but rows of pots crowded together, and as most of their contents were not even green, I found myself on the whole rather disappointed. I mean as regards the flowers—but for what was wanting there, the beautiful and rare birds made ample amends. About in the centre of the garden is the Aviary—from the summit of two large rocks is thrown a wire grating painted green—covering several large trees—a fountain, and two or three little grottos. In this beautiful and novel aviary, are hundreds of the most splendid Birds, here enjoying comparative freedom. They seem as happy as can be—some perched on the trees, sweetly tuning their little notes—others walking stately and grand, under the branches—nor was the fountain forgotten—for on the brink were some, dipping their little bills into the water—and then turning up their heads to the skies, while many of the tribes had ventured in, and were frolicking and flapping their wings in the sparkling fountain.[25]

The text also distinguishes the different Chinese social groups, identifying the richer and the poorer based on the observation of their clothes and general appearance. The Portuguese and Chinese dimensions of the enclave, both unknown and unfamiliar to the American traveller, are presented as parallel in the urban tissue:

> scattered among these lofty hills are the dwellings of the Portuguese—English and American residents—and separated from the near communion with Barbarians, may here and there be seen the closely packed huts of a Chinese village, toward which many of the inhabitants were pursuing their way with their little string of fish, or baskets suspended on a stick, thrown over the shoulder, containing either the gleanings of the streets, or refuse from some foreigner's table, while parties of Lascars—Caffres and Chinese —may also be seen winding among the hills.[26]

The diarist-flâneur reveals her growing knowledge of the Portuguese and Chinese realities of Macao, and exoticism becomes a recurrent presence during the daily walks to Penha Hill, the Praia Grande, the A-ma Temple, the Chinese hills and fields, the Loyal Senate, and the Barrier Gate, strolls that mark the passage of time in Macao. When visiting the Casa Garden, a Portuguese villa that had been rented to English traders for a long time, Caroline mentions the orphan teenager who owned it. Portuguese sources reveal that the owner was Maria Ana Josefa (1825–1901), who was not fifteen years old but twelve and the daughter of Manuel Pereira, who had died on March 1826.[27] Next to the residence stands the famous Camões Grotto or Cave, where, according to a legend, the sixteenth-century bard wrote part of his epic poem *Os Lusíadas* (1572). After describing the grotto and the summer house on top of it, Caroline includes a short biography of the Portuguese writer, showing that throughout the centuries Macao has been a Lusophone place where Anglophone visitors and residents had their first contact with the life and literary work of Luís Vaz de Camões.

The final section of the diary complements the main text by filling in voids with information that Caroline had previously left out. She adds the description of the Chinese village that she had only mentioned before:

> at almost every turn a new and beautiful view was presented to us. From one quarter, rose the majestick [*sic*] Lappa—the waters of the Inner Harbour gently laving its base—while the numerous Portuguese and Chinese craft, floating idly on its bosom, were plainly reflected in the calm transparence. Again, you are looking down as from a precipice, upon the busy tumult of a Chinese village with its gay decorations of coloured and gilt paper hung around the doors and walls, as propitiatory offerings to "JOSH." The hum of voices—the yelping of their ugly yellow dogs—the beating of the Gong, and cries of children come "full and thick upon the ear." From another quarter the island of Hean-shan stretches far in the distance, and over the narrow neck of land which connects it with Macoa, a party of English and American gentleman and ladies were gaily galloping along the beach, until they arrived at the Barrier or Boundary Wall, beyond which according to Chinese law no "Barbarian" must pass, when turning their ponies as is "old custom," they as gaily gallop back again.[28]

The ellipsis in the diary entries that is revealed by this final section shows how the selection of information to be inserted in a travel narrative is always an ongoing process. On her way back home, onboard the *Roman*, Caroline concludes that Anglophone female residents in Macao—where there were only eight or ten British and four American families—did not really mingle:

> yet in this small circle, and in a foreign land too, where one would suppose the utmost good feeling and sociability would exist—the case is different—there is all the etiquette and ceremony of a city life to be found here, and the only rational thing they do is to join together in walking or riding—but as for intimacy in any other way, c'est une chose impossible—parties and Balls are very common—as also Dinner parties, which serve to enliven the tediousness of a life in Macoa, which every inhabitant of English or American growth pronounce to be most "dreadful."[29]

Regarding the Lusophone community, the diary mentions both the Macanese and Portuguese who administrate the city. Caroline's picturesque enclave of Macao is composed of Western architecture and peopled by the mixed-blood population, the Macanese, whom the author identifies (erroneously) as being Portuguese: "very unprepossessing in their appearance—their complexions very swarthy—and features flat and insipid—they are a mongrel race—half Portuguese—half Chinese—but I think their whole appearance vastly inferior to the Chinese. Most of the Portuguese in Macoa are of this description—they are but a few pure blooded."[30] The diary also portrays another aspect of the multicultural frame of the city, a group of Macanese ladies covered by their black veils, or *dós*, most likely on their way to church. This image gives place to an interesting comparison between Macanese and North-American (dressing) habits:

> By and by approach a party of Portuguese women—Their walking dress is singular. They wear no bonnets or caps—but in lieu they have large square shawls, of very gay colours, and made stiff with glazing—these they open to their full size, and pin one end on the top of their heads—slightly projecting over their faces, while the rest falls around them like a mantle—This has not an ungraceful appearance—on the whole it is rather pretty to see one of these women walking along—you would almost expect to see a beautiful face with rosy cheeks and sparkling eyes, peeping from under this close covering but alas—you find on the contrary, the dark and unmeaning features of the Portuguese—I must confess however they are better looking than the men—they have good eyes, and very red lips, which I am told they paint.[31]

Caroline describes the Portuguese as:

> a miserable race, and with the exception of the Governor and family, there are not many persons of rank and respectability. Even the priests seem to be equally degraded, without the least sanctity of aspect, they

> may be seen parading the streets at all hours, in their long black robes—while the Bells of the different churches are most of the time pealing forth for some ceremony, pass one of these churches at what time of day you will, and you invariably encounter groupes of Shawled Portuguese women, pouring in and out, with their long rosarys suspended from their necks.[32]

These excerpts and the diary in general show the different ways that male and female residents experience the city through their clothes, physiognomies, and even makeup, in the case of women.

The Chinese fluvial/maritime population is Caroline's first sight of the country, and from the balcony of her hostess, Mrs King, and of other American ladies, she observes many other Chinese figures who walk the streets of Macao, namely Chinese ladies with bound feet, a social and cultural practice she comments on:

> a Chinese woman came hobbling along with the true genuine little feet—how ridiculous it looks, to see such a large frame supported by such small props—still her walk was more easy than I should deem possible—the Chinese lovers, compare this unsteady gait in their mistresses, to the graceful moving of the willow. The dress of this woman very similar to that of men—no covering on her head, which she protects from the sun, by holding over it a parasol formed of black bamboo & palm.[33]

A long procession of typical figures of nineteenth-century Macao marches through the diary. These figures include priests, compradors, worshippers, beggars, and Chinese street sellers with their typical cries. The drawings of another nineteenth-century North American traveler, Lucy Cleveland (1929), who has been recently studied and published on, offers some illustrations.[34] Rich Chinese residents and Chinese beggars who make New York beggars look like kings, as well as local monks, and especially the Tanka or boat women are, as in Rebecca Kinsman's letters, anthropological elements of Caroline's diary.[35] Commenting on the Tanka women, she writes:

> they seem to be a sort of amphibious animal—almost web footed I doubt not, they are born and die in these boats—frequently we see these women, skulling their boats, with an infant of a few weeks old, slung over their shoulders in a bag—while the bottom of the boat holds three or four other little creatures [...] in case however that a child should fall overboard, they have gourds, or a frame of Bamboo around their necks to buoy them up.[36]

Regarding this topic, we can compare Caroline's text with other Macao-based trade narratives that record the common interests of female authors. For instance, Rebecca Kinsman also describes the Tanka women:

> as I raise my eyes from my paper, and see this beautiful roadstead with the numberless boats, so near us, that the voices of the boatmen are distinctly heard [...]. At this moment, a little tankah-boat is before the window, looking almost like an egg-shell upon the waters, from its smallness and frailty of appearance. Here lives a family—here probably they were born, and will perhaps die. The mother has *her baby fastened to her back, and as she pulls the oar, the motion rocks the little one, who seems to enjoy it*. I cannot see how many this boat contains, as it is covered or roofed over one end, but frequently a mother, with one or even two grown-up daughters, and two or more little children, live on the boat, and sometimes two women join their means and take a boat together. They are managed entirely by women, whose husbands are either coolies on shore, or more probably fishermen of the larger boats. But it is really interesting to watch with what skill they manage these little cockshells.[37]

These different China diaries and Canton narratives form a network of Old China Trade intertexts that communicate with and influence each other, creating an interesting process of intertextuality or intertextual travel.

Gender influences how authors write and the contents of these writings on/in Macao. Unlike women, male writers rarely describe the decoration inside and outside the Portuguese houses in detail. Like Rebecca Kinsman and Harriett Low, Caroline Butler enumerates the duties of her comprador, the Chinese "butler" in Western homes/ships/factories, before sending him to the Chinese bazaar to buy "curiosities" to take back to United States:[38]

> the Steward or head of the establishment [house]—he procures all the other servants, who are subservient to him—he purchases every thing for the use of the family—in short he has the whole control of every thing. The servants are all men. Every service is performed by them—they act as cooks—waiters—chambermaids etc—the errand boys—or those under the Compredores [*sic*] are called Coolies. Every foreign resident must have their Compredore—he takes all care from the lady of the house—who is as it were, as free from anxiety regarding her household affairs, as any visitor—for all the accidents which may happen thro' the neglect or carelessness of the coolies—for thefts etc.[39]

The Chinese Other is just as unfamiliar to the American traveler as the Portuguese Catholic Other, so the female authors we have been referring to find not just one exotic Other in Macao, but two different, distant communities: the Chinese and the Portuguese, as well as residents from other countries like Great Britain, Sweden, and India. Macao is therefore exotic both for the Westerner because of its Chinese dimension, and for the Chinese visitor because of its Portuguese dimension—a "double" city that has been referred to as a cultural Janus.[40] The diary acquires a stronger ethnographic dimension when it describes the Festival of the Hungry Ghosts and the irrigation systems that the Chinese farmers use in Mongha to water their crops, but the author is well aware that she cannot generalize or develop any idea based on her limited "first impressions" of Macao's Chinese reality.[41] One thing she safely concludes is that the Chinese defend the "old custom" (Chinese tradition) and reject any attempt to change: "They all heartily despise [*sic*] the "Barbarians" and hold all their customs in "contempt."[42] Caroline compares the Patane fields ("Paddy Fields") to a more familiar American landscape, Hadley Meadows in Northampton.[43]

The Butlers left Macao on a fast boat to board the *Roman* on March 17, 1837, and the enclave became a place of memory. Caroline resumes her writing on March 26, and these later writings revisit the friends, landscapes, soundscapes, monuments, and daily practices that she has left behind. The previously mentioned final section enumerates, just like Kinsman's letters, the different dishes of Macao, where butter, milk, and cows are scarce and expensive, and where shops do not exist at all. As a mother, Rebecca Kinsman also mentions the high value of the cow that the family brought from the United States and how hard it is to find milk and dairy products in the enclave.[44]

The most important section of Caroline's journal is this final one, unique in the corpus of the Anglophone Old China Trade literature, as it describes the solitary everyday life of the North American women in Macao, almost to the hour. This section recovers several themes from the main text of the diary and is divided into four parts: "Cameons [*sic*] Cave," "beautiful Garden at Macoa" (Thomas Beale's garden), "The Penha," and "Life of Foreign Ladies at Macoa."[45] The section also shows that the hectic *negotium* of the male community in Canton contrasts with the monotonous *otium* of their female relatives in Macao:

> the life of the foreign ladies at Macoa, admits of but little variety—one day may serve as a very fair specimen of all. Banished from the society of their liege lords [in Canton] by the ungallant mandates of the Celestial Emperor, they enjoy (pardon the word ye husbands) a life of single

> blessedness. The first sound in the morning, is the heavy dashing of the surf upon the beach—the next, the brisk notes of a Fife, and beat of drum and in a few moments the measured tread of the Governors guards, is heard beneath the window wending their way toward the Monte Fort.[46]

The pleasant mornings of the Anglophone ladies start with a walk in the balcony to the sound of the hawkers' cries and Catholic bells, as Robert Bennet Forbes also described in 1839.[47] Other typical figures, such as musicians, Portuguese priests, mandarins in their sedan chairs, and noisy children, stroll along the Praia Grande and are part of another cultural *Bildgedicht* in which images of the Chinese that were painted on the chinaware imported to the US seem to have gained a life of their own again, giving the text thematic circularity.[48]

According to the diarist, until 2:00 p.m. the thirty American and English ladies take care of their homes, and write notes ("chits") to friends. From 2:00 to 4:00 p.m. they visit each other. At 5:00 p.m. the lady of the house enjoys the luxuries of the East during a rich but lonely dinner in the company of the comprador, as her husband is in Canton. After dinner, a walk or a horse ride to the Barrier (Campo), the Penha, Cacilhas Beach, or around the city finishes the day, while the Chinese stare (back) at the exotic and strangely dressed Western women. It is as if there is a game of mirrors or cultural reflections during which the visitor realizes she is the Other in a foreign country. Just like the diaries and letters of Harriett Low and Rebecca Kinsman, and the drawings of Lucy Cleveland, this personal narrative describes the human and cultural frames of the urban tissue of nineteenth-century Macao, female worries, experiences, priorities, domestic occupations, the luxurious dinner parties, the city's toponimy, its Anglophone, Chinese, and Lusophone communities, as well as the cultural and religious distance that characterizes the relations between the above-mentioned national groups.

Although Macao has been regarded by researchers as a multicultural city, in the nineteenth-century Macao was multicultural only to a certain degree, as its different communities did not interact as much as one could suppose; maybe that was the only possible level of interaction at that time in a generally tolerant "contact-zone" shared by people from China, Catholic Portugal, Protestant England, and the United States of America—four communities separated by cultural, political, linguistic, and religious "borders" as well as by economic interests.[49] Caroline Butler's unpublished and peripatetic diary describes the city's everyday life, focussing mainly on its Portuguese and Anglophone spheres. She depicts the Chinese as trade partners, servants, or exotic inhabitants with whom communication is almost impossible and whom she therefore judges mainly on their physical appearance. The territory administrated by the Portuguese was a feminine space of suffering and learning where North American female travelers acquainted themselves both with the Catholic and exotic Others, while their husbands wrote their own personal narratives of trade in the (also) isolated space of the foreign factories in Canton.

7 The Face of Diplomacy in Nineteenth-Century China

Qiying's Portrait Gifts

Yeewan Koon

> When exchanges become closer there must be greater precautions [...]. If presents are sent one should firmly refuse them. If they are ambiguously accepted, the laws of the Heavenly Dynasty are very strict. Not only is it contrary to the constitution, it is also very difficult to evade the statutory regulations. The said envoys respected the instructions and obeyed. But when we met, small gifts were given, such as foreign wines or perfumes, their value being slight, and as the intent was sincere it was improper to reject them. Your slave gave only personal accessories such as snuff bottles and pouches in return—to give the idea of returning more than was received. Furthermore, the four countries: Italy, England, the United States, and France asked for my portrait. These were made and presented to all [...].
>
> Excerpt from memorial dated November 23, 1844 to Emperor Daoguang[1]

So reported Qiying (耆英 1787–1858), the imperial commissioner who was responsible for negotiating the Treaty of Nanjing (1842) with England's Henry Pottinger in Hong Kong, the Treaty of Wangxia (1844) with Caleb Cushing of the United States, and for the other trade treaties between China and the West in the mid-nineteenth century. In this memorial, Qiying refers to several points of protocol when exchanging diplomatic gifts: In the act of giving, one should give more than what is received; the nature of gifts should be understood as political etiquette and cannot be excessive in value; and personal relations between the diplomats were not to be encouraged. Qiying's account also includes a remarkable comment, not least because of the unremarkable way in which it is delivered: "The four countries: Italy, England, the

United States, and France asked for my portrait. These were made and presented to all."

Qiying's casual delivery belies the gravity of his conduct. First, the gifting of portraits was not part of the customary diplomatic exchange in China; when, in 1816, Lord Amherst offered a portrait of King George IV in royal robes to the emperor, it was rejected it.[2] Furthermore, there is a damaged and incomplete letter to a foreign trader from one of the most influential Cohong merchants in Canton, Wu Bingjian (more popularly known as Howqua, 1769–1843), who dissuades the trader from commissioning George Chinnery (a famous portraitist based in Guangdong and Macau) to copy a portrait of the king as gift to the Daoguang Emperor.[3] The general sentiment toward such portraiture seems that of suspicion, as implied by the comments of Zhang Xi (fl.1800–42), a member of Qiying's team, when he observed that "The barbarians secretly brought artists who sketched the likeness of the three officials."[4]

Rejections, dissuasion, and secrecy seemed to have beleaguered the use of portraits in political contexts, so why did the foreign envoys request these particular ones of Qiying? Can we begin by trusting his insistence that the portraits were responses to requests? Moreover, when compared to the expected snuff bottles and pouches of diplomatic routine, a portrait implies greater personal value and a stronger attempt to establish intimacy with the recipient. Would not requesting a portrait risk insensitivity to the terms of diplomatic courtesy?

This paper investigates a moment in Chinese diplomatic history when portraiture played a complicated role in sustaining and negotiating political relationships.[5] In a general sense, gifting was a means whereby networks of patronage and friendships were set up, obligations reciprocated, and political and economic interests advanced.[6] In the specific context of China's treaty negotiations with the West in the decades after the First Opium War (1839–42), gift-giving suggests the terms of intimidation and war through which England and the United States were attempting to establish policies of what they called free trade. Interpreting the gift requires a careful consideration of culturally specific ideals regarding identity and a realization that the terms peace, friendship, and property were part of a treaty discourse through which China and the countries of England and the United States confronted each other over the control over land and commerce.

The gifted portrait mentioned by Qiying enabled him to present himself to its recipients as a minister to the emperor of China, but the portrait also symbolized a more personal connection with the recipients. Because the painting absorbed the image of the subject (Qiying), the painting blurred the distinction between persons and things and between official diplomacy and personal friendship, thus dangerously violating the restrictions set by the emperor on the exchange of gifts. At the same time, the terms of connection between the parties involved in the gift exchange seems simultaneously both reinforced and rendered more ambiguous. In giving a portrait of himself to Western powers in 1844 after the Opium War, is Qiying inviting the West into closer communication or establishing terms of reciprocity that enforce a buffer zone, keeping them at arm's length? An understanding of social practices and cultural codes suggests that such gifts both highlighted profound differences between cultural ideas of self and were haunted by the apprehension of violent confrontations between two systems with very different definitions of what "free trade" would mean.

This paper is set in two parts: The first examines the portrait as an object reflecting the social conventions of patronage and the blend of Chinese and Western pictorial conventions that lend it form and legibility in the Sino-Western diplomatic relations of the first half of the nineteenth century. The second part of the paper compares the British and American attitudes toward gifts, to examine more closely the political context in which China negotiated the terms of free trade. I look at the exchange and reception of the portraits to illuminate how Qiying attempted to balance his dependency on established networks and practices of local merchants with the directives he had received from the emperor and with relationships to the Western trading nations. A brief coda considers the legacy of a portrait that he gave to the American minister Caleb Cushing, and thereby highlights Qiying's sad frustration in maintaining the balance of contrary diplomatic expectations.

The Portrait Object in Guangdong

As a preface to the historical contexts of portrait-gifting, a few words about the cultural differences in the making and receiving of portraits in the mid-nineteenth century are necessary. The eighteenth- and nineteenth-century Euro-American portrait is often described as an expression of a hierarchic status in a society whose members believed in their right to civilized rule over a world regarded as less developed, barbaric, and even savage. The grandness and scale of the Western Empire generated wealth that enabled the patronage of the arts and cultivated the "genius" of individuals who were celebrated in pictorial styles expressing the spirit of the age. The production and display of portraits were often poignant examples of this imperial attitude. With the establishment in 1856 of the British National Portrait Gallery, the imperial, noble, literary, and artistic worked in concert to set up a visual narrative that told the story of imperial advancement in the arts and science.[7] The aura of this gallery's display of faces permeated the private environments of middle-class homes and, in the form of miniatures, even reached into men's and women's pockets and purses. Out of these imperial origins of painting, buying, and hanging portraits of the aristocratic and elite evolved a new practice. The middle class began likewise to utilize the portrait, as those with the money and inclination strived to establish their own social visibility in a market-based world. The romantic terms of a faded aristocratic age provided commercial investors with a template by which to present themselves as the new heroes of their commercial nation.[8]

In Qing China, broadly speaking, there were also portraits, but the social assumptions behind them imply major and important differences in the structure of Chinese society and its attitude to the self and the world. There were two main types of Chinese portraits. The most common form was that of an ancestral portrait that would be hung for commemoration at certain times of the year.[9] Anonymous artists produced these and followed the conventional rules of physiognomy, reproducing standardized images for ritual occasions.[10] A second type is the informal portrait that was used to affirm close relationships; these portraits were shared among members of the same family, kin, and small groups of friends and associates.[11] By 1500, the variety of informal portraits had expanded and typically would portray the semi-private side of the sitter at leisure and would serve as parting gifts on which friends could write farewell messages. Richard Vinograd's pioneering study of Chinese portraiture distinguishes between Chinese portraits that moved in relatively closed social circuits, and European and American portraits that circulated more publicly in the marketplace and in exhibition spaces.[12]

One of the key representational requirements in late imperial China was fabricating a "likeness" that also asserted the sitter's social position in relation to the artist or viewer. It was this closed circuit that made Chinese portraits a particularly complicated form of cross-cultural diplomatic gift. Portraits of

Chinese emperors were never given as gifts outside of the Imperial Court, because the emperor transcended the coordinates of ordinary social status and thereby troubled the way in which portraits conventionally positioned sitters, artists, and viewers in relation to one another. Who could possibly be intended as the audience for the informal portrait of a Son of Heaven? Whereas the informal stance of many of these portraits depicted the Qing emperors at leisure, the political message was anything but casual. These portraits were a highly codified design that reaffirmed the emperors' position as rulers who stood above the social circuit of gift-giving. These portraits were not intended for public display or private consumption but to stand as historical markers tracing a line of sacred authority.

In the context of eighteenth-century international commerce, the philosophies of Chinese and European portraiture collided. The early exchange of portraits in international trade relations can be traced to the British East India Company in South Asia. Within certain areas of India, excessive gifts such as bejewelled robes and money often changed hands as forms of tributes. In the late 1760s, the company's directors were concerned about the growing corruption and expense of the Mughal gift rituals. They imposed the Regulating Act of 1773 that prohibited British officials from receiving land, money, and jewels from Indians. The governor-general of India, Warren Hastings (serving from 1772 to 1785), was among the first to replace his expensive gifts with a token of potentially stronger personal symbolism—the painted portrait.[13] Subsequently, this practice was widely adopted and spurred a colonial market for portraits in both the Indian and the British public.

Hastings expanded the practice of gifting portraits from the mercantile negotiations to the political world of diplomacy. He encouraged the British rulers of Bengal to follow those diplomatic policies that were followed in Europe and to adapt the policies where necessary to the Indian practices of gifting. In the place of giving expensive presents (and risking appearances of bribery), government representatives presented a portrait gift along with messages of friendship when requesting things like access to land and other favours. The timing of the gift exchange was important, and some observers have equated the portrait-giving practice as equivalent to the exchange of turbans in Indian court circles.[14] As a result of the expansion of British India Company into China, the practice of portrait-gifting continued among merchants. However, unlike the social practice in India, the exchange of portraits was conducted after negotiations were completed, and often functioned as farewell gifts. Thus those farewell portraits exchanged between the Westerners (diplomats and entrepreneurs) and the Chinese (Cohong merchants and government representatives) adapted a Western material, style, and format to the commemorative functions of the Chinese context.

The arrival of George Chinnery in Guangdong was a watershed moment for the world of Chinese portraiture. Chinnery had long served in India before coming to Macau to escape from debt collectors and a needy wife. He arrived on September 29, 1825, and stayed in Guangdong for short spells between 1826 and 1832.[15] Despite the brevity of his stays, the repercussions of his style were considerable. He was instrumental in fanning the popularity of full-length portraiture, and his influence accounts for a general rise in the production and quality of this genre in Guangdong, where portraits began to include dramatic shadows and rich hues of great contrast that covered the expanse of the canvas and shimmered under the gloss of oil paints.

Chinnery's portraits of Wu Bingjian (Howqua) are perhaps the most famous, not least because of Wu's own reputation (Figure 7.1).

Moreover, the portraits reveal another layer of intercultural negotiations at the level of pictorial conventions. A typical portrait of Wu by Chinnery shows a man with a knowing gaze, seated in a relaxed cross-legged position. The cross-legged posture was the typical stance used to connote the Western gentleman at leisure, usually depicted in three-quarter view that cultivated an air of gentlemanly ease. Chinese portraits favor the formal iconic posture following physiognomic regulations concerning the authority of the sitter. In this instance, we see both conventions seamlessly combined as Wu appears in a frontal cross-legged pose. Such a pose demands the skills of a good artist in capturing this unusual foreshortened perspective. The casual formality in Chinnery's portraits is more than the result of artistic conventions; it also mitigates the cultural distance between the three parties of the painter, sitter, and patron. The European conventions of class markers seem to model a presentation of Wu's foreign differences, making him appear familiar and accessible despite the potential racial Otherness that a Western viewer of the nineteenth century might have registered.

We see a similar balance of the familiar against the strange in the background and in the arrangement of the scene's props—an arrangement that conflates material wealth with the sitter's body. The Western column represents Rome and ideals of civilization; the high-back chair carries associations of nobility by its similarities to a throne; the tea cup refers to one of the main items of the China trade; and the glimpse of a foreign landscape indicates an exotic far-off territory. These interiors and exteriors should not be taken literally but instead as inscriptions of wealth, high social status, and as emphasis on Chinese cultural, racial, and political identity. In this painting, Wu belonged to the same polite world as his patron.

The official robe was a consistent feature of the diplomatic portraits and held various and sometimes contradictory meanings for the different audiences of the portrait. In Western portraits and others by Chinnery, the robe indicated that the sitter was part of an exotic landscape. For the Western artist, the crest on the robe could serve as a central motif that simultaneously displayed exoticism and denoted authority while tying together the formal elements and meaning of a portrait. For the Western patron, it was an element that distinguished his trading partner as both foreign and rich. However, for the Chinese sitter, the robe was a form of personal vanity that asserted his social standing within the mercantile community. Furthermore, for the sitter, the presentation of himself as a gentleman in an official robe followed the formal conventions of ancestral portraiture.[16]

Although extant examples and textual records indicate that there was a large market for oil portraits of Cohong merchants, there are surprisingly few images of Qiying, the Manchu official who negotiated with the West after the Opium War and whose quote begins this essay.[17] This may reflect the political sensitivity of making images of Qiying, as it transgressed diplomatic practices. However, in a rare record, we have documentation showing that Qiying commissioned portraits of himself in Guangdong by a local artist called Lamqua, who may have been trained by Chinnery. Jules Itier (1802–77), a customs official and amateur daguerreotypist who was part of the French ambassadorial team tasked with negotiating the Treaty of Whampoa in Guangdong, wrote a diary of his journey to Asia and took photographs of his trip. In his diary, Itier recalled a visit to Lamqua's studio in Macau on August 27, 1844:

> It is also on this street where the painter Lamqua is. This is the official painter of Chinese and European diplomats. When Sir Henry Pottinger and Qiying exchanged portraits, it is his [Lamqua's] brush that fixed their strokes on the canvas. As for the work, as he took oil painting lessons from an English artist, there is no trace of his Chinese style of painting. He sold a copy of the portrait of Qiying. It is a curious sample of a new school of painting in China.[18]

Lamqua was the same artist who made numerous high-quality oil portraits of the Cohong merchants, many of which were given as part of the gift exchange between merchants—exchanges that established connections of friendship as well as business. Here we have in Itier's account a glimpse at how some of these conventions of friendship, first employed by the merchants, were also adopted in diplomatic negotiations of free trade.

The Portrait Gift as Event

Prior to his role in the negotiation of the trade treaties with England, France, Italy, and the United States, the Manchu official Qiying had very little to do with the local and international affairs of the Canton trade.[19] His previous foreign policy experience had been as a Tartar general at Mukden, where he drew up defence regulations. Despite his lack of diplomatic experience, in July 1842, the emperor sent him to Nanjing to make peace with the British. In the wake of the war's devastation, he met with Sir Henry Pottinger (1789–1856). In August, a treaty was agreed upon and copies were sent to the respective rulers for ratification. Qiying was only one of several officials involved in the treaty meetings, but within a year he rose to become the most influential of the Manchu representatives.

The 1842 Nanjing Treaty was relatively brief, and it was agreed that further discussions were needed to negotiate extraterritorial claims and tariff controls. When the elderly Manchu official Yilibu passed away on March 4, 1843, the talks came to a standstill, testing the patience of the British Commission. Consequently, Qiying was promoted to imperial commissioner and once again went to Guangdong in May. By June he had settled the matter. Hereafter, we see evidence of what has been described as Qiying's "appeasement policy." His strategy was to conduct acts of conviviality as means of defusing hostile impulses. By maintaining intimate relationships with Western envoys, he achieved a sort of personal ascendancy and thus influenced their attitudes and the ultimate course of their policies in regards to China. Courting intimacy was a dangerous game. His predecessor, Qishan (d.1854), had been denounced for letting friendship with the barbarians lead him to concede too much to the British.[20]

It is in this context that Pottinger wrote to the Earl of Aberdeen a letter (July 5, 1843) in which he recalls a remarkable feast with Qiying after the Nanjing Treaty had been ratified by both the Daoguang Emperor and Queen

Victoria. Pottinger hosted the feast in Hong Kong and welcomed the imperial commissioner Qiying and his advisors.[21] The feast was probably not just a celebration; it had been agreed that negotiations would continue and finer details would be added, leading to the supplementary Bogue Treaty of 1843.

In Pottinger's letter we have the first evidence of the gifting of portraits between Pottinger and Qiying. The letter also exposes Qiying's braggadocio, which both impressed and bewildered his British counterpart. The relevant sections of the letter register the many layers of meaning to the gift-giving economy:

> During this short period Keying's [Qiying] attention was attracted to the miniatures of my family which happened to be on the table, and he desired Mr. [John Robert] Morrison to explain to me that he had no son himself and therefore wished to adopt my eldest boy and to know if I would allow him to come to China. To this I replied that the lad's education must be first attended to, but that stranger things had happened than his seeing Keying. Hereafter to which His Excellency rejoined "Very well, he is my adopted son from this day, his name—which he had previously ascertained—shall henceforth be Frederick Keying Pottinger and until you send him to me after he is educated you must allow me to keep his 'likeness.'" To this proposal I could make no objection and I accordingly gave him the picture. Immediately after His Excellency expressed a strong wish to have Lady Pottinger's miniature also, but [...] before the matter was either way settled, dinner was announced and we went to table.
>
> I supposed the thing would be forgotten, but when dinner was partly over, Keying again introduced his request, said that he would send me his wife's likeness in return, and that he wanted my whole family to take back with him when he went to Nanking (Nanjing) and eventually to show to his friends at Peking (Beijing). I felt it was impossible to refuse this flattering request, and I had the miniature brought and put it into his hands. He immediately rose, placed it on his head—which I am told is the highest token of respect and friendship—filled a glass of wine, held the picture in front of his face, muttered some words in a low voice, drank the wine, again placed the picture on his head and then sat down [...]. He then delivered the miniature to his principal attendant, who was standing behind him and directed him to send it home in his state chair.

We might surmise that Qiying, by adopting the images of Frederick, Lady, and Sir Henry Pottinger, sought to weave himself into the British envoy's family network. He continued with his flattery by claiming that he would carry the portraits with him on his travels back to the capital.[22] By insisting on Frederick's portrait, renaming him, and offering to adopt him, Qiying was not only maintaining ties over distance but also over time—Pottinger's and his relationship would grow into the next generation.

Qiying's extravagant reception of Lady Pottinger's portrait must have baffled Pottinger. Qiying treated her miniature as if it were a real person, offering the portrait wine and had "her" taken back with him on a state chair. Other than inebriation, is there an explanation for Qiying's rather bizarre behaviour? An explanation of this particular moment of portrait-gifting is complicated by the political tensions that frame the potential for intercultural communication in the shadow of the unequal treaty that suspended the open hostilities of the First Opium War. As foreign women had previously been banned from entering China, the appearance of the diplomats' wives caused much ado. Perhaps Qiying was trying to honor Pottinger's wife in a way that he thought would be fitting. It is difficult to overlook the potential erotic charge in the way Qiying treats the portrait of Pottinger's wife. In European custom, the exchange of miniatures between men and women was usually an act of private affection. In general, the diminutive size of the miniature enabled the owner to hold her beloved in her hand, or wear his image around her neck, thus promoting a hope that affections would retain durability in the absence of the beloved. When Qiying takes the painting as a literal incarnation of Lady Pottinger, offering wine to the portrait and putting the portrait in a carriage for the ride home, he is also pushing this connection to a point of challenging Pottinger's supposed own possession of his wife. In short, by taking the portrait of the lady, he was taking to his home the wife of another. It demonstrates, whether self-consciously or not, the absurdity of diplomatic codes that could use the language of friendship to annex parts of China to foreign control. Qiying later made a miniature of his second wife as a gift for Pottinger, thus closing the circle of reciprocity on this symbolic gesture of swapping images of wives.[23]

Overt displays of friendship with foreigners could be dangerous. Given the Chinese imperial regulations that sought to quarantine the West, even at the price of giving up Hong Kong, Qiying had to walk a tightrope during these diplomatic endeavours. Qiying seems to have used the giving of portraits as a way of maintaining a double role in a masquerade whereby he sought to negotiate with the West effectively while at the same time appearing strong for the Chinese emperor. In an 1844 memorial to the Daoguang Emperor, Qiying explains his gifts of portraits and gestures of friendships as part of an appeasement strategy:

> Certainly, we have to curb them by sincerity, but it has been necessary to control them by skilful methods. There are times when it is possible to have them follow our directions, but not let them understand the reasons. Sometimes we expose everything so that they will not be suspicious, whereupon we can dissipate their rebellious restlessness [...] truly it would be of no advantage in the essential business of subduing and conciliating them. To fight them over empty names and get no substantial result would not be so good as to pass over these small matters and achieve our larger scheme.[24]

In cultivating this impression of friendship and connection, Qiying goes as far as to transliterate in Chinese the word for "intimate" (因地密特) or "yin-di-mi-te"—a word he uses in his correspondence when addressing Pottinger.[25] In light of this, the extravagant display of placing the miniature of Pottinger's wife on a sedan chair and adopting of Frederick Pottinger strategically blurs both the boundaries of subject and object and Chinese and British, thus highlighting the ways in which the giving of portraits set up familial intimacy as a political tool in the contest for control over land and commerce.

American Gifts

When compared with the exchange of portraits between China and England, exchange between China and the United States was more formally conducted. Caleb Cushing, the high commissioner for the United States, was more cautious about the use of gifts and the appearance of overly friendly relationships. In particular, Cushing was skeptical of extravagant exchanges, perhaps reflecting the puritanical attitudes of his New England background. In any case, it echoed the nation's diplomatic protocol at the time. According to Constitution of the United States (Article 1 Section 9), no "Person holding any Office of Profit or Trust under them, shall, without the Consent of the Congress, accept of any present, emolument, Office, or Title, of any kind whatever, from any King, Prince or foreign State."

Cushing's anxiety over presents can be understood in relation to his own sense of civilizing purpose. Prior to his departure, he announced at a meeting that included President John Tyler: "I go to China, sir, if I may so express myself, in behalf of civilization," to become "teachers to our teachers."[26] In regard to gifts, Cushing was keen to insist that:

> the usage among Asiatic States of giving and receiving presents has been the source of much inconvenience to the United States in those cases even when it has been a mere matter of courtesy. But the receipt of presents by the Chinese government has always hitherto been assumed by the latter as act of tribute on the part of the giver. About making such presents, it seemed to be still more desirable to abolish the principle at once by a provision of the treaty.[27]

Cushing's austere approach to diplomacy set the tone for the exchanges made between Qiying and his American counterpart. It is telling that in the correspondence between the two men, Qiying never refers to Cushing as his "yindimite" friend.

In the case of the Americans, it was only after the signing of the Treaty of Wangxia (1844) that gifts were presented. At the banquet held in celebration of the event, Peter Parker recorded the following episode:

> The gentleman being seated, the American minister took from his finger a ring presented by the honourable mother and addressing himself to Keying alluding to the serious objection to the exchange of valuable presents as they might be construed as tribute, but to the exchange of trifles as keepsakes there could be no objection. In pleasantry, he remarked that the ring he received the preceding day was an emblem of war as the Chinese use it in drawing the bow, but it was of no consequence, he had received it as a token of peace and friendship. Keying, smiling, replied it had never been used for that purpose. Mr. Cushing then remarked that the ring be held in his hand was presented by his honorable mother that he had nothing more sacred that he could present him as a memento of his esteem and friendship and as such, begged that he would permit him to place it upon his fingers.[28]

By placing his mother's ring on Qiying's fingers, Cushing was initiating a bond of intimacy, but the exchange was double edged. On one level, Cushing's joke mitigates any implied aggression of Qiying's gifted ring, and exerts his own authority as he places his mother's ring on Qiying's finger. With great political savvy, Cushing focuses on the personal nature of his gift to ensure that the ring cannot be interpreted as a bribe or a tribute. In this way, his mother's ring appeals to feelings of family as "retaliation" to Qiying's own gift of a Manchu "war ring." He asserts intimacy as a form of power that at the same time may not seem entirely appropriate to a mission of securing from China the concessions that England had demanded after winning the war.

Portraits were also exchanged after the meeting. This time it was initiated by Cushing, who sent an etching of President Tyler. In response, Qiying sent a large Chinese hanging scroll on which he was portrayed formally in the style typical of Chinese ancestor portraits.

The scroll (Figure 7.2) is a full frontal iconic portrait of Qiying in his blue winter court robe with a boldly displayed crane motif, symbolizing an officer of the first rank. The decision to present an image of himself in a formal Chinese mode rather than an intimate miniature may be telling of the different relations forged between China with Great Britain and United States.

How effective was Qiying in his negotiations with the British and the Americans? In both cases, the process of giving portraits is inflected with Qiying's challenge to create a feeling of intimacy with the West but also to hide from the Qing Emperor his actions in fear of being accused of being too friendly. Political gift-giving was a balancing act, both sides exercising caution and not wanting to appear too friendly or to appear to be paying tribute.[29] Qiying, borrowing practices established in the trading communities, used strategies of intimacy, including the gifting of portraits, to jostle for positions of power during the discussions of new trade terms. The British treaties set up the template for all later negotiations, but a comparison of the gifting practices between China and the United States and Britain reveal differences. Qiying used overt strategies of intimacy, as appeasement, with the British, to prevent the threat of further forced entry into the country. With the United States, it was Cushing who used intimacy as a form of power positioning, as seen in the exchange of rings. Cushing also initiated the gifting of portraits, and Qiying returned the most formal type of Chinese portraits that mitigated the intimacy of the gift. Peter Parker reported how Chinese officials feared Britain's imperialist ambitions, as demonstrated with India, and sought out friendship with the French and the United States (both countries having fought back against the British) to strengthen their own position. Qiying might have held back with extravagant gestures of intimacy, ironically, to cultivate friendship. In both cases, what is evident is paralleling the discussions of new trade agreements; the language of intimacy and friendship, seen in the presentations of gifts, played a role in the jostling for power.

For a time, Qiying succeeded in preventing the Western powers from gathering together to coordinate access to the capital. By granting equal footing to each Western trading partner, Qiying forestalled a coalition between the Western nations that would penetrate into the Chinese mainland. The 1844

Treaty of the Bogue supplemented the earlier Treaty of Nanjing and granted the British extraterritorial rights to complement the opening of five designated ports. However, it proved to be difficult to implement the terms in Guangzhou because the general populace resisted British entry. Discussions regarding the opening of Guangdong were delayed until 1847, by which time local militia groups led by local elites and scholars had rallied together against the British. There were fears that the British wanted to penetrate deeper into Guangdong's hinterlands and capture the profitable inland routes of interregional trade connecting southeast China with the Yangtze regions. Finally, Qiying managed to negotiate a two-year grace period and promised to have Guangdong opened by April 1849. Between 1847 and 1849, Guangdong was a volatile region that saw xenophobic protests, local uprisings, and violent clashes. It was only with the daring tactics of Ye Mingchen (1807–59) that Guangdong was able to bluff its way out of another military showdown with the British. Meanwhile, the growing mistrust at the Imperial Court, fuelled by reports of the growing alienation of the local Guangdong populace and of violence among the local militia, made his strong overtures of friendliness an increasingly dangerous game. By 1850, the Daoguang Emperor had passed away and rumors of the new emperor's diplomatic plans incited more local uprisings, especially in Guangxi, where the vision of a young man changed the course of history when he saw himself as the brother of Christ. The ensuing rebellion of the Taiping Army against the Manchu court would cost tens of millions of lives.

By the mid-1850s, France and Britain had joined forces in the Second Opium War (1856–60), proceeding to the capital and looting the Summer Palace. It appears that in the end, Qiying's strategy of coordinating appearances of intimacy with European trading powers had run its course and become ineffective.

The Afterlife of Portrait Gifts

In the wake of the First Opium War (1839–42), Cushing pursued opportunities for introducing into China methods of shipbuilding and innovative weaponry produced by US artillery manufacturers. He sent letters to Qiying outlining proposals that would have led to lucrative deals with US manufacturers, but there are no records of Qiying accepting Cushing's proposals. Nonetheless, the United States' attempts were not entirely futile. He had included in his diplomatic envoy a young engineer, John Peters, Jr., who stayed in China after Cushing's departure, in part to collect Chinese artifacts for his father, John Peters, Sr., who was assembling a massive collection on China to exhibit in the United States. It was unlikely that Peters knew what and where to buy artworks, and he may have had help from Pan Shicheng, a rich and influential salt merchant in Guangzhou who built a warship with help from foreign friends, perhaps including Peters.

One of the terms in the 1842 Treaty of Nanjing called for abolishing the Canton System and ending the Cohongs. However, this did not deter the Cohong merchants from becoming actively involved in the negotiations between the officials and being eager to reposition themselves in the new free trade market. Pan Shicheng was the cousin of one of the most powerful Cohong families, and he often acted as part of Qiying's advisory team during the negotiations of treaties with France and the United States. Many of the negotiations and meetings that led to the treaty signings were held at the homes of Pan Shicheng and his coterie of merchant friends, including Howqua's successor, Wu Shaorong.

When Cushing returned home to the US, he gave his portrait of Qiying to John Peters, Sr., who had purchased a plot in Manhattan where he pursued plans to erect the large exhibition of China wares obtained through his son.[30] When the building of a venue was delayed, the elder Peters rented a space for display in Boston, and the Boston Chinese Museum opened to the public in 1845. The opening was attended by curious thousands who consulted the handbook *Guide to the Descriptive Catalogue of the Chinese Museum in the Marlboro Chapel, Boston* (1845–47). The Boston Chinese Museum followed in the steps of Nathan Dunn's successful exhibition, "Ten Thousand Chinese Things," which had opened in 1838. Dunn's and Peters's exhibitions were both large-scale projects offering a form of theatrical showcase. In both exhibitions, real Chinese figures walked among the exhibits, offering a chance for visitors to see, meet, and even talk to these ethnographic performers.

By the mid-nineteenth century, numerous publications on China were available, but Peters's exhibition was able to offer visual experiences that included a vast number of objects. The exhibition catalogues picked up words that flanked the entrance of Chinese temple doors as a motif that described the experience of interpreting the scene. Written in bold Chinese characters and with English translation were the phrases "Words may deceive" on the right, and on the left, "the eye cannot play the rogue." Through this gateway visitors entered a reconstructed world, walking a path through a reality and performance of China. Peters, like Dunn before him, was seeking to create a more sympathetic image of China. What is noteworthy about his exhibit is the ways it seems to distrust words and yet suggest that fanciful portraits misrepresent China. To counter this misrepresentation, Peters opted for tangible and practical objects of everyday life, showcased in exhibits that emphasized how things were used, worn, and consumed. As a collection, it presented a hermetic Chinese world, transported to Boston and saturated with the materiality of day-to-day experience. Visitors came, visited, discussed the show, and savored an experience that disciplined their vision, while exciting the imagination to inscribe material objects with cultural meaning. It was in this context that Qiying's diplomatic gift found an afterlife.

According to the broadside advertisements that announced the opening of Peters's "The Great Chinese Museum, Largest Collection of the Kind in the Nation," the key attractions of the show were the Chinese people—dressed up as everyone from emperors to empresses, to lawmakers and lawbreakers, and from the rich to the poor.

In a hall measuring 100 feet by 70 feet, groups of life-size mannequins were used to portray dioramas of life in China and quotes from long-term inhabitants of missionaries and merchants, emphasizing the authenticity of the portrayals (Figure 7.3). The exhibition opened with the image of the emperor holding a brush as reference to the signing of the Treaty of Wangxia. According to the exhibition, the face of the emperor was based on that of Qiying, as it was believed that the two, only tenuously related, looked alike. Cushing's portrait of Qiying was thus transformed into a metonymical tool that figured the emperor as actually signing a treaty that Qiying had negotiated through his tightrope walk over the abyss of appeasement.

As for Pan Shicheng (Figure 7.4), a salt merchant and part of Guangdong's elite, who had helped with the negotiations of the treaties with the Americans, British, and French, his subsequent affairs and angry encounters with the British tainted his friendships with the foreign traders.

In an 1851 postscript to a manuscript of inscriptions from a famous eighteenth-century Chinese ink painting entitled "Ghost Amusements" (Figure 7.5) in Pan's art collection, he penned a long poem in which he berates the Western traders for their part in the Opium War.

In the poem he plays on various meanings of the popular meaning of "ghost" (鬼 gui), which by the mid-nineteenth century in Guangdong had begun to refer to "foreigner" or "foreign devils" (番鬼 *fan gui*).[31] The poem entitled "Writings to Curse Ghosts," 《罵鬼書》 references the Han Dynasty practice of chanting rhymes as a form of exorcism. In the poem, he bitterly reflects on the consequences of trading with the West, and on his sense of betrayal after having worked alongside these men. Part of the poem reads as follows:

> [I have] also heard of ghost worlds at the four frontiers, where the people roam at night and hide during the day. At the extreme, they are like Ye Cha and Luo Cha in their ghostly caves.[32]
>
> These ghosts are not ghosts, and they come from ten thousand *li* across many oceans. When the ghosts first came to set up their ghost markets, their assortment of wares dazzled our eyes and ears. With valuables on the one side and fire on the other, they went upriver and downriver. Bales of cloth were transported using carts and boats. With the changing of the winds, their steam-powered ships sailed away in haste.
>
> Ghost-manufactured objects possess a divine ingenuity, [but] the ghost chief's money is as worthless as paper. In the beginning we embraced the ghosts, admiring and trying each other's wares. All the while, they plotted their ghost plans to spy on us.
>
> The slanderous ghost and the flattering ghost—they rape with force; the poor ghost and the hungry ghost—their teeth gnaw [at us] on behalf of the ghost commissioner. The superiors do not believe in the principles of Heaven; those below them do not have the principles of men. Now we realize that these non-ghosts are ghosts [all the same]. We call them ghosts on account of their lies.[33]

For his faith in trade with the West, Pan Shicheng paid a very heavy a price. For Qiying, his double-dealing bravado (on the one hand claiming intimacy with the West and on the other, dismissing them as foolish) landed him in danger. What Qiying had feared during his earlier negotiations came true in 1856, when the British joined forces with the French in the Second Opium War. When the Xianfeng Emperor ordered Qiying to once again negotiate treaties, the British interpreters Horatio Nelson Lay and Thomas Francis Wade exposed Qiying by producing a translation of the 1844 memorial by Qiying to the Daoguang Emperor, cited at the beginning of this essay. Humiliated, Qiying abandoned his post, only to be later arrested. On June 29, 1858, Qiying committed ritual suicide by strangulation.

An earlier version of this paper was delivered in Chinese at the Guangdong 20th Century Chinese Fine Arts International Conference in 2005. Further research was made possible with access to the Peter Parker Collection at Yale University, Philips Library at the Peabody Essex Museum, and the Boston Anthenaeum. My gratitude extends to Kendall Johnson for his editorial guidance.

8
To Make a Way

Telling a Story of US–China Union through the Letters of Henry Adams and John Hay

Paul A. Bové

One consequence of what American intellectuals and journalists call the *culture wars* is a deepened interest in the racial dimension of US relations with people from China.[1] Literary and cultural scholars have produced most of the important work in this field, sometimes aligning themselves with, while at other times needing supplementation by, the work of more specialized historians or state political thinkers.[2] Innumerable books and articles have illuminated the history of US/China relations while, increasingly in recent years, American authors have made sustained efforts to *explain* China to the US, often for ideological reasons, but more important, for the best purposes of understanding and exchange. Some of the ideological efforts belong to a genre I call *anxiety over American greatness* books. They are a subgenre of American "End of History" thinking and have, in turn, especially on the self-defined academic left, their own subgenre in the *movement of capital West stories*—all of which, no matter whether fearful or celebratory, mark the migration of power from New York to what *The Financial Times* headlines as, "If China Loses Faith the Dollar Will Collapse."[3] Even some serious recent efforts to write the history of China for a US audience judge harshly elements of China's internal policies while describing the extraordinary advances China has made economically, with the cooperation of the US on matters of trade and exchange.[4]

It is impossible to write a history of the US' understanding of its own relations and intentions regarding China, but the US State Department has made an effort to produce an official narrative of diplomatic relations between the two countries.[5] The State Department does not hesitate to say that US actions were "important factors in building animosity and resentment toward Western imperialism."[6] The first treaty between the US and China was The Treaty of Wangxia (Wang-hsia), signed in 1844. It followed the First Opium War, and it largely duplicated the British-imposed Treaty of Nanjing but added specific codicils reflecting American interests, which appear to be as early as this in conflict with those of Great Britain.

Given worldwide knowledge of America's unrelenting religiosity, it does not surprise us that one difference between the US and UK versions of these first *Open Door* treaties had to do with freedom of religion. This freedom, guaranteed by the First Amendment to the Constitution of the United States, should apply to US missionaries in China. Article 17 of the treaty insisted on this. More surprising, perhaps, for what is even now, despite migration, an intensely monolingual dominant US culture, is Article 18, which forced the Imperial Court in Beijing to end its ban on foreigners learning Chinese with the help of tutors. Historians seem to agree that the US typically followed the British expansionist policy towards China early in the nineteenth century, but there were clearly conflicting tendencies within US thinking and practice. Put simply, the conflict was between those for whom trade was the sole determining factor of US action and policy and those who thought more of US state ambitions and not surprisingly chose to bide their time in developing US strength and interests.[7]

Classic materialist accounts invariably align the interests of capital and the state. Since Marx adapted Hegel and classical economics, increasingly sophisticated analyses of this alignment have made it difficult to imagine that the state might have interests different from those of capital. It is exceedingly difficult to conceptualize such a difference, especially when dealing with the most advanced capitalist states, such as the US. A more limited view would admit that the state, in the form of its leading intellectuals and planners, take a position that state interests are not the same as capital's and that the state has purposes independent and, at times, in conflict with those of capital itself. The representational history of US/China interaction tests this hypothesis.

The State Department's timeline of US/China relations attempts to sustain a double narration, but it cannot obscure its self-understanding that US state interests controlled the ambitions of trade and capital. "American trade with China began as early as 1784," it asserts, "relying on North American exports such as furs, sandalwood, and ginseng, but American interest in Chinese products soon outstripped the Chinese appetite for these American exports."

The British especially decided to use force to manage the problem of uneven trade flows, and following the Opium Wars, US negotiators demanded arrangements that kept open Chinese markets for US goods.

The State Department's narrative gives more space to the economic motives of these various wars, treaties, and arrangements, but just as with its notice of US demands in culture and language, it notes valuable geopolitical consequences of these actions: "The treaty system also marked a new direction for Chinese contact with the outside world." The State Department believes the Treaty of Wangxia was the most important consequence of Western violence in China. It forced China to "adhere to Western diplomatic practices." In other words, it tried to force China into the form of a nation-state as dictated by the Treaty of Westphalia, at least as far as international relations were concerned.[8] Even as, following the British model, Western nations were dividing China into spheres of economic interest, these treaties also made internal Chinese political coherence a concern for those powers intent on maintaining a global order of state politics developed along that seventeenth-century model. By 1868, the Chinese were especially upset with American involvement (meddling?) in China's internal politics, resulting in the Burlingame-Seward Treaty that showed how US/China relations had evolved from the early nineteenth century, when the US essentially followed Britain's lead. As the State Department notes, "The new treaty established some basic principles that aimed to ease immigration restrictions, and represented a Chinese effort to limit American interference in internal Chinese affairs."[9] As we know, the Chinese Exclusion Act of 1882 abruptly and one-sidedly abrogated Chinese freedom of emigration to the US, while retaining US rights within China.

While the State Department emphasizes, perhaps surprisingly, the role of cultural and social racism and economic anxiety in US domestic politics as an important point in US/China relations, it explicitly notes that US state action toward China continued nonetheless. Whereas US actions had the effect of making Chinese markets and goods available to US commercial interests, China also became an important element in growing US state dominance throughout the world. The traditional "Open Door" policy embraced by the US towards China is a continuation of the UK's imperial military and commercial interests, but the modern form of the Open Door aims as much at the UK geopolitically as it does at the expansion of US trade with China.

A brief comment from John Hay suggests the context for these actions on the part of the US. Writing from the State Department on February 1, 1899, then Secretary of State John Hay reports to his correspondent, E.A. Abbey, of a typical evening he had with his friend and advisor, Henry Adams. Hay and Adams, the closest of friends for decades, regularly walked for an hour late each afternoon when Adams was in Washington and Hay was secretary. Hay tells Abbey that Adams soothes his "loneliness here": "I get out of the Department an hour or so before dinnertime, and we then walk through a triangle of back streets discoursing on the finances of the world, and the insolent prosperity of the United States."[10] Edward Chalfant has argued that Adams was, in effect, a co-secretary of state, so influential was his thinking on Hay. This is a very difficult claim to defend, but that Chalfant, the author of an original three-volume biography of Adams, makes it suggests the importance of these exchanges between the two friends and intellectuals.

There are two components in this seemingly tossed-off social remark that matter: the wealth of the US and the concern with global finance. Hay would issue the First Open Door Note on September 6, 1899. Hay and Adams had no doubt that the US was the dominant global economic power although they understood that the US did not have military power commensurate with its economic force. They also knew that European competition, especially between a rising Germany and a declining England, threatened world order. They clearly saw this time of US overseas action—the Spanish–American War of 1898 had given the US dominance in the Caribbean and in the Western Pacific—as the chance to remake the global order to suit the nature of US power. Undoubtedly, the US saw its expansive policies as serving its interests in gaining export markets. It judged its economic power greater than other nations' productive systems, and so it theorized that in an Open Door world its traders would dominate.

However, as the Hay-Adams alignment suggests, the export of what Adams called "The American System" was just as important to the policy of US expansion.[11] In his recent book, *Henry Adams and the Making of America*, Garry Wills gives an excellent account of Adams's deepening thinking about the political nature of the US and its proper world role, including important thinking about US military and geopolitical strategies.[12] We could think of this export as the start of a new model of empire. Adams thought that American inertia was, paradoxically, a destabilizing form of energy that expanded the US arrangement of republican government and market capitalism without careful social regulation across the globe. Ironically, this meant that the center of this American system could constantly shift, including the possibility that it might move entirely away from the US to other places in the world. Discussing what he called the coal economy, Adams hypothesized that, at some point, China would become the center of this American System.

In *The Education of Henry Adams*, the author makes very clear that John Hay's success in the modern Open Door policy at the turn of the twentieth century rearranged the global order of politics and economy. Like all such changes, this one occurred suddenly and surprisingly. Only after the fact did it appear to be a coup long prepared and much needed. The final chapters of *The Education* contain several passages noting the fictional Henry Adams's anxieties over the movements of history and the possible success or failure of the US System's expansion. In Chapter XXVI, for example, Adams elaborates on how society and the intellectuals cannot determine by comparison the value of contemporary events. Society erroneously indexes value on the model of the commodities market, a fact best represented by fashion and design: "The fall of China was chiefly studied in Paris and London as a calamity to Chinese porcelain. The value of a Ming vase was more serious than universal war."[13] Implicit in Adams's condensed scorn of Western understandings of China's importance is the old conflict between those who imagine China and relations to it only as regards trade, as opposed to those who understand and worry about the long secular historical interests of the human species itself.

Adams describes the imperceptive and trivializing European response to the political events in China around 1899–1900 as an example of measuring events in "money-value."[14] Moreover, Adams disapproved of how Westerners interested themselves in China in narrative that imitated the popular novels of Alexandre Dumas—presumably the great adventure stories *The Three Musketeers* and *The Count of Monte Cristo*. Adams's point, of course, is that Western societies and perceptions had no mode of understanding or organizing the meaning and sequence of historical events, save those offered by the myopic forms of the bourse and popular culture. In other words, thinking or narrating about China in relation to trade, which means in indexes or popular forms, entirely misunderstands the world-historical significance of the events centering on the readjustment of US global relations at the turn of the century as these play themselves out around what Adams takes to be the central global fact of China.

In 1902, John Hobson's *Imperialism* had considered the Western imperial powers' relations to China in rather dire ways. Hobson, an Englishman, had assumed that Western imperial dominance would remain a fact of eternal life and expressed deep concern that Western control of China would result in a cultural debacle that left the West in a state of moral and cultural decay, dependent upon the enslaved productivity of massed Chinese labor. In this popular story, China remained in a subservient world-historical position although it recovered what some economists refer to as its position as the world's workshop.

Americans Adams and Hay had a different perception, the traces of which we see in the State Department's timeline of US/China relations. As the quotation from Hay's letter makes clear, the political intellectual leadership of the US understood the possibility if not necessity of the US assuming a leading position in international affairs—because of its comparative advantages in wealth and systemic modernity of state and economy. As Hay and Adams make clear, too, for much more than a century, US concern has centered not only on US relations to China but on the key task of organizing a world in which China would play a major if not a dominant role consequent upon its size and wealth.

The US position on China had always differed from that of the UK. In the modern form of the Open Door, Hay insisted that no country should quarter foreign troops on Chinese territory. He not only challenged the traditional British position on China, but he specifically defined a difference between US and British forms of empire. Although the US fought a long war of occupation against independence fighters in the Philippines after 1898, it did not adopt the colonial model of imperialism that the British had favored in India, South Africa, and elsewhere. Nor did it actively garrison large territories as protectorates, as the UK assumed control over Egypt. Rather, the US theory required a generally decolonized global space across the face of which the US could, as it would, project power and influence. Adams understood this matter as thoroughly as any intellectual of his generation. In Chapter XXX, "Vis Inertiae," of *The Education*, Adams elaborates his sense of the stakes involved in the US/China relation and does so by a counterpoint that he often uses to discuss modernization, that is, the contrast between American activity and Russian inertia.

In this chapter, Adams's anxiety over the historical fate of China takes the form of a more profound anxiety that US energy and intelligence is inadequate to tip the balance of power against Russian traditionalism that aspires to draw China into its own inert system of arrogation. Adams always saw Russia as the definitive European problem: "The history of Europe for two hundred years had accomplished little but to state one or two sides of the Russian problem."[15] He recounts how the Adams of that time thought that drawing Russia into a modern world-system, an aspiration shared by the first President Bush and his allies some ninety years later, would be the highest accomplishment. Making cosmopolitan the often-told Russian myth of a conflict between modernizers and traditionalists, between Europhiles and Slavophiles, Adams writes, "The last and highest triumph of history would, to his mind, be the bringing of Russia into the Atlantic combine, and the just and fair allocation of the whole world among the regulated activities of the universe." The Adams of 1900 thought he could foresee the "chart of international unity."[16] America would be the agent of these utopian accomplishments, but he feared that "the fatalism of Russian inertia meant the failure of American intensity" and the stakes were high—namely, China, without which the species future could not be settled.[17]

Adams understood that, in 1900, the UK was receding from the global stage and that Germany and the US were the most active and rising agents. Russia, however, he understood as competing with the US to influence China, and he took the construction of the Trans-Siberian Railway as Russia's technological card played against the expansion of the American system. In Adams's view, and likely in Hay's as well, the railway allowed "the enormous bulk of Russian inertia to roll over China" to create a "single mass which no amount of new force could henceforward deflect."[18]

While Adams's analysis presents the US as the potentiality of the future and Russia as the negation of all futurity, the keystone of world history is understood to be China. Unlike Hobson, whose Eurocentrism denies China primacy of place or historical agency, Adams, the historian with an enormously long worldview and a deep historical sense of the species' capacity to struggle over its own self-definition, realized (as Hay likely did) that the movement of historical forces had momentarily deposited the greatest power in the hands of the US state and economic formation to attempt to assure the species its own right to its futures. Significantly, when Adams reaches the nadir of his confidence that US force can overcome Russian inertia, he turns to the movement of energy to understand the species' limits and capacities. He adapts a Newtonian idea to think this through: Inertia can take the form of movement as much as it does rest. Minds that move without novelty are inert. Mental movement depends on motive and, as Adams insists, when motives are habitual, the mind is inert, no matter how active. To deflect inert minds from their habitual path required greater and greater force as the motives underlying habit ossified and regularized. Adams's thinking is uniquely anti-pragmatist at moments like this, and it allows him to understand the conjunction between thought and geopolitical or world-historical forces in any momentary configuration. John Hay becomes Adams's ideal figure for overthrowing the inertia of idea and mass, a fact explained by Hay's adroitness in dealing with the China question.

Hay had written to Adams on May 18, 1899, to assure him that "You are wrong—as usual—about the open door. It is wider than ever for us."[19] He agreed with Adams, however, about the inadequate social and intellectual grasp of world events, adding on December 26, 1899, that Americans "are wallowing in a fat and stupid prosperity that gives occasion for nothing but sleep and scorn."[20] Hay and Adams jointly judged that the average American politician, intellectual, and entrepreneur had no sense of the "occasion" the moment embodied. Hay, despite all the institutional inertia this habituated dullness posed—most often in the form of the US Senate— managed a series of consistent policies embodied in statements and acts that ruptured world historical relations, all of which gestures concerned China.

In a contemporary letter to Whitelaw Reid, publisher of *The New York Tribune*, Hay expressed the complex opportunities inherent in US/China relations:

> About China, it is the devil's own mess. We cannot possibly publish all the facts without breaking off relations with several powers. We shall have to do the best we can, and take the consequences—which will be pretty serious [. . .]. We are to limit as far as possible our military operations in China, to withdraw our troops at the earliest day consistent with our obligations, and in the final adjustment to do everything we can for the integrity and reform of China, and to hold on like grim death to the open door.[21]

Unlike the UK and Russia, the US had no interest in the military occupation or political division of China afforded by the Boxer Rebellion. Hay's grand strategy depended on sea power, not land forces, and so while he negotiated with Russia and the UK over interests in Alaska and their impingement on the Pacific as forming part of the international political order, he also negotiated with the US Senate to pass the Clayton-Bulwer Treaty that would fund the Panama Canal, itself the result of a brazen act of US aggression.

Implicit in all of these actions is a clear narrative of US intent: to control the ordering of the Pacific in contest with European powers and Russia, in order best to enable the emergence of China into the essentially European-defined arrangement of nation-states, the profitability and stability of which the US saw itself as best able to defend. Hay makes this very clear in a comment on the canal in 1899: All will admit "that the canal ought to be built, that the United States alone will build it, [. . .] that when built it will be to the advantage of the entire civilized world."[22] That this world-historical perspective justified and enabled horrendous abuses of especially non-European lands and peoples, that it rings of the self-righteousness of US ideological confidence in its own exceptional nature and position must not obscure the US intent to seize a chance to order the world along the lines of an American System, the final goal of which was China's entry into that world order—even if, as Henry Adams suspected, China might itself someday become the center of that system.

Hay's correspondence throughout this period of his greatest success and action as secretary of state contains explanations of and allusions to his grand strategy, the narrative effect of which was that the US lacked appropriate political institutions and understanding to grasp intelligently and imaginatively the national obligations afforded logistically to the state to ensure the continued emergence of a peaceful and stable order that, in the long view, depended on preparing China for its emergence and stabilizing the system for China's major role. Hay characterized China as a world-historical necessity that by weight, intellect, and tradition would necessarily dominate a modern world order into which it might emerge as a modern nation. Adams's fear, clearly shared by Hay, concerned the Russian inertia, that is, the possibility that US force and power could not properly shape the world in which China would play its essential and insuperably weighty role.

At stake in these anxieties were not just limited materials concerns over the relative power of the US to achieve its ends. There were more restraints on US power, especially the ability to project power, than critics of US empire-building admit. Writing to Adams on September 25, 1900, Hay mentions his view in passing, which suggests he and Adams shared this opinion, that in regard to China the US could not "force the other powers to follow our lead, when we have no army and no central government."[23] Any fantasy of US aspiration and order ran aground in the minds of these grand strategists on the realism of institutions and structures. As Adams might say, inertia of mind was everywhere and demanded original ideas and tactics to overcome it. Hay is Adams's hero in the final chapters of *The Education* precisely because, against overwhelming inertia, by mind, skill, and imagination he achieved goals aimed at the success of the grand vision. Adams imagined the politician on the model of artist as the only possible figure of success inside such masses of inertia. The artist politician could, with proper conditions, coax the needed coupure in history, an achievement based on analytic perception of real possibilities that itself grounds the active imagination of a future. Of course, lest utopians of all stripes object here, we admit that such realism-based imaginings are constrained by actually existing conditions—a claim easily made against utopians and all others who object from what predetermined positionality they might embrace.

Adams and Hay together embody a political adaptation of a late-Romantic Euro-American commitment to individualized aesthetic accomplishment moved to the arena of geopolitics understood as a matter of world history with species-wide importance. Their anxiety about the success of US aspirations, which we might as well call their own aspirations for the species—to be achieved through the exercise of US instrumentalities—were placed within two other conflicting narratives of state theory that underlay their own remaking of the aesthetic politician.

In "Twilight," Chapter XXVI of *The Education*, Adams opens with a characteristic analytic mockery of a social world that "jogged" past what it judged to be the "futilities of St. Gaudens, Rodin and Besnard."[24] Just as the Western world's habits of indexing and measuring by money value made China part of only the trivial forms of popular literature, so the same world's inability to measure the seriousness of its aesthetic accomplishments made it impossible to weigh the potential they afforded in the political and strategic fields. The value of art was never more strongly defended than here, when Adams insists that it provides the better training for strategic imagination than Wall Street or politics! The author Henry Adams notoriously portrays the character "Adams" as close to his own thinking and experience while making use of the character to reveal developments in thought and history. Normally, the text portrays "Adams" as failing to perceive and understand but gradually coming, by surprise, to see something others had already seen.

In this instance, "Adams" misjudged Hay's chance of success, and "Like them [Europe's politicians] all, he took for granted that the [Foreign] Legations [in Beijing] were massacred, and that John Hay, who alone championed China's 'administrative entity,' would be massacred too, since he must henceforth look on, in impotence, while Russia and Germany dismembered China, and shut up America at home."[25] Great art comes as a sublime surprise to its audience, often with the effect of retrospective recognition that makes the invisible obvious. Hay had brought a New World Order into being: "History broke in halves," says Adams.[26] Hay had acted independently of European powers, asserted US leadership, "rescued the Legations, and saved China." For "Adams," still acquiring education, the event was sublime, "meteoric," absolutely original in "American diplomacy." The aesthetic effect was simple: "the world was struck dumb." Civilization "submitted" to US leadership because Hay had discovered the secret that the inert had a "mere instinct of docility" ready "to receive and obey his orders." This aesthetic coup achieved the political effects of legitimation and pleasure; society approved what it had not seen or understood and "burst into almost tumultuous applause." Hay had pursued a dramatic gesture that in an instant supervened against all extended narratives of ostensible decay and drift. Word and act incarnated themselves as the result of mind and power. History broke in two; amnesia set in, and all stories and affects of decay were forgotten. Success was the measure of Hay's apotheosis and it renewed him: "Hay was too good an artist not to feel the artistic skill of his own work, and the success reacted on his health, giving him fresh life."[27] Hay's success in preserving China from European predation and in extending the American system settled the competition between competing narratives or theories of history and political power that undergirded Adams's and Hay's anxieties about the likely success of US force.

As many historians of US imperialism have made clear, Alfred Thayer Mahan's great books on sea power have provided the blueprints for US grand strategy at least since the 1890s.[28] Mahan's near contemporary, H. J. Mackinder, presented a competing narrative of geopolitical history, known as "The Heartland Theory," according to which Adams's nightmare of inertia's victory was assured.[29] On one level, these theories raised the question of whether land or sea afforded the surest role to world power and dominance. Mackinder's theory might at first seem odd as the position of a state intellectual of a naval power, but in his time, the UK had already fought an important war over the heartland and was engaged in a ruinous struggle in Africa. The effort to control Egypt to assure access to India imposed greater demands on the UK to muster control of the ground and to deploy land forces in addition to colonists. The US, acting on Mahanian theories of sea power, chose not to occupy land but to project power, building in those days a battleship navy, followed in the last half-century by a submarine and carrier fleet. Mahan argued that coaling stations mattered more than colonies, and in his analysis French empire fell to English competition because the French found themselves using their naval power to protect colonies and shorelines rather than controlling sea lanes through the aggressive projection of concentrated force.

Mahan imagined the global order as a sort of smooth surface over which the US would exert influence by projection and unimpeded movement. Rather than imagining the world as a smooth surface, Mackinder presented it as an uneven surface with, as his title suggests, a Pivot around which forces moved and achieved order. Whoever controlled this pivot controlled the world. As the *National Geographic* put it, Mackinder "asserted that the pivot around which the destiny of nations has revolved in the past has been the great steppes of interior Asia—of Siberia and Mongolia—and that the history of future centuries will revolve even more dependently around these enormous plains, whether dominated by the Russian, Chinaman, or Japanese."[30] Adams's language affords us the chance to retheorize Mackinder's concept. The geographical story was fatalist: "the social movements of all times, past and future, have played and are to play around the same physical features, the heart of Asia." Such stories not only assert the facts of history to be inert, as tied to geological time, but they removed history from the meaningful sphere of human action and agency. They were the legitimation of the great inert that Adams called Russia and that he feared US resources could not overcome.

Hay's great coup proved human history was more than the record of the relative deployment of force in relation to the heartland. Innovation, especially the forms of modernity called "America," could transform geopolitics so that the inertia articulated by a narrative of historical persistence and repetition would yield to the higher power of intellect and imagination intent on smoothing the world for purposes of order achieved by modernization and sustained by the projection of power. Reconsidered in terms specific to China, the competition between Mackinder and the Hay/Adams/Mahan combine appears as the difference between the development of internal resources and coastal development of external trade. To put it technologically, we might say the competition is between the priority of the railroad and the steamship.

Adams's anxiety over the Trans-Siberian Railway was a nightmare about the likelihood that, as Mackinder argued, "The land power, the steppes of the Russian Empire and Mongolia, dormant while the oceans were being overrun, will now reassert itself."[31] China would be relegated to a marginal role, indeed, would be made tributary as under the Mongols, while the US would be overmatched, since naval power could not reach Central Asia but it, in turn, using its periphery, "would permit of the use of vast continental resources for fleet-building, and the empire of the world would then be in sight."[32] Mackinder imagines a vast new population fixed and permanent, secure and immobile, in the Heartland. This is the elaborated vision Adams calls inertia, and it is the dead weight against which Hay achieves his coup. Mackinder, as a result, saw the Atlantic as the border between civilizations, between East and West. This extraordinary and bold vision saw the US drawn permanently to the Oriental periphery of the Heartland, its diminishment the result of its Pacific Strategy. Adams saw the game similarly: "The last and highest triumph of history would [. . .] be the bringing of Russia into the Atlantic combine." As we have seen, for Adams, this aspiration had China's freedom from the land empires of Central Asia, from the seeming fatedness of geopolitics that Mackinder theorized. Adams and Mackinder alike believed it unlikely "that any possible social revolution will alter her [Russia's] essential relations to the geographical limits of her existence."[33] Put differently, in nineteenth-century terms that recent events in Iraq and Washington have reactivated, Mackinder saw the end of European imperial hegemony and knew the US inadequate to picking up the task and burden, because the Heartland was active and thriving again. "The westward march of empire," he wrote, "appears to me to have been a short rotation of marginal power round the southwestern and western edge of the pivoted area."[34] Hay and Adams attempted nothing less than a coup against this understanding of history and against the inert, whether it is called Russia or old thought.

Adams wrote, "Instantly the diplomacy of the nineteenth century [...] was forgotten."[35] Hay's boldness has an intellectual parallel in Adams's daring assertion that this single act could so transform the world, without extended allegorization, that inert thought could also be forgotten. There is something nearly Nietzschean in Adams's sense that forgetting is a result and means of creativity. Imagination dies unless activated in a struggle against the presumed to be already known, the analytically evident, as much as the unmeasured and untried fantasies of power and its explicators. Consider Hay's great act as a dramatic gesture, and it shows how active agency embodying emergent intellect can make and remake. What had not been, suddenly, was. In this case, the Pacific became the extension of the Atlantic, a violent act with enormous and threatening consequences for millions, but an act that remade the world away from the inert stories of European failure that had extended themselves into endless elaborated allegories of necessity and ruin.

China and the US had become the foci of the new world order not merely in geography but thought and imagination. Mackinder could only imagine history as more of the same, as a return with small differences; the future was merely a repetition. The US/China link shaped original thinking and action with consequences still not completely known. A simple point stands out: The major strands of US state political imagination rested upon the question of China—its importance and its capacities. Never did the US state imagine itself except in relation, perhaps even in a sort of subtending relation, to the great question of China. The game for China had to be played at the highest levels of concept and boldness, far in excess of mundane matters such as money and trade. This fact gives critics an opportunity to see how to reach beyond the confines of culture to use their skills in national and international understanding and explication. The Hay/Adams combine, while certainly not the last answer to the question of theorizing strategy or power, affords an interesting case for those formed in the humanities, as they were formed in the arts, to expand rather than diminish their importance into mere allegories of belatedness.

9
The Flow of the Traders' Goddess

Tianhou in Nineteenth- and Twentieth-Century America[1]

Khun Eng Kuah-Pearce and Yedan Huang

Introduction

As Chinese laborers and traders migrated during the eighteenth and nineteenth centuries, they moved with various cultural icons that helped them to cope emotionally with the challenges ahead and to maintain a sense of connection to the places and people whom they had left. Among these icons was Tianhou (天后), also known as Tin Hau in the Cantonese dialect of Guangdong Province, the region of origin of most of the Chinese who headed to North America. In the United States, a belief in Tianhou helped many emigrating workers and traders to re-establish a sense of communalism at their destination and to maintain a connection to the families and kin whom they had left behind. At times, the worship of Tianhou proved controversial, as Chinese immigrants tried to find common ground between traditional Chinese religious practices and the Christian denominations of a dominant American society. Over the past century, the worship of Tianhou has changed and endured. Today Tianhou faithful in the United States continue both to shape the culture of the United States and to generate political and cultural influences in diasporic networks that reach back to China and other East Asian countries where Chinese immigrants have established temples dedicated to the worship of this deity.

Significance of Tianhou in the Fishing and Trading Industry

Tianhou literally means "Heavenly Empress/Queen." She is also known as Mazu (Matsu, Ma-Tsu, Machor, 妈祖) in Fujianese. Thus, in Hong Kong,

Macau, Taiwan, Southeast Asia, and North America, we often find temples dedicated to this goddess who is believed to protect fishers, sailors, and migrants (laborers and traders) when they travel the oceans.

The cult of Tianhou emerged as a deity of the water within the Chinese pantheon of gods and goddesses in the early Northern Song Dynasty (ca.960–1127). Prior to her deification, Tianhou was born into a humble fishing family on Meizhou Island in Putian County, Fujian Province, in 960.[2] She was born mute and hence named Lin Moniang (林默娘 literally, the "mute maiden"). Although mute, she was renowned for possessing supernatural power that enabled her to assist people in need, particularly fishers, whose survival depended on safe guidance through storms. Because of this, fishers and migrants who crossed the ocean built temples in her honor.

Through the centuries, from the late Song Dynasty to the late Qing Dynasty, the role of Tianhou was recognized not only by local fishing and migrant communities but also by the Imperial Courts. As such, she was granted posthumous titles by the imperial officials who elevated her status from one of "lady" to "mother ancestress," and eventually to the "Empress of Heaven" (Tianhou). Her high status within the Chinese pantheon of gods and goddesses is reflected in the material culture associated with her. The iconography of Tianhou includes full royal regalia consisting of an imperial robe of yellow silk, richly embroidered with floral and even dragon motifs; she is generally shown wearing a crown.[3] Anthropologically, the details of the costume and the headdress reflected her high status in past centuries and contemporary times (Figure 9.1).

From the sixteenth through nineteenth centuries and onwards, migration from China to Southeast Asia and America caused a corresponding rise in Tianhou worship within the emigrant villages and the migrant communities. Even after the development of trading and commerce in the early migrant communities, the migrants continued to worship her for wealth and prosperity, revering Tianhou as "a goddess of commerce and wealth."[4] In many overseas communities, Tianhou continued to play a prominent role in the migrants' lives, even as they became more land bound as laborers who remained in one place for a long time.

As the early Chinese migrant communities took shape, the migrants established social organizations and re-created various Chinese cultural arrangements to provide them with a sense of community and identity. Here again, Tianhou became the guardian goddess for some of these communities, and she was revered by members of specific clan associations, *huiguans* (会馆), of immigrant merchants and traders. As early as the late Ming Dynasty (ca.1572–1644), the temple expenses that were associated with her rituals were often shared by "officials, merchants and the local villagers."[5] Within each *huiguan*, there was an incense committee (*xianghui* 香会) whose members were responsible for the purchase of religious paraphernalia. The worshipping of Tianhou within the *huiguan* was a periodic affair, during which the immigrants gathered for both religious and social purposes. Such social interactions tended further to reinforce business and trading partnership among the participants.[6]

The Migrational Flow of Tianhou Worship

Whereas the imperial bureaucracy promoted Tianhou by bestowing on the goddess titles that popularized her in Chinese society, it was the global migration of the traders from south China that spread the communal practices of Tianhou worship throughout the world. During the early years of emigration from China, there were essentially two groups that left. The first were the poor farmers for whom life was harsh. Facing starvation, and lacking land holdings or other durable resources, they were willing to risk the uncertainty of moving to unknown parts of their world. The second group was composed of emigrating traders, who were generally looked down upon by the mandarinate, the gentry, and the landlords.[7] The conventional Confucian prescription for social class ascension in the early centuries called for successful traders to groom a son for the mandarinate by preparing him to become a scholar. In a rigid Confucian social hierarchy, wealth by itself did not offer families an avenue to class respectability. To wealthy traders looking to find more respect from those around them, emigration became an option.

Furthermore, during the late Qing Dynasty the First Opium War destroyed the Canton Trade System, and the internal chaos of the Taiping Rebellion forced many Chinese to take the risk of migrating abroad to seek opportunities. Again in the late nineteenth century and the first half of the twentieth, there were massive waves of migration from south China to Hong Kong, Taiwan, Southeast Asia (Singapore and Malaysia), and to a lesser extent the United States, where the Chinese Exclusion Act dramatically curtailed the immigration of Chinese people in 1882.

Throughout the nineteenth century, the majority of these migrants were indentured laborers, known as "coolies," who worked in mines, on plantations, and in railroad construction. After their indenture expired, some became traders in the places where they had relocated. There were also a small number of Chinese traders who migrated independently of an indenture to pursue trade. All of the migrants brought with them their culture and traditions, including religious beliefs, and Tianhou worship played an important role in the developing communities of what would become the Chinese Diaspora.[8]

Belief in Tianhou provided psychological support during dangerous sea journeys, when it was necessary to cope with stressful living conditions. Many who braved the oceans did not survive the voyage. Upon arrival at their destination, those who did survive paid respects to Tianhou as a way of offering thanks, of mourning those who had died, and of gathering their strength to look ahead. As the sojourners adapted to their new social environment, they built Tianhou temples where the faithful gathered to pray and seek emotional and spiritual comfort in their new lives. Most temples started out as modest structures, and as the immigrant community prospered, they expanded these temples. The Chinese who first settled in Taiwan during the seventeenth and eighteenth centuries offer a fine example of those who "brought the worship of Tianhou with them" and adapted its practice as their lives continued.[9]

Temples to Tianhou also played a role in the communities' broader economic and social experiences. Jacobs outlines the fundamental cultural significance of a temple to Tianhou or Mazu:

> The village temple, in its most important political function, gives the village a focus for solidarity. Village residents do not simply burn incense together as they pray for personal and village peace and prosperity; they also cooperate in numerous activities such as festivals in which the interests of the gods, the temple, and the village's residents coincide.[10]

Furthermore, many Tianhou temples that were constructed in new places functioned not only as sites for merchant and clan associations but also as a physical place from which to imagine reconnecting to the village cultures, thus maintaining and renewing clan affiliations over vast geographical distances. For newly arrived Chinese immigrants, these temples would be a home base from which they could create "symbolic meanings" of a *huigan* space as they began to negotiate their new social space and created a sense of belonging.[11] For example, nineteenth-century Chinese migrants to Singapore erected two temples: Thian Hock Keng (天福宫 built by Fujianese) and Yueh Hai Ching Temple (粤海清庙 built by immigrants from Chaozhou). Both were dedicated primarily to Tianhou and are now regarded as the oldest and best-known Chinese temples in Singapore. Here, "the Chinese temple serve[d] primarily as a center for individual worship, as well as a symbol of and focus for community identity."[12]

Tianhou in Early America

As a result of the spread of migration of Chinese to the West, Tianhou also became established as a significant deity in the United States, beginning in nineteenth-century California. Whereas a majority of the Chinese migrants from Canton who arrived in California usually worked in the gold mines or on railroad construction, some found trading opportunities in seafaring and commercial activities based on the West Coast of the United States.[13] Given the history of American and Chinese commerce, it is not surprising that over the next century Chinese trading companies developed solid trading relationships with American traders and networks that reached across the United States. After all, in the first decades of the nineteenth century, Howqua of the Wu family had been a very wealthy and influential trader developing close relationships with American companies from his headquarters is Canton. In the mid-nineteenth century, the Wu family became involved in the American railroad companies.[14] (See the essay by Haddad in this volume.)

The oldest Chinese temple in the US is Tianhou (Tin Hau) Temple in the Chinatown of San Francisco, California. The original location of Tianhou Temple was believed to be at Waverly Place.[15] Founded in 1852, two years after California became a state, it catered to the increasing number of Chinese migrants from the districts of Sze-yap and Haining (Taishan) in Guangdong Province.[16] The number of migrants from Haining alone numbered 75,000, almost half of the 151,000 Chinese who were in California in the 1860s.[17] These migrants were also served by the various Chinese benevolent organizations and *huiguans* (会馆). The early Tianhou Temple was closely associated with these organizations. It is believed that the Sanyi District Association was the first owner of Tianhou Temple. But by the turn of the twentieth century, ownership had transferred to the Sue Hing Benevolent Association (肇庆总会馆).[18]

Beginning in the 1860s, there were at least six visible companies that facilitated emigration from China to the United States: Ning Yeong Company, Hop Wo Company, Kong Chow Company, Yeong Wo Company, Sam Yap Company, and Yan Wo Company. The membership in these companies was based on the territorial proximity of members in China or to the members' specific clan networks. As territorial-based and clan-based associations, they generally appealed to the immigrants who were from their respective districts in Guangdong and who shared common surnames.[19] By the mid-nineteenth century, San Francisco's Chinatown was a bustling trading town with an array of stores engaged in import and retail businesses. Stores imported and retailed Chinese products such as ham, tea, dried fish, and dried duck to the Chinese immigrants. There were also sales of copper kettle, pots, and all kinds of curios.[20]

Chinese businesses and trading houses established other socio-business networks in San Francisco and throughout California, in order to service the emerging remittance economy of a large majority of immigrants who sent money back to help rebuild the home from which they had emigrated and support family that had remained. The development of financial services became an important aspect of the Chinese business. Here, postal services, financial companies, import and export companies known as *jinshanzhuang* (金山庄), as well as individual couriers emerged to meet the demand for this lucrative service. *Jinshanzhuang* literally means the "Gold Mountain firms." The *jinshanzhuangs* grew out of the small grocery businesses whose owners launched remittance businesses and grew into large companies.[21] Often these companies forged networks with those in Hong Kong, where the remittances were dispatched throughout the Pearl River Delta region.[22] Another lucrative business was the transportation of immigrants to San Francisco. In 1860, each immigrant paid US$50 for the passage from Hong Kong to San Francisco. In 1860 alone, 73,890 Chinese immigrants were cleared by the San Francisco Customs House. Between 1860 and 1873, a total of 112,362 migrants arrived in San Francisco. Given the large number of immigrants, shipping companies and labor brokers made huge sums, and the business benefitted the merchants in Hong Kong and San Francisco as well as the British and American entrepreneurs who operated the steamship companies.[23]

The local merchants and grocery owners in San Francisco benefitted greatly from the influx of the Chinese migrants, as their arrival also led to an increase in the demand for Chinese foodstuffs and products[24] that would provide soul food and emotional comfort for immigrants who felt socially and emotionally alienated. These import and export firms were known as *nanbeihang* (南北行), meaning north-south firms (*nam pak hong* in Cantonese), and they proliferated from the 1850s onwards.[25] But in North America, they became commonly known as *jinshanzhuang*, along with those firms involved in transport and financial services. In the last few decades of the nineteenth century, the volume of trading was very brisk between Hong Kong and the United States. In 1867, trade volume between across the Pacific Ocean mounted to $11.4 million, and it jumped to $26.8 million in 1872.[26]

Along with the increase in trading was also an expansion of the trade networks that involved more groups of people in the rural areas of the Guangdong region where importers and exporters began to seek out more sources for all types of Chinese goods that could be exported to San Francisco. At the same time, Chinese grocery store owners living in other parts of America established trade links with the *jinshanzhuang* in San Francisco in order to procure food and other items for the Chinese immigrants in other North American cities, from Honolulu to Los Angeles, Washington to Houston, and Vancouver to Winnipeg.[27]

Once in the United States, the Chinese community extended and cultivated a rich cultural and religious tradition. Dragons, which are an important symbol in Chinese religious practices, could be seen frequently in San Francisco's Chinatown. At the same time, the dominant community of a young California State registered their impressions in newspaper articles that labeled the religious worship of the "joss house" as mere superstition and denigrated Tianhou Temple as a "heathen temple."[28] Nevertheless, there was also a vibrant spirit of adaptation in the Chinese community; in 1868, *The Overland Monthly* reported that the original Tianhou Temple, which had been primarily devoted to the Queen of Heaven, had become home to other deities who catered to the varied needs of the Chinese immigrants. The neighborhood gradually gained the nickname Tianhou Temple Street, *Tianhou Miaojie* (天后庙街) (pronounced in Cantonese *Tien Hau Miu Gau*).[29] Like other Chinese temples, Tianhou Temple in San Francisco displayed an assortment of gods and deities and thus reflected the Chinese cosmological worldview. Guarding the temple's entrance was the Earth God, *tudigong* (土地公), and on the inside one could find Guanyin (观音), the Goddess of Mercy, to whom Chinese women went for blessings (especially blessings of children and for the safe delivery of a child), and the Warrior God Guandi (关

帝), whom merchants worshipped in a commitment to loyalty and brotherhood. In addition to Tianhou Temple, more temples dedicated to Guanyin and Guandi emerged as the Chinese population grew. Furthermore, each of the six major companies erected its own temple where its members would worship their more specific clan-based guardian deity.[30]

From the 1870 onwards, rivalry developed between Chinese temples and Christian churches. Despite the ample resources of Christian churches, a surprisingly small group of Chinese people were drawn to the practice of Christianity. Chinese children might have attended Sunday School to learn English, but they left the church after having acquired elementary language skills. When pursuing business, many potential Christian converts returned to "the pagan practices which they carried with them [and that] [...] remained unmodified by the touch of [so-called] loftier ideals."[31] When, in 1879, the first bill attempting to limit Chinese immigration passed Congress and nearly became law (it was vetoed by President Rutherford B. Hayes), Chinese religious practices intensified.[32] In addition to Tianhou Temple, other temples emerged to cater to the substantial Chinese communities scattered in many towns.[33] In San Francisco, Waverly Street became known as "Queen of Heaven Street" because of the religious activities associated with Tianhou Temple and Tianhou.[34] Chinese migrants and traders also worshipped Guanyin, who was also known as Guandi, Guangong (关公) or Guanyu (关羽).[35] Besides worshipping in the temples, the Chinese organized religious processions and paraded their gods in public for all to see.

These religious associations also inspired overt political activism over the terms of immigration. Throughout these difficult years, the Chinese community in the United States worked to increase the immigration of Chinese women to the United States. When, in 1882, US President Chester Arthur signed into law the Chinese Exclusion Act, severely curtailing the number of Chinese who were legally allowed to immigrate to the United States, many of the men who had immigrated by themselves in search of work were potentially cut off from family and friend networks that usually facilitated marriage. It is worth noting that the exclusion laws did not result in total exclusion, although the merchants, students, teachers, diplomats, and travelers who were allowed travel to and reside in the United States were carefully monitored.[36] In 1883, as a result of the Chinese Exclusion Act of 1882, the six major companies (Ning Yeong Company, Hop Wo Company, Kong Chow Company, Yeong Wo Company, Sam Yap Company, and Yan Wo Company) formed a confederation known as the Chinese Consolidated Benevolent Association (CCBA) (in the east coast the Chinese name is 中华会馆; in the West coast, it is 中华公所) that was dedicated to protecting a sense of cultural identity for the Chinese migrants.[37] The CCBA, which today has chapters in many cities throughout the United States, played a leadership role in championing causes that were important to the Chinese community.[38] Furthermore, between 1882 and 1843, the *jinshanzhuang* also facilitated the movement of Chinese immigrants into the United States. During this period when the Chinese Exclusion Act was in effect, the companies of the *jinshanzhuang* helped Chinese to immigrate under the legally allowed categories of merchants, family members of merchants, diplomats and their dependents, tourists, teachers, and students. As such, most who immigrated did so under these categories.[39]

In 1910, immigrants who were wives and daughters of merchants accounted for forty-three percent of the 344 Chinese women admitted.[40] The arrival of more women also seems to have had an impact on the religious landscape of the early Chinese American community.[41] Whereas the wealthy trading class had become the elite of the Chinese community and embraced Confucianism, there was an increasing move towards Christianity among the women and youth of the working class. Women and youth found Christianity less oppressive than Confucianism, and it provided many with a sense of liberation and enabled them to enjoy social rights on a basis more equal to that of men.[42] By the 1910s and 1920s, there was an increasing number of Chinese Christians. The emergence of various Christian groups, including the Young Men's Christian Association (YMCA) and the Young Women's Christian Association (YWCA) in San Francisco's Chinatown, directly challenged the influence of Tianhou and other Chinese temples on the Chinese community. The YMCA and YWCA aggressively discouraged Chinese Christians from practicing traditional Chinese customs and engaging in religious practices, including Chinese weddings and funeral rituals. They introduced Western-style church weddings and funeral rituals.[43] Christian churches often offered social services that were designed to appeal especially to women, such as provision of day care, instruction of English, and the assistance of widows.[44]

However, Chinese women found ingenious ways of combining their newfound Christian faith with traditional Chinese beliefs. They often continued to practice Confucianism, Buddhism, and Daoism while allowing their children to attend Sunday School and Christian celebrations.[45] The syncretic nature of the Chinese belief system tended to incorporate in traditional beliefs a version of a Christian God who could address people's everyday spiritual needs.

By 1900, the Chinese in the city and county of San Francisco had branched out into different types of occupations, which can be categorized into seven broad types: (1) primary producers and extractors that included agriculturalists, agricultural laborers, miners and fishers; (2) professionals; (3) skilled artisans; (4) entrepreneurs and their assistants, such as merchants, other entrepreneurs, clerks, and shop assistants, factory workers, and agents and supervisors; (5) laundry workers; (6) cooks; and (7) other personal services. Within these seven occupational categories, one-third were entrepreneurs and their assistants. In this entrepreneurial category, China-born merchants stood at around 18.6% and American-born Chinese merchants at 17%.[46]

From the 1930s onwards, ships from China sailed regularly to the American Pacific coast, where Chinese traders traded in sea otter skins. San Francisco became an increasingly important center for trade in a range of commodities including granite, furniture, wood planks, rice, Chinese curios, and other products. It was reported that Chinese traders in the United States furnished the J.L. Riddle and Company with "nearly all the furniture [that] was of Chinese importation."[47]

As commerce took hold in the United States, the flow of money and people increasingly went in both directions. The flow of transnational capital back into the immigrants' hometowns enabled many of these villages to prosper relative to those that did not received remittances. By the turn of the twentieth century, some Chinese immigrants had become successful enough in the United States either to contribute substantially to the infrastructural development of China or to return to China, where they started up various types of business. Fong Joe Guey was the first aviator to return to China, where he started the Guangdong Aviation Company in 1911.[48] Another Chinese American, J.K. Choy, left his native home of Honolulu for China and became head of the Chinese Merchants Navigation Company.[49] A Seattle labor contractor, Chin Gee Hee, raised capital from the Chinese community in the US and Canada to help finance the construction of the Sunning Railroad that ran from Taishan District to Xinhui District in Guangdong.[50] One spectacular result can be seen in the three- to four-storey buildings built in the Kaiping region of the Pearl River Delta during the 1920s and '30s. These buildings, known as the Diaolou (碉楼), combine Eastern and Western styles and were listed as a cultural heritage by UNESCO in 2007. Since then, other Chinese American entrepreneurs have invested in various factories, department stores, and utilities, primarily in Guangdong Province.

As a by-product of this influx of capital back into the emigrant villages, Chinese Americans were also able, despite their absence, to exert political influence on their home villages. In one case, the Chinese Americans in San Francisco and Los Angeles who had emigrated from the district of Enping protested against the incorporation of Enping District into another district. Their protests prompted the district governor to communicate to the Chinese American community in California and explain the rationale for such action.[51] In another incident, the intervention of a Chinese American originally from Xinning District prevented the local magistrate of the district from being forced out of office.[52]

As Chinese Americans searched for footing in both the United States and in their homeland, they became increasingly vocal in their support of economic initiatives and political causes. In the 1920s and 1930s, when the Republican government threatened to abolish Confucianism, the expatriates advocated its preservation by highlighting the centrality of Confucian values to Chinese who were not only in the homeland but also in the United States.[53] Scholars such as Yong Chen have argued that many of these economic ventures and political protests were expressions of national affiliation on the part of Chinese emigrants who wanted to live in the United States and yet continue to shape China's economic and political engagement with the world.[54]

Tianhou in the United States during Recent Decades

Chinese gods and goddesses continue to offer new immigrants to the United States ways not only of coping with life but also of reshaping American culture. The worship of Tianhou has been strengthened by continuing waves of migration from mainland China and Hong Kong and from communities of the Chinese Diaspora located in Taiwan, Singapore, Malaysia, Vietnam, and other places. Often they relocate to the United States with wealth and skills that enable them to lead middle- to upper-middle class lifestyles there. Their urbane and cosmopolitan experiences make it less necessary for them to rely on social programs offered by Christian organizations, and they often continue uninterrupted in their practice of religious and cultural beliefs.

The practice of Tianhou worship in the United States continues to reflect the international politics of Chinese identity. In 1986, Taiwanese immigrants built a new Tianhou temple called Ma-Tsu Temple U.S.A. in San Francisco. The temple was first located on Vienna Street and then relocated to Grant Avenue. Finally, in 1996, the trustees of the temple purchased a three-storey building at the present location of 30 Beckett Street in San Francisco's Chinatown. Within the temple, the main Ma-Tsu Shrine Hall houses three Ma-Tsu goddesses. The central figure is a replica of the original Ma-Tsu from Taiwan. She is flanked on the right by the second Ma-Tsu, *er-ma* (二妈), and on left by the third Ma-Tsu, *san-ma* (三妈). The temple is also home to other gods and goddesses such as Guanyin, the Earth God, and a variety of other guardian gods.[55] This temple plays a vibrant role in the community, hosting a variety of religious functions that coincide with events of the lunar calendar. Jonathan H.X. Lee traces the development of this temple from its original home in Beigang, Taiwan, and examines how this particular Ma-tsu temple developed a transnational reach with its branch in San Francisco. In 2005, it was estimated that there were 1,500 fee-paying lifetime members and 800 non-fee-paying registered members, primarily of Taiwanese origin.[56] The temple is now a standard part of processions that celebrate Chinese New Year. On the first day of the lunar New Year, it provides a space for the devoted to praying and asking for blessings.[57] In the seventh month of the lunar calendar, the temple organizes rituals, *pudu* (普渡), dedicated to the Hungry Ghosts. These rituals watch over the lonely, hungry, and orphaned spirits who are not cared for by any kin.[58] In addition to this specific site, Tianhou features prominently in attempts by Taiwanese Americans to stay connected to their homeland. For example, many believers in Tianhou embark on pilgrimages to the main Ma-Tsu Temple in Beigang to honor Mother Tianhou; and, during the 2008 presidential election, over 10,000 Taiwanese majority entrepreneurs from California returned to cast their votes in elections.[59] As such, Tianhou is regarded as a transnational deity.

In California, there are other major temples to Tianhou, including two in Los Angeles. One is located in the relatively poor district of Lincoln Heights and the other in Chinatown.[60] Furthermore, in the early 1980s, the Elderly Indochinese Association's Tianhou Temple was built to serve the Chaozhouese and Cantonese-speaking Chinese from Southeast Asia.[61] In September 2005, another Tianhou Temple costing US$2 million was built in Los Angeles. It is known as Thien Hau Temple, or as Chùa Bà Thiên Hậu in

Vietnamese. Thien Hau Temple in Los Angeles is affiliated with the Camau Association, a charity organization that supports and caters to Vietnamese refugees from the Camau region in Vietnam as well as to communities of Sino-Vietnamese, Sino-Khmers, and Sino-Thais who speak Chaozhouese and Cantonese.[62]

The Tianhou temples organize various religious activities on the first and fifteenth days of the lunar month, ceremonial ringing of bells, and vegetarian dinners and festivals. On Chinese New Year's Eve, various Chinese communities come to make offerings to Tianhou and other gods and goddesses, asking for blessings from these supernatural beings. Ma-Tzu Temple U.S.A. also participated in other Chinese religious ceremonies dedicated to related deities and another making Ma-Tzu's presence felt in the wider American Chinese community.[63] On such occasions, the temple comes alive with many worshippers, creating a festive atmosphere of "heat and noise" (热闹) that delights the diverse Chinese American community, whose members come from China and Southeast Asia.

Conclusion

The flow of Tianhou to the United States began in the mid-nineteenth century and continues in the present. There are many stories yet to be written of the varied experiences of Chinese migrants who prayed to Tianhou as they adapted to a new environment and looked to the future with a heart filled with memories of villages and hometowns to which they hoped to contribute after achieving prosperity in the United States. The relative economic strength of recent migrants from communities of the Chinese Diaspora continues to extend the legacies of Tainhou worship. This traditional Chinese worship does not merely endure but thrives in vibrant religious communities such as those of the Tianhou and Ma-Tsu Temples in San Francisco and Los Angeles, providing the Chinese with a transnational social space to craft a sense of American identity that keeps them reconnected to their original home.

Today, the various Tianhou temples throughout the United States stand as testimony to generations of Chinese who have worked their way into the fabric of American society. At these sites of worship, ancestral memories remain alive to those who are keen to know their past. For others, the experience of relocation may seem a distant family legend and an experience that they might not want to revisit. For many mainstream non-Chinese

Americans, Tianhou and other Chinese temples stand as a testimony to the influx of the Chinese migrants who have helped shape American culture.

The Christianization of Chinese Americans at the turn of the twentieth century greatly influenced the worshipping of Tianhou and other traditional Chinese gods and goddesses. As Chinese Americans became rooted in American society, it became more practical for some of these migrants—traders, laborers, and intellectuals—to adopt the Christian faith as a means of gaining acceptance into American society at large. Similar to China's early so-called "rice Christians," those in nineteenth- and early twentieth-century America often needed the assistance extended to them by Christian organizations. Like the waxing and waning of the moon, belief in Tianhou and all the other gods and goddesses has faded in and out of the lives of many Chinese Americans.

Today, as a result of continued flows of new migrants who include wealthy entrepreneurs and traders from China, Hong Kong, Taiwan, and Vietnam, Tianhou is benefiting from renewed interest of believers. The monthly lunar cycle has taken on significantly vibrant meanings as temples now conduct regular religious services. In addition, the large religious processions and celebrations during the lunar New Year are a visible testimony of the continued importance of Tianhou in the American Chinese Diasporic community.

Notes

Introduction

1. Brantz Mayer, "China and the Chinese," *Southern Quarterly Review* 12.23 (July 1847): 6.
2. ———, 48. Mayer is quoting from John Quincy Adams, "December 1841, Lecture on the War with China, Delivered before the Massachusetts Historical Society," *Chinese Repository* 11.5 (May 1842): 274–89.
3. John Gallagher and Ronald Robinson, "The Imperialism of Free Trade," *Economic History Review* 6.1 (1953): 1–15.
4. Bernard Semmel, *The Rise of Free Trade Imperialism: Classical Political Economy, the Empire of Free Trade and Imperialism, 1750–1850* (Cambridge: Cambridge University Press, 1970).
5. Elizabeth Malcolm, "The Chinese Repository and Western Literature on China 1800 to 1850," *Modern Asia Studies* 7.2 (1972): 168.
6. David Todd, "John Bowring and the Global Dissemination of Free Trade," *The Historical Journal* 51.2 (2008): 385.
7. Adams, 277.
8. ———, 281.
9. American involvement in the opium trade is well documented (Fairbanks 1953; Goldstein 1978; Downs 1997); Michael Greenberg notes that, because of the British monopoly on India, Americans trucked "Turkey opium from Smyrna (in practice generally imported *ex bond* from London)" (108). See Michael Greenberg, *British Trade and the Opening of China, 1800–42* (Cambridge: Cambridge University Press, 1951).
10. *The Oxford English Dictionary* (OED) traces the English word *stereotype* to the French *stéréotype*, which derives from the Greek components *stereo-*, meaning solid, and *-type,* from the root of the word meaning to beat or to strike. The OED records the first usage of the word in the 1798 *Annual Chronicle Register; or a View of the History and Politics of the Year* in an article announcing the "new discovery in printing." In an interesting echo of the points of reference in this introductory essay, the OED traces the first figurative usage as "something continued or constantly repeated without change; a stereotyped phrase, formula, etc.; stereotyped

diction or usage" to William H. Prescott's *History of the Conquest of Peru* (1850), as quoted in George Ticknor's *Life of William Hickling Prescott* (1864).

The related meaning of *cliché* followed later, at the end of the century. The French word for a stereotype block is *cliché*, originally the past participle of *clicher*, a variant of *cliquer* and "applied by die-sinkers to the striking of melted lead in order to obtain a proof or cast." The OED finds the first literal English usage in Charles Babbage's *The Economy of Manufacturers* (1832) and the figurative usage as "a stereotyped expression, a commonplace phrase" in the December 1892 issue of *Longman's Magazine*, in an article by the Scottish historian and poet Andrew Lang.

11. The VOC obtained its charter not from a king or queen but from the States-General of the Dutch Republic on March 20, 1620. See Leonard Blussé, *Visible Cities: Canton, Nagasaki, and Batavia and the Coming of the Americans* (Cambridge, MA: Harvard University Press, 2008).
12. Paul A. Van Dyke, *The Canton Trade: Life and Enterprise on the China Coast, 1700–1845* (Hong Kong University Press, 2005).
13. There is evidence, however, of an extensive network of informal trade, junk trade, and smuggling; see Van Dyke.
14. See Peter C. Perdue, "Rise & Fall of the Canton Trade System – III, Canton & Hong Kong," http://ocw.mit.edu/ans7870/21f/21f.027/rise_fall_canton_03/index.html, MIT Visualizing Cultures, (accessed May 23, 2011).
15. On the impact of opium in China, see Yangwen Zheng, *The Social Life of Opium in China*. (Cambridge: Cambridge University Press, 2005); and, Hsin-pao Chang, *Commissioner Lin and the Opium War* (Boston, MA: Harvard University Press, 1964).
16. On the impact of Adam Smith's writings on the young American nation in the 1780s and 1790s and, specifically, on John Adams, Thomas Jefferson, and James Madison, see Samuel Fleischacker, "Adam Smith's Reception among the American Founders, 1776–1790," *The William and Mary Quarterly* 59.4 (October 2002): Fleischacker argues that the founders read Smith closely and did not reduce him to the slogans of "free trade" by which Smith's theories would be foreshortened in the nineteenth century.
17. Adam Smith, *Inquiry into the Nature and Causes of the Wealth of Nations* (1776; New York: Prometheus Books, 1991).
18. ———, 28.
19. ———, 9.
20. See K. Scott Wong, "The Transformation of Culture: Three Chinese Views of America," *American Quarterly* 48.2 (June 1996): 201–32.
21. The historical work on the China Trade is vast. In affording the basis for this introduction's overview, most important have been work by Jonathan Goldstein, Jacques Downs, Paul A. Van Dyke, John Haddad, P.C.E. Smith, John M. Belohlavek, John Fairbanks, Michael H. Hunt, George Souza, Leonard Blussé, and James R. Fichter.

As for the precedent of historical work on the China Trade, the work of Hosea Ballou Morse is perhaps the most influential in providing accounts of how the system of trade functioned. To trace a scholarly thread through twentieth-century work, please note James Callahan (1907), Kenneth Latourette (1917), Tyler Dennett (1922), Sydney and Marjorie Barstow Greenbie (1925), Foster Rhea Dulles (1930), George Danton (1931), Michael Greenberg (1957), Walter Cohen (1971), Margaret Christman (1984), and A. Owen Aldridge (1993).

22. Sydney and Marjorie Barstow Greenbie, *Gold of Ophir; or The Lure that Made America* (1925; New York: Wilson-Erickson, 1937), xiii.
23. Edward Said, "Orientalism Reconsidered," in *Literature, Politics and Theory: Papers rom the Essex Conference, 1976–84*, ed. Francis Barker, Peter Hulme, Margaret Iversen, and Diana Loxley (London: Methuen, 1986), 211.
24. For definition of "competency" and its distinction from "affluence," see James R. Fichter, *So Great a Proffit: How the East Indies Trade Transformed Anglo-American Capitalism* (Cambridge, MA: Harvard University Press, 2010), 116–8.
25. The romance of free trade was not limited to the nineteenth century. In *American Diplomacy in the Orient* (1903), the prominent late nineteenth-century diplomat John Watson Foster looks back over the previous century to characterize the United States as a civilizing force in Asia. Foster served in the Mexican–American War (as had Brantz Mayer) and in the Union Army during the United States Civil War, after which he became an influential United States diplomat in Europe, South America, and Asia. At the end of the First Sino–Chinese War (1894–95), Foster was the American advisor to General Li Hongzhang (李鴻章), the powerful viceroy of Beijing who brokered a costly end to the conflict with Japan (Vol. 4, p. 161). Consider Foster's following characterization as it seemingly echoes the sentiments of Mayer and President Adams:

    "The people of the United States of America, as soon as they had achieved their independence in 1783, manifested a notable spirit of commercial maritime adventure. Within two years after peace was secured the flag of the new nation had been carried by American ships into all the waters of the globe. When they reached the Pacific Ocean in quest of avenues of trade, they found almost all the ports of Asia closed against them. Within the brief lifetime of this young nation, a great transformation has been wrought in that region of the globe, which is vitally affecting the political and commercial relations of many nations. In this transformation the United States has borne a conspicuous and honorable part" (1).

    Foster goes on to credit the "government of the United States" with "bringing [the Orient] out of their seclusion and opening them up to commercial and political intercourse with the outside world" (2). In this narrative of national development, the United States joins the civilized Christian cultures of the West in competitive enterprise and industry as each nation pursues its own self-interests. Foster's appreciation of American distinctiveness gauges the degree to which the nation has opened up the disrespectfully recalcitrant patriarch to commercial intercourse. See John W. Foster, *American Diplomacy in the Orient* (Boston and New York: Houghton, Mifflin and Company, 1903).

26. Mayer, 1.
On Mallalieu, Margaret Oliphant writes "apparently editor, or at least principle contributor, of various London papers, dating his letter from one newspaper office after another, and apparently also engaged in official work of some description in connection with the Foreign Office. His special department was politics and political economy, and his pretension to superior knowledge were very high" (Vol. 2, p. 201). On Mallalieu's political views and reputation, see Margaret Oliphant ("Mrs. Oliphant"), *Annals of a Publishing House: William Blackwood and His Sons, Their Magazine and Friends*, 3 vols (Edinburgh and London: William Blackwood and Sons, 1897), Vol. 2, 201–5.
27. Consider Edward Said's more general description of Orientalism: "From roughly the end of the eighteenth century, when in its age, distance and richness the Orient was rediscovered by Europe, its history had been a paradigm of antiquity and originality, functions that drew Europe's interests in acts of recognition or acknowledgement but *from* which Europe moved as its own industrial, economic and cultural development seemed to leave the Orient far behind. Oriental history—for Hegel, for Marx, later for Burkhardt, Nietzsche, Spengler and other major philosophers of history—was useful in portraying a region of great age, and what had to be left behind. Literary historians have further noted in all sorts of aesthetic writing and plastic portrayals that a trajectory of 'westering,' found for example in Keats and Hölderin, customarily saw the Orient as ceding its historical pre-eminence and importance to the world spirit moving westwards from Asia and towards Europe" ("Orientalism Reconsidered," 215).
28. Arif Dirlik, "Chinese History and the Question of Orientalism," in *Genealogies of Orientalism: History, Theory, Politics*, ed. Edmund Burke III and David Prochaska (Lincoln: University of Nebraska Press, 2008), 401.
29. John K. Fairbank, *Chinese-American Interactions: A Historical Summary* (New Brunswick, NJ: Rutgers University Press, 1975), 12.
30. See John Ledyard, *The Last Voyage of Captain Cook: The Collected Writings of John Ledyard*, ed. James Zug (Washington DC: National Geographic Society, 2005). As Zug explains, John Ledyard's *A Journal of Captain Cook's Last Voyage to the Pacific Ocean* (New Haven: CT, 1783) was crucial to early attempts to secure copyright protection when Ledyard secured from the Connecticut Assembly a fourteen-year guarantee of sole rights of publication. Zug regards this as ironic, charging that Ledyard's book is "marred by plagiarism," particularly from an account of Cook's first voyage published by John Hawkesworth (see bibliography) and from the anonymously published *Journal of Captain Cook's Last Voyage to the Pacific Ocean on* Discovery; *Performed in the Years 1776, 1777, 1778, 1779* (1781). In 1921, Frederick W. Howay attributed authorship of this text to John Rickman, a British Lieutenant aboard Cook's ship *Resolution* (Zug, p. xxii). However, Zug's charge of "plagiarism" overlooks the printing conventions of the era when the

precise nature of authorial proprietorship was being formulated, and many books appeared anonymously and were published by multiple printers. Ledyard's letter to the Connecticut Assembly was a bid for control over rights of republication and not necessarily a claim of originality.

31. In the late 1780s, the *Columbia Rediviva* and *Lady Washington* embarked from Boston en route to Cape Horn and Nootka Sound on the Northwest Coast and then on to Canton. In the early 1790s, the *Columbia* performed the voyage again. The first voyage, lasting from 1787 to 1790, included both the *Columbia* and the *Washington*. The ships embarked on September 1787, to collect furs throughout the Northwest Coast and eventually split up. The *Lady Washington* arrived in China on January 26, 1790, where its captain, John Kendrick, altered it and sold it. Only the *Columbia*, under the command of John Gray, returned to Boston on August 17, 1790. On the second voyage that began in September 1790, John Gray captained the *Columbia* to the Northwest Coast of North America, where he negotiated with the Native peoples for furs before proceeding to China. He returned to Boston on June 29, 1793. Frederick Howay's *Voyages of the Columbia to the Northwest Coast 1787–1790 & 1790–1793* collects the journals and logs of these voyages. Howay also notes that the first United States ship to engage in "maritime trade on the Northwest Coast" with a destination in Canton may have been the *Eleanora*, which arrived in Canton on August 12, 1788; there is no paper trail to that voyage (x).
32. Martin I. J. Griffin, *Commodore John Barry, Father of the American Navy: The Record of His Services for Our Country* (published by the author: Philadelphia, 1903), 259.
33. ———, 276–7.
34. On the full extent of American companies dealing in opium, see Jacques Downs, *The Golden Ghetto: The American Commercial Community at Canton and the Shaping of American China Policy, 1784–1844* (Bethlehem, PA: Lehigh University Press, 1997). Fichter (2010) includes Elias Derby (pp. 132–5) of Salem, and William Bingham (pp. 136–8) of Philadelphia among the merchants who made fortunes (often precarious ones) from the Indies trade.
35. On the distinctive logic behind the development of United States corporations of this period, see Chapter 10 ("American Capital and Corporations") of Fichter's *So Great a Proffit* (2010), especially pages 254–7.
36. David Shavit, *The United States in Asia: A Historical Dictionary* (New York: Greenwood Press, 1990), 537-38.
37. David Abeel, *Journal of a Residence in China, and the Neighboring Countries, from 1829 to 1833* (New York: Leavitt, Lord & Co., 1834), 7.
38. Samuel Wells Williams became the first Chair of Chinese Language and Literature at Yale University, where he and son, Frederick, who became a professor of modern Oriental history also at Yale, revised *The Middle Kingdom*, first published as two volumes in 1847 (Haddad 25). The missionary foundations of Chinese studies at Yale are evident in the early twentieth-century scholarship of

Kenneth Scott Latourette, on the faculty of the Yale Divinity School, who wrote on China and the history of Christianity, and who served as president of the American Historical Association in 1948.

39. The most complete edition of Low's letters is Hodges and Hummel, 2002. Harriett's daughter Katherine Hilliard edited her mother's letters to publish *My Mother's Journal: A Young Lady's Diary of Five Years Spent in Manila, Macau, and the Cape of Good Hope from 1829–1834* (1900). This edition was greatly abbreviated and filtered by Low's daughter. There is another version, edited by Elma Loines: *The China Trade Post-Bag of the Seth Low Family of Salem and New York* (1953). Also, Rosmarie W. N. Lamas has recently published an account of Low's life in Macao by editing Low's letters and journals; see *Everything in Style: Harriett Low's Macau* (Hong Kong University Press, 2006). For more on Low, see Puga 2002, 2003.
40. Lucy Cleveland accompanied her husband on his trading voyages throughout Asia. In 1829, she lived in Macao and was a friend of Harriett Low. Her journal and sketchbook are held at the Peabody Essex Museum. For more on Cleveland, see Puga 2007. Mary Parry Sword accompanied to Macao her husband, John Dorsey Sword. She resided in Macao from 1841 until her death in 1845. Her letters are held in the Sword family papers at the Historical Society of Pennsylvania. Rebecca Kinsman accompanied her husband to Macao in 1843 and lived there with her niece and two daughters until 1847. For more on Kinsman, see Puga 2004, 2006, 2008.
41. See Hsin-pao Chang, *Commissioner Lin and the Opium War* (Cambridge, MA: Harvard University Press, 1964) and Peter Ward Fay, *The Opium War 1840–1842: Barbarians in the Celestial Empire in the Early Part of the Nineteenth Century and the War by Which They Forced Her Gates Ajar* (Chapel Hill: University of North Carolina Press, 1975).
42. John M. Belohlavek, *Broken Glass: Caleb Cushing and the Shattering of the Union* (Kent, OH: Kent State University Press, 2005), 163.
43. David Hunter Miller, *Treaties and Other International Acts of the United States of America* (Washington, DC: Government Printing Office, 1931–34), Vol. 4, 566.
44. Teemu Ruskola, "Canton Is Not Boston: The Invention of American Imperial Sovereignty," *American Quarterly* 57:3 (September 2005): 874.
45. John Lauritz Larson, *Bonds of Enterprise: John Murray Forbes and Western Development in America's Railway Age*, expanded ed. (1984; Iowa City: University of Iowa Press, 2001), 21.

Chapter 1

1. This list and summary of the differences between company and private bookkeeping practices is based on many years of work in those respective archives. It is impossible to list all of the documents and archives here, but in general, they include the company archives of the EIC, VOC, DAC, SOIC, GIC, and CFI; Portuguese records in Macao; and the American China Trade records in

numerous libraries and archives in Salem, Boston, Providence, Mystic Seaport, Philadelphia, and several other cities in the United States. For a more complete list of archives and sources consulted, see the bibliography in Paul A. Van Dyke, *The Canton Trade: Life and Enterprise on the China Coast, 1700–1845* (Hong Kong University Press, 2005; reprint, 2007).

2. The EIC consultations and diaries of the eighteenth century, for example, were kept in duplicate, and the VOC diaries (called *dagregisters*) were kept in triplicate. The DAC kept duplicate and/or triplicate copies of their trade journals (the sections that cover the time the Danes were in China). The GIC often kept multiple trade journals for each ship, and sometimes in three languages (Dutch, English, and French). These companies and others regularly copied many other documents from their China Trade as well.
3. For a summary analysis of the decline of the East India companies in China and the rise of private traders in the early nineteenth century, see Van Dyke, Chapter Six.
4. A recent study has shown that Chinese junk ratios stood at about 2.5 tons-per-man, whereas Western ships sailing to China had ratios ranging from 1.8 to 11 tons-per-man. The overwhelming majority of Western vessels operating in East Asia were much more labor-efficient than Chinese junks, only a few falling below 2.5 tons-per-man. The number of cannons a junk could carry was tightly restricted by the Chinese government, often only allowing a couple to each, so they had no choice but to minimize their armaments. The number of men in junk crews was also regulated according to the size of the vessel, but the enforcement of this policy does not appear to have been as uniform as the one restricting cannons. Paul A. Van Dyke, "Operational Efficiencies and the Decline of the Chinese Junk Trade in the Eighteenth and Nineteenth Centuries: The Connection," in *Shipping Efficiency and Economic Growth 1350–1800*, ed. Richard Unger (Leiden: Brill, forthcoming in 2011), Table 4: "Tons-per-man ratios of vessels in Asia."
5. The small American vessels that sailed to China in the early nineteenth century were often the targets of pirates. Company ships, in contrast, were usually free from such threats as they were much too large and heavily armed for pirates to overcome them. For examples of small private ships being attacked in China, while company ships sat safely at anchor, see entries in Hosea Ballou Morse, *The Chronicles of the East India Company Trading to China, 1635–1834*. 5 vols. (Cambridge, MA: Harvard University Press, 1926; reprint, Taipei: Ch'eng-wen Publishing Co., 1966).
6. The post of an American consul in Canton was often a voluntary assignment with little or no pay involved, so there were no regulations requiring the keeping of extensive records. In fact, the documents that have survived from the American consuls are anything but complete or sophisticated, often being a simple note, receipt, or letter. These documents have no order to them, no page or document numbers, and many have no title or date. They can be correctly

described as nothing but a box full of miscellaneous notes. Washington, DC, National Archives: "Despatches from United States Consuls in Canton, 1790–1906." In contrast, the Dutch consular records in Canton are fairly complete and sophisticated. See examples in National Archives, The Hague: Canton 265–74, 378, and 389–90.

7. For examples of the EIC diaries, see Morse. For VOC diaries translated into English, see Paul A. Van Dyke and Cynthia Viallé, *The Canton-Macao Dagregisters*, 1762 and 1763 (Macau: Macau Cultural Institute, 2006 and 2008, respectively).
8. The American "shoe box" style of accounting is still visible today, as those records are now kept in the archives using the same method (one box of loose papers per ship or voyage). For examples, see the many private archives of China traders in the Phillips Library at Peabody Essex Museum, Massachusetts Historical Society, Rhode Island Historical Society, the John Carter Brown Library at Brown University, and the Barry-Hayes Papers in the Independent Seaport Museum in Philadelphia. In contrast, the VOC put all of the original receipts and papers together from each voyage, in a systematic sequence, and then sowed them together into very large bound bundles with leather covers. The GIC and DAC recorded most of their information into bound books. The DAC entered original documents from China into these bound books, including contracts, receipts, and agreements. Each type of document was entered in the books in a predetermined sequence and order. The EIC followed a similar practice but used bound booklets instead of books. Unlike the Danes, English officers copied documents into the booklets and then discarded the originals, which was the practice of the GIC as well. As a result, there are now very few original documents from Chinese merchants in the EIC and GIC archives, whereas the VOC and DAC archives are full of them. The American archives have some of those types of records but nothing compared to what is in the VOC and DAC archives. There are also a few original contracts from the Canton merchants in the SOIC and CFI archives. Understanding these different bookkeeping practices of the China traders is essential in explaining why those archives contain different documents today.
9. These observations are based on analyzing several hundred American logbooks and thousands of European journals and diaries. For a list of the specific records and archives, see the bibliography at Van Dyke, *The Canton Trade*, 2005.
10. Printed Price Currents for major ports in Asia were fairly widespread by the 1820s. For an example of one from Canton in 1823, see Van Dyke, *The Canton Trade*, Plate 24.
11. In the latter half of the eighteenth century, the EIC often charged Chinese merchants each year for goods that they delivered in previous years that were found to be deficient. For examples, see Morse. Look for entries of "rubbish teas."
12. For examples of the Canton junks consigning cargo space, see Van Dyke, *The Canton Trade*, 145–50.
13. The Shreve family papers at Peabody Essex Museum and the Carrington papers at the Rhode Island Historical Society are exceptions, as they contain

ledger-type books. But when comparing them to those of the companies, they fall far behind, as the latter contain multiple cross-referencing to other books and documents and are very consistent in the type of information they contain. The overwhelming majority of the American China traders created no such documents. In bookkeeping, Shreve and Carrington were among the best of the Americans. They created trade ledgers and did a fairly good job of balancing their accounts. But both of them also employed the shoe box method, throwing all the receipts from a ship or voyage into a box or folder, and their ship logbooks are very simple documents. There are no financial records in the American China Trade collections consulted for this study that can compare to the sophisticated accounting systems of the East India companies.

14. For a couple of examples of these privately kept journals and expense books of the EIC ships, see British Library, India Office Records: Mss Eur D 1199 "Journal of accounts of Capt. John Hamilton to Canton 1800–1801"; and the many private journals and records of Captain John and Archibald Hamilton in the National Maritime Museum Archive in Greenwich. Because the ships these captains commanded were not owned by the EIC (even though they were employed by the EIC), those documents were not the company's property and are therefore not in the company archives today. Because all the other East India companies owned their ships, those documents appear in their archives today.
15. For a discussion of the differences in the port fees that companies and private traders paid in China, see Van Dyke, *The Canton Trade*, 104–8.

Chapter 2

1. The first ship to embark for China was probably the sloop named *Harriet*. See James Fichter, "American History on Other Continents," *Common-Place* 7.1 (October 2006), http://www.historycooperative.org/journals/cp/vol-07/no-02/tales/ (accessed July 20, 2010. Also see Tyler Dennett, *Americans in Eastern Asia: A Critical Study of United States' Policy in the Far East in the Nineteenth Century* (1922; New York, Barnes and Noble, 1963), 9.
2. See Chen Jianhua, "Eighteenth Century Guangzhou—A Witness to the Prelude to the Friendly Exchanges between China and the United States," Prologue to *Empress of China* (Chinese version) (Guangzhou: Guangzhou Publishing House, 2006), 9. Another major financier of the voyage was Robert Morris, who had been the major financial architect of the Revolutionary War. In his later years, he miscalculated in land speculation that bankrupted him, and he spent time in prison for his debts. For the financing of the voyage, see Clarence L. Ver Steeg, "Financing and Outfitting the First United States Ship to China," *Pacific Historical Review* 22.1 (1953): 1–12.
3. Samuel Shaw, *The Journals of Major Samuel Shaw, the First American Consul at Canton: With a Life of the Author by Josiah Quincy*, ed. Josiah Quincy (Boston, MA: Wm. Crosby and H.P. Nichols, 1847), 229.

4. Jonathan Goldstein, *Philadelphia and the China Trade, 1682–1846* (University Park: Pennsylvania State University Press, 1978), 33.
5. Shaw, 232.
6. Dennett, 9.
7. Shaw, 129.
8. Anon, Review of *The Journals of Major Samuel Shaw, the First American Consul at Canton: With a Life of the Author, by Josiah Quincy, North American Review* CXXXVIII (January 1848): 250.
9. On character, see Martin Price, *Forms of Life: Character and Moral Imagination in the Novel* (New Haven, CT: Yale University Press, 1983).
10. Shaw, 105.
11. For Adam Smith's influence on the young American nation in the 1780s and 1790s and, specifically, on John Adams, Thomas Jefferson, and James Madison, see Samuel Fleischacker's "Adam Smith's Reception among the American Founders, 1776–1790." *The William and Mary Quarterly* 59.4 (October 2002): 897–924.
12. Quoted from Philip Chadwick Foster Smith in Jean Gordon Lee, *Philadelphians and the China Trade, 1784–1844* (Philadelphia, PA: Philadelphia Museum of Art, 1984): 23. Also see Goldstein, 17.
13. Quoted from Smith, *The Empress of China* (Philadelphia, PA: Philadelphia Maritime Museum, 1970), 70.
14. Shaw, 183.
15. See Francis Paul Prucha, *American Indian Policy in the Formative Years: The Indian Trade and Intercourse Acts, 1780–1834* (Cambridge, MA: Harvard University Press, 1962); *American Indian Treaties: The History of a Political Anomaly* (Berkeley: University of California Press, 1994); *Documents of United States Indian Policy* (Lincoln: University of Nebraska Press, 2000). Also see, Vine Deloria and Clifford M. Lytle, *The Nations Within: The Past and Future of American Indian Self-Government* (New York: Pantheon Books, 1984).
16. Shaw, 231–2.
17. Smith, 203; Shaw, 232.
18. See Kristen Johannson, *Ginseng Dreams: The Secret World of America's Most Valuable Plant* (Lexington: University of Kentucky, 2006); Jerry Bradley Knox, *History, Geography, and Economics of North American Ginseng* (Ann Arbor, MI: UMI, 2000); David A. Taylor, *Ginseng, the Divine Root* (Chapel Hill, NC: Algonquin Books of Chapel Hill, 2006); and Alexandra Cook, "Linnaeus and Chinese Plants: A Test of the Linguistic Imperialism Thesis," *Notes & Records of the Royal Society* 64 (2010): 121–38.
19. See Lydia Liu, "The Question of Meaning-Value in the Political Economy of the Sign," in *Tokens of Exchange: The Problem of Translation in Global Circulations* (Durham, NC: Duke University Press, 1999), 19. Also see Eric Cheyfitz, *The Poetics of Imperialism: Translation and Colonization from The Tempest to Tarzan* (1991; Philadelphia: University of Pennsylvania Press, 1997).

20. Jean Baptiste Du Halde, *A Description of the Empire of China and Chinese-Tartary, Together with the Kingdoms of Korea and Tibet: Containing the Geography and History (Natural as well as Civil) of those Countries. Enrich'd with General and Particular Maps, and Adorned with a Great Number of Cuts.* From the French of P. J. B Du Halde, Jesuit: With Notes Geographical, Historical, and Critical; and Other Improvements, particularly in Maps, by the Translator [R. Brookes]. 2 vols. (London: Printed by T. Gardner in Bartholomew-Close, for Edward Cave, at St. John's Gate, 1738, 1741), Vol. 1, 322.
21. ———, 322.
22. Chris Parsons, "Ginseng in Canada?" John Carter Brown Library (August 2008), http://brown.edu/Facilities/John_Carter_Brown_Library/I%20found%20it%20JCB/august08.html (accessed November 17, 2010).
23. For the translation of "Garent-oguen" and the standardization of Linnean nomenclature, see Cook, who quotes from *Mémoire présenté à S. A. R. Mgr le duc d'Orléans, Régent du Royaume de France: Concernant la précieuse plante du Gin seng de Tartarie, découverte en Canada par le P. Joseph-François Lafitau, de la Compagnie de Jesus, Missionaire des Iroquois du Sault Saint Louis* (Joseph Mongé, Paris, 1718), 11–2.
24. Quoted from Edwin Wolf and Kevin J. Hayes, *The Library of Benjamin Franklin* (American Philosophical Society, 2006), 262. Wolf quotes Franklin from the *Pennsylvania Gazette,* July 27, 1738.
25. See final page of John Green's "Receipts, Canton in China, 1784–1786," Archival Materials in the Rare Book and Ms Library Manuscripts of the Van Pelt Library, University of Pennsylvania (Ms. Coll. 499).
26. See Shaw, 207–8.
27. ———, 140–1.
28. Goldsmith's overview of six races holds true in the 1774, 1782, 1795, and 1823 editions of *History* that I have consulted. See Oliver Goldsmith, *A History of the Earth and Animated Nature*, Vol. 2 (Dublin: Printed by James Williams, No. 21, Skinner-row, 1782).
29. Shaw, 178–9.
30. In Benjamin Franklin, *Writings*, ed. J. A. Leo Lemay (Library of America, 1987), 735.
31. From the University of Notre Dame Libraries, Coin and Currency Collections in the Department of Special Collection: http://www.coins.nd.edu/ColCurrency/CurrencyText/CC-05-10-75a.html (accessed June 2, 2010).
32. Shaw, 10.
33. ———, 21, 54.
34. ———, 58; emphasis in the original.
35. ———, 77; emphasis in the original.
36. ———, 100.
37. ———, 91.
38. ———, 91; emphasis in the original.

39. ———, 111.
40. ———, 111–2.
41. Benson J. Lossing, *Pictorial Field-Book of the Revolution; or, Illustrations, by Pen and Pencil, of the History, Biography, Scenery, Relics, and Traditions of the War for Independence*. 2 vols (1853; New York: Harper & Brothers, 1860), Vol. 1, 695.
42. Shaw, 198–9.
43. Amasa Delano, *Delano's Voyages of Commerce and Discovery: Amasa Delano in China, the Pacific Islands, Australia, and South America, 1789–1807*, ed. Eleanor Roosevelt Seagraves (Stockbridge, MA: Berkshire House Publishers, 1994), 6.
44. Delano, 6.

Chapter 3

1. This essay contains material previously published by the author in *The Romance of China: Excursions to China in U.S. Culture, 1776–1876* (Columbia University Press, 2006).
2. Caroline Howard King, *When I Lived in Salem, 1822–1866* (Brattleboro, VT: Stephen Daye Press, 1937), 28–30. Walter Muir Whitehill, *The East India Marine Society and the Peabody Museum of Salem, a Sesquicentennial History* (Salem, MA: Peabody Museum, 1949), 37–8, 45–6.
3. William Goetzmann, *New Lands, New Men: America and the Second Great Age of Discovery* (New York: Penguin, 1986), 1.
4. *Chinese Repository* (January 1843), 6. According to the historian Kenneth Latourette, China in the early part of the nineteenth dentury "was almost as remote from ordinary American life as the planet Mars." Kenneth Scott Latourette, *The History of Early Relations between the United States and China 1784–1844* (New Haven, CT: Yale University Press, 1917), 124.
5. William Wood, *Sketches of China* (Philadelphia: Carey & Lea, 1830), vii, x–xi.
6. Gideon Nye, *The Morning on My Life in China* (Canton, 1873), 4.
7. Nancy Ellen Davis, "The American China Trade, 1784–1844: Products for the Middle Class" (Ph.D. Dissertation, George Washington University, 1987), 114.
8. ———, 67, 122. Ping Chia Kuo, "Canton and Salem: The Impact of Chinese Culture upon New England Life during the Post-Revolutionary Era," *New England Quarterly* 3 (1930), 431. In the early nineteenth century, a Boston or Salem dwelling might have as much as one-tenth of its "effects" originating in China, and Philadelphia would not have fallen too far short of that figure. Jonathan Goldstein, *Philadelphians and the China Trade, 1682–1846* (University Park: Pennsylvania State University Press, 1978), 6. In Charleston, South Carolina, Chinese export porcelain is one of the most commonly found ceramics at archeological sites, accounting for twenty-four percent of all ceramics uncovered. The majority of these are shards of the blue and white inexpensive dinner and tea wares. Robert A. Leath, "After the Chinese Taste: Chinese Export Porcelain and Chinoiserie Design in Eighteenth Century Charleston," *Historical Archeology* 33 (1999), 50.

9. Crosby Forbes, *Hills and Streams: Landscape Decoration on Chinese Export Blue and White Porcelain* (International Exhibition Foundation, 1982), preface.
10. Whereas all Chinese ceramics were hand painted, the British employed this mechanical technique. A design engraved on copper was printed onto a piece of tissue paper, which was then transferred onto the ceramic object. Forbes, preface; Davis, 119.
11. Harry Barnard, *The Story of the Wedgwood Willow Pattern Plate* (Hanley, England: Catalogue Printers), 2–7.
12. In this version of the story, the father, not the duke, finds the lovers on the island. Ada Walker Camehl, *The Blue-China Book* (1916; New York: Dover Publications, 1971), 287.
13. David Quintner, *Willow! Solving the Mystery of Our 200-year Love Affair with the Willow Pattern* (Burnstown, ON: General Store Publishing House, 1997), 152.
14. Perhaps realizing that Americans preferred to think of the willow legend as of Chinese origin, the Buffalo China Company, the first American pottery company to produce Willow Ware, misinformed potential customers in its 1905 catalogue: "The legend illustrated by the Blue Willow ware decoration is centuries old. It originated in China and forms a love story so alive with human interest that it never grows old." Quintner, 128. Similarly, Ada Walker Camehl wrote that what she believed was a Chinese story had inspired Thomas Minton to make the original Willow Pattern. Camehl, 287. Finally, Amy Carol Rand, in an article instructing women how to design table linen using the Willow Pattern, also wrote under the misconception that the pattern was Chinese in origin. *The Modern Priscilla* (July, 1910), 4.
15. Benjamin Silliman, *American Journal of Science and Arts* (January, 1839), 392–3; *Public Ledger* (December 28, 1838). Also see Dunn's obituary in that same newspaper (October 24, 1844).
16. Philadelphia Directories, *Nelson B. Gaskill Papers*. Historical Society of Pennsylvania.
17. Arthur Hummel, "Nathan Dunn," *Quaker History* 59.1 (1970): 34–8.
18. Yen-P'ing Hao, "Chinese Teas to America—A Synopsis," *America's China Trade in Historical Perspective,* ed. John King Fairbank and Ernest May (Cambridge, MA: Harvard University Press, 1986), 29.
19. Goldstein, 51–3. Elma Loines, ed., *The China Trade Post-bag of the Seth Low Family of Salem and New York* (Manchester, ME: Falmouth Publishing House, 1953), 7 and 298.
20. Patrick Conner, *George Chinnery, 1774–1852: Artist of India and the China Coast* (Woodbridge, UK: Antique Collectors' Club, 1993), 227.
21. John Curtis Perry, *Facing West: Americans and the Opening of the Pacific* (Westport, CT: Praeger, 1994), 41. John Murray Forbes and John Cushing in just a few years each made enough money to retire and invest their substantial profits in American industry. Yen-P'ing Hao, 29–30. The trader Benjamin Shreve of Salem listed his priorities in life: "approving conscience...irreproachable character,

good health, a good wife, and plenty of money!" Carl Crossman, *The China Trade: Export Paintings, Furniture, Silver & Other Objects* (Princeton, NJ: The Pyne Press, 1972), 7.

22. *Poulson's American Daily Advertiser* (January 3 and February 16, 1820).
23. *Isaac Jones, Richard Oakford, and Samuel T. Jones Vs. Nathan Dunn, Defendant, February 1832* (Philadelphia, PA: Brown, Bicking & Guilbert, Printers, 1835), 34–5. Library Company of Philadelphia.
24. Letter from Nathan Dunn (November 19, 1821). The Quaker Collection, Haverford College.
25. *Isaac Jones, Richard Oakford, and Samuel T. Jones Vs. Nathan Dunn*, 33–4.
26. ———, 37.
27. Perry, 29. Loines, 300–1.
28. Tyler Dennett, *Americans in Eastern Asia* (New York: Macmillan, 1922), 59.
29. Perry, 29. Loines, 300–1. Howqua's fortune would translate into over US$1 billion in current terms and represent a very high percentage of the United States' gross domestic product (GDP) in the 1840s.
30. The events surrounding the fire of 1822 also impressed upon Dunn a favorable view of China's poorer citizens. For in the midst of all the chaos, an elderly Chinese gentleman walked away with about ten bags of silver belonging to Dunn, each worth $1,000. As well as being poor, the man possessed a large family and could easily have kept the small fortune without getting caught. However, in an act of honesty that, according to Dunn, "says something for the poor people of China," he returned the bags of silver to the pleasantly astonished owner. *Isaac Jones, Richard Oakford, and Samuel T. Jones Vs. Nathan Dunn*, 34–5. Library Company of Philadelphia. Joan Kerr Facey Thill, "A Delawarean in the Celestial Empire: John Richardson Latimer and the China Trade" (M.A. Thesis, University of Delaware, 1973), 40.
31. *Isaac Jones, Richard Oakford, and Samuel T. Jones Vs. Nathan Dunn*, 33–4. William Wood, a friend of Dunn, explained the economic situation and England's retaliatory measures: "The extensive importation of British goods in American vessels had been materially detrimental to the Company's trade in China, and, as they found it impracticable to prevent the exportation from England by Americans, they resolved to thwart them, by using their influence to affect their sales in Canton." Wood, 64.
32. For Dunn's collecting, see Brantz Mayer, *A Nation in a Nutshell* (Philadelphia, PA: Brown, Bicking, & Guilbert, 1841). Pamphlet in the Rare Books Department, Library of Congress. E.C. Wines, *A Peep at China in Mr. Dunn's Chinese Collection* (Philadelphia, PA: Ashmead and Co., 1839), 10. J. S. Buckingham, *Buckingham's America: Eastern and Western States*, Vol. 2 (London: Fisher, Son, & Co., 1842), 44.
33. Silliman, *American Journal of Science and Arts*, 393.
34. Joseph Kastner, *A Species of Eternity* (New York: Alfred A. Knopf, 1977), xii–xiv, 3–5.

35. Peale was organizing his museum in 1792, two years after Franklin's death. Charles Coleman Sellers, *Mr. Peale's Museum* (New York: W.W. Norton & Company, 1980), 60.
36. William H. Goetzmann and William N. Goetzmann, *The West of the Imagination* (New York: W.W. Norton & Company, 1986), 15–35.
37. Dennett, 49. Foster Rhea Dulles, *The Old China Trade* (Boston, MA: Houghton Mifflin Company, 1930), 18–9.
38. Letter from Nathan Dunn (April 13, 1824). The Quaker Collection, Haverford College.
39. Mayer, *A Nation in a Nutshell.*
40. Wines, 10–1.
41. Silliman, *Mr. Dunn's Chinese Collection.*
42. Buckingham, 44.
43. Daniel Bowen, *A History of Philadelphia...Designed as a Guide to Citizens and Strangers* (Philadelphia, PA: Daniel Owen, 1839), 85–6.
44. "Chinese Collection," *Philadelphia Saturday Courier* (December 22, 1838).
45. Wood, 243.
46. Hummel, 34–8.
47. According to Bowen's 1839 guide to Philadelphia, Dunn was one of the city's "most wealthy and respectable citizens." Bowen, 82.
48. Sellers, 273.
49. ———, 15, 19, 60, 215. Neil Harris, *Humbug: The Art of P.T. Barnum* (Boston, MA: Little, Brown and Company, 1973), 35. Edward Alexander, *Museum Masters* (Nashville, TN: American Association for State and Local History, 1883), 5.
50. Wines, 12.
51. Dunn, *Descriptive Catalogue of the Chinese Collection in Philadelphia* (Philadelphia, PA, 1838), 92.
52. Letter dated November 23, 1838. The Quaker Collection, Haverford College.
53. Wines, 10, 15; *Public Ledger* (December 28, 1838).
54. "Chinese Collection," *Philadelphia Saturday Courier* (December 22, 1838).
55. Sellers, 294–5.
56. Wines, 15.
57. *Chinese Repository* (November 1843), 567–8. Since Nathan Dunn's friends and acquaintances in Canton were intrigued by his museum, he sent the *Repository* a packet of press clippings that it used as the nucleus of an article.
58. William Wood described the same shrine. Wood, 87.
59. Buckingham, Vol. 2, 46–7. Buckingham probably appreciated Dunn's anti-opium stance, having himself brought before Parliament on June 13, 1833, an invective on the demoralizing tendency of opium. R.B. Forbes, *Remarks on China and the China Trade* (Boston, MA: Samuel N. Dickinson, 1844), 51.
60. Silliman, *American Journal of Science and Arts,* 394. Crossman, 205.
61. *Chinese Repository* (March 1840), 583–4.
62. Mayer, "China and the Chinese," 6–7; Mayer, *A Nation in a Nutshell.*

63. Mayer, *A Nation in a Nutshell.*
64. Alexis de Tocqueville, *Democracy in America* (Chicago, IL: University of Chicago Press, 2000), 485–92. The original work was published in France in two volumes, 1835 and 1840.
65. Dunn, *Descriptive Catalogue*, 7, 13, 97, 100.
66. ———, 30–3, 105.
67. Silliman, *Mr. Dunn's Chinese Collection in Philadelphia.*
68. Dunn, *Descriptive Catalogue*, 118–20.
69. Mayer, *A Nation in a Nutshell.*
70. ———.
71. Bowen, 86.
72. Buckingham, Vol. 2, 55.
73. Joseph Sturge, *A Visit to the United States in 1841* (London: Hamilton, Adams, and Co., 1842), 62.
74. *Public Ledger* (December 28, 1838).
75. "Chinese Collection," *Philadelphia Saturday Courier* (December 22, 1838).
76. "Curiosities in Philadelphia," *The Farmers' Cabinet* (August 14, 1840).
77. Mayer, *A Nation in a Nutshell*; Mayer, "China and the Chinese," 6–7.
78. *Chinese Repository*, v. 12, 570.
79. Williams's residence in China did not overlap with Dunn's. However, in the pages of the *Chinese Repository*, the English language newspaper that he published in Canton, Williams mostly lauded the museum and its proprietor, pronouncing Dunn "a true Friend of the Chinese." *Chinese Repository* (March 1840), 585 and (November 1843), 582.
80. This poem apparently enjoyed a wide circulation. A Dr Scott (whose first name is not given) cited it in his "Lecture on the Chinese Empire," delivered in New Orleans before the Mechanics' Institute, January 26, 1854. New York Public Library. The poem is also quoted in an adventure novel set in China. Harry French, *Our Boys in China: The Thrilling Story of Two Young Americans Scott and Paul Clayton Wrecked in the China Sea, on their Return from India, with their Strange Adventures in China* (New York: Charles Dillingham, 1883), 45.
81. Frederick Wells Williams, *The Life and Letters of Samuel Wells Williams, LL.D.* (New York: G.P. Putnam's Sons, 1889), 144–6. Samuel Wells Williams, *The Middle Kingdom* (New York: Wiley and Putnam, 1848), xiii–xvi. In the mid-1840s, Osmond Tiffany, who visited China in 1844 and admired the Chinese, decried the same rampant mockery observed by Williams: "Their manners, their habits, language, dress, and sentiments, have all been made the butt of witless ridicule." *The Canton Chinese* (Boston, MA: James Monroe & Co., 1849), 266.
82. According to Stuart Creighton Miller, China received national attention for the first time during the Opium War because the conflict coincided with the rise of the penny press. And since these widely read newspapers portrayed China's military efforts as futile and its leadership as pompous, many Americans grew to be

more critical of Chinese culture. *The Unwelcome Immigrant: The American Image of the Chinese, 1785–1882* (Berkeley: University of California Press, 1969), 83–4.

83. Smyth wrote his detailed description of current views towards China to set up an analogy with the Episcopal Church. He likened the pomp and ceremony of that denomination to the Chinese empire. Thomas Smyth, "The Prelactical Doctrine of Apostolical Succession Examined," *Princeton Review* (January 1842), 139–41.
84. Smyth, 139–41.
85. ———, 139–41.
86. ———, 139–41.

Chapter 4

1. John Gallagher and Ronald Robinson, "The Imperialism of Free Trade," *Economic History Review*, Second series, 6.1 (1953). 1–15.
2. Derek S. Linton, "Asia and the West in the New World Order—From Trading Companies to Free Trade Imperialism: The British and Their Rivals in Asia, 1700–1850," in *Asia in Western and World History*, ed. Ainslie T. Embree and Carol Gluck (New York: M.E. Sharpe, 1997), 83–116.
3. On this voyage, see Philip Chadwick Foster Smith, *The Empress of China* (Philadelphia, PA: Philadelphia Maritime Museum, 1984); and Samuel Shaw, *The Journals of Major Samuel Shaw, the First American Consul at Canton* (Boston, MA: Wm. Crosby and H. P. Nichols, 1847).
4. Leonard Blussé, *Visible Cities: Canton, Nagasaki, and Batavia and the Coming of the Americans* (Cambridge, MA: Harvard University Press, 2008).
5. Foster Rhea Dulles, *The Old China Trade* (Boston, MA: Houghton Mifflin, 1930), 210; Blussé, 64.
6. For the United States' early contact with Siam, see Edmund Roberts and W.S.W. Ruschenberger, *Two Yankee Diplomats in 1830s Siam* (Bangkok: Orchid Press, 2002). For development of the US Canton trade, see Jacques M. Downs, *The Golden Ghetto: The American Commercial Community at Canton and the Shaping of American China Policy, 1784–1844* (Bethlehem, PA: Lehigh University Press, 1997), 128; Paul A. Van Dyke, *The Canton Trade: Life and Enterprise on the China Coast, 1700–1845* (Hong Kong University Press, 2005), 135–7. For the rice trade, see also Benito J. Legarda, *After the Galleons: Foreign Trade, Economic Change and Entrepreneurship in the Nineteenth-Century Philippines* (Quezon City: Ateneo de Manila University Press, 1999), 157–78; and Huang Zisheng and He Sibing, *Feilübin Huaqiao Shi* [*History of the Philippine Chinese*], rev. and enlarged ed. (Guangzhou: Guangdong Gaodeng Jiaoyü Chubanshe [Guangdong Higher Education Press], 2009), 262–3.
7. "Copartnership Agreement between Cyrus Butler, Edward Carrington and Co., B. and T. C. Hoppin and Samuel Russell" (December 26, 1818), Russell and Company Records, Manuscript Division, Library of Congress.
8. P. Ammidon to his brother (December 27, 1823), Russell and Company Records.

9. Robert B. Forbes, *Personal Reminiscences*, 2nd ed. (Boston, MA: Little, Brown and Company, 1882), 128–30; Carl Seaburg and Stanley Paterson, *Merchant Prince of Boston: Colonel T. H. Perkins, 1764–1854* (Cambridge, MA: Harvard University Press, 1971), 368–70.
10. He Sibing, "Qichang Yanghang Yu Shijiu Shiji Meiguo Dui Guangzhou Maoyi" ["Russell and Company and American Trade with Canton in the Nineteenth Century"] *Xueshu Yanjiu* [*Academic Research*] 6 (2005): 109–16; "Russell and Company, 1818–1891: America's Trade and Diplomacy in Nineteenth-Century China" (Ph.D. Dissertation, Miami University, 1997).
11. On the Canton System, see Randle Edwards, "The Old Canton System of Foreign Trade," in *Law and Politics in China's Foreign Trade*, ed. Victor H. Li, (Seattle: University of Washington Press, 1978): 360–78; and Van Dyke, *The Canton Trade*. For the origins and ramifications of the Cohong, see Kuo-tung Anthony Ch'en, *The Insolvency of the Chinese Hong Merchants, 1760–1843* (Taipei: The Institute of Economics, Academia Sinica, 1990); W.E. Cheong, *Hong Merchants of Canton: Chinese Merchants in Sino-Western Trade* (London: Curzon Press, 1997); Patrick Conner, *The Hongs of Canton: Western Merchants in South China, 1700–1900, as Seen in Chinese Export Paintings* (London: English Art Books, 2009); and Zhang Wenxin, *Guangdong Shisan Hang Yu Zaoqi Zhongxi Guanxi* [The Thirteen Hongs of Guangdong and the Early Sino-Western Relations] (Guangdong Jingji Chubanshe [Guangdong Economics Press], 2009).
12. William Hunter, *"The Fan Kae" at Canton before Treaty Days, 1825–1844* (London: Paul Trench and Co., 1882; reprinted, Shanghai: Oriental Affairs, 1938), 24; Sarah Forbes, Hughes, ed., *Letters and Recollections of John Murray Forbes*. 2 vols. (Boston, MA: Houghton Mifflin, 1900; reprinted, New York: Arno Press, 1982), Volume 1, 86.
13. Paul G. Pickowicz, "William Wood in Canton," *Essex Institute Historical Collections* 107 (January 1971): 3–14.
14. *Canton Register*, 15 November 1827.
15. ———, 30 November 1827; 4 February 1828.
16. William W. Wood, *Sketches of China; with Illustrations from Original Drawings* (Philadelphia, PA: Carey and Lea, 1830), 63–4.
17. Michael Greenberg, *British Trade and the Opening of China, 1800–1842* (Cambridge: Cambridge University Press, 1951), 179, 184.
18. *Canton Register*, 19 February 1831.
19. Rosmarie W. N. Lamas, *Everything in Style: Harriett Low's Macau* (Hong Kong University Press, in conjunction with Instituto Cultural do Governo da R.A.E. de Macau, 2006), 292.
20. *Chinese Courier and Canton Gazette*, 28 July 1831.
21. ———, 4 August 1831.
22. ———, 18 August 1831.
23. ———, 13 October 1831.

24. ———, 31 August 1833.
25. W.E. Cheong, *Mandarins and Merchants: Jardine Matheson & Co., A China Agency of the Early Nineteenth Century* (London: Curzon Press, 1979), 5–8.
26. Yen-p'ing Hao, *The Commercial Revolution in Nineteenth-Century China: The Rise of Sino-Western Mercantile Capitalism* (Berkeley: University of California Press, 1986), 31, 215.
27. Te-kong Tong, *United States Diplomacy in China, 1844–60* (Seattle: University of Washington Press, 1964), 22.
28. Robert B. Forbes to Rose Forbes, 31 March 1839, in Phyllis Forbes Kerr, ed., *Letters from China: The Canton-Boston Correspondence of Robert Bennet Forbes, 1838–1840*, (Mystic, CT: Mystic Seaport Museum, 1996), 114–5.
29. B. and T. Hoppin to S. Russell & Co. (25 April 1819), Russell and Company Records.
30. Robert B. Forbes to Rose Forbes, 21 May 1839, Kerr, *Letters from China*, 142.
31. A Memorial from the American Merchants at Canton (25 May 1839), US House Document, No. 40, 26th Congress, 1st Session, Serial Number 364, in *United States Policy Toward China: Diplomatic and Public Documents, 1839–1939*, ed. Paul Clyde (New York: Russell and Russell, 1964), 3–6. This document was signed by eight members of the Russell firm: Russell Sturgiall, W. Delano, Jr., Gideon Nye, Jr., R.B. Forbes, A.A. Low, Edward King, S.B. Rawle, and Jas. Ryan.
32. Jules Davids, ed., *American Diplomatic and Public Papers: The United States and China*. Series 1: *The Treaty System and the Taiping Rebellion, 1842–1860*. 21 vols. (Wilmington, DE: Scholarly Resources, 1973): Vol. 1, xxxviii. P. W. Snow was US consul in Canton from 1835 until 1843 when he was forced to leave China because of ill health.
33. Quoted in Geoffrey C. Ward, *Before the Trumpet: Young Franklin Roosevelt, 1882–1905* (New York: Harper & Row, 1985), 74.
34. Hunter, 146–9; Ward, 75–6.
35. Stuart Creighton Miller, "Ends and Means: Missionary Justification of Force in Nineteenth Century China," in *The Missionary Enterprise in China and America*, ed. John K. Fairbank (Cambridge, MA: Harvard University Press, 1974), 249–82.
36. For Bridgman, see Michael C. Lazich, *E.C. Bridgman (1801–1861), America's First Missionary to China* (Lewiston: Edwin Mellen Press, 2000).
37. "Intercourse with the Chinese," *The Chinese Repository* 1 (August 1832): 141–7.
38. "Free Trade," *The Chinese Repository* 1 (December 1833): 355–73.
39. "Free Intercourse with China," *The Chinese Repository* 3 (July 1833): 128–37.
40. "Promulgation of the Gospel in China," *The Chinese Repository* 3 (January 1835): 428–37.
41. "Universal Peace," *The Chinese Repository* 3 (March 1835): 516–27.
42. "Christian Missions in China," *The Chinese Repository* 3 (April 1835): 559–68.
43. "Treaty with the Chinese," *The Chinese Repository* 4 (February 1835): 441–9.
44. Message (December 30, 1842), *The Papers of Daniel Webster: Message and Papers*, ed. Kenneth E. Shewmaker (Hanover, NH: Dartmouth College and University Press of New England, 1983–88), Vol. 4, 211–4.

45. Charles Hall to John C. Calhoun (November 30, 1844), *The Papers of John C. Calhoun*, ed. Robert L. Meriwether and W. Edwin Hemphill. 21 vols. (Columbia: University of South Carolina Press, 1963–1993): Vol. 20, 405–11.
46. Jules Davids, ed., *American Diplomatic and Public Papers*, Vol. 1, xlii.
47. Circular (March 20, 1843), Shewmaker, *The Papers of Daniel Webster: Diplomatic Papers*, Vol. 1, 901–2.
48. Sarah Forbes Hughes, ed., *Letters and Recollections of John Murray Forbes*, 2 vols. (Boston: Houghton, Mifflin & Co., 1899; Reprinted, New York: Arno Press, 1981), volume 1, 115.
49. John Murray Forbes et al. to Daniel Webster (April 29, 1843), in Shewmaker, *The Papers of Daniel Webster: Diplomatic Papers,* Vol. 1, 917–21. The letter was signed by John M. Forbes, Robert B. Forbes, Thomas H. Perkins, Samuel Cabot of the firm of Thomas H. Perkins, William Appleton, a merchant and later a congressman from Suffolk, Massachusetts, Nathan Appleton, a textile manufacturer and congressman from Boston, and John Lowell Gardner, East Indian merchant and railroad magnate.
50. John Green and N. Alsop Griswold to Daniel Webster (13 May 1843). Quoted in Qiao Mingshun, *Zhongmei Guangxi De Diyi Ye: 1844 Nian Wangxia Tiaoyue Qianding De Qianqian Houhou* [The First Page of Sino-U.S. Relations: The Signing of the Wangxia Treaty of 1844] (Beijing: Shehui Kexue Wenxian Chubanshe [Social Sciences Documentation Press], 1991), 68.
51. Kenneth E. Shewmaker, "Forging the 'Great Chain': Daniel Webster and the Origins of American Foreign Policy Toward East Asia and the Pacific, 1841–1852," *Proceedings of the American Philosophical Society* 129.3 (1985): 225–59.
52. In 2005, the *American Quarterly,* the journal of the American Studies Association, published international law scholar Teemu Ruskola's essay on Cushing's invention of American imperial sovereignty in the Treaty of Wangxia. Historian Belohlavek's new biography of Cushing was also published in the same year. A chapter of this book is devoted to the China mission, which provides new insights into Cushing's diplomatic endeavors in Macao. See Teemu Ruskola, "Canton Is Not Boston: The Invention of American Imperial Sovereignty," *American Quarterly* 57.3 (September 2005): 859–84; and John M. Belohlavek, *Broken Glass: Caleb Cushing and the Shattering of the Union* (Kent, OH: Kent State University Press, 2005), "The Road to China, 1843–1844": 150–80.
53. Macabe Keliher, "Anglo-American Rivalry and the Origins of U.S. China Policy," *Diplomatic History* 31.2 (April 2007): 227–57.
54. ———, 228–9.
55. See Letters 183, 198, and 201 in *China Trade and Empire: Jardine, Matheson & Co. and the Origins of British Rule in Hong Kong, 1827–1843,* ed. Alain Le Pichon (Oxford: Published for the British Academy by Oxford University Press, 2006); and Cheong, *Mandarins and Merchants.*
56. Lamas.

57. Murray A. Rubinstein, *The Origins of the Anglo-American Missionary Enterprise in China, 1807–1848* (Metuchen, NJ: Scarecrow Press, 1996).
58. Downs, 292.
59. Davids, *American Diplomatic and Public Papers*, Vol. 1, Documents 48–51.
60. Hunter, 146–7.
61. Forbes, 152–3, 155.

Chapter 5

1. This article is an outcome of the research project entitled "Jindai Sheng-Gang-Ao Dazhong Wenhua yu Dushi Bianqian" [Popular Culture and Urban Transformation of Modern Canton, Hong Kong, and Macau], granted by the Ministry of Education, PRC, for the Centre for Historical Anthropology, Sun Yat-sen University (Project No. 2009JJD770032). The author would like to thank the two anonymous reviewers for their comments and suggestions.
2. In 1664, the French made their first organized attempts to enter the trade of the Indian Ocean with the foundation of the French East India Company. They maintained a low profile for the greater part of the seventeenth century. See Lakshmi Subramanian, ed., *The French East India Company and the Trade of the Indian Ocean* (New Delhi, India: Munshiram Manoharlal Publishers, 1999), "Introduction." The Swedish came even later. The 1732 departure of the *Fredericus R.S.*, the first vessel staffed and armed by the newly established Swedish East India Company, marks the beginning of regular relations between Sweden and India and more particularly China. See Paul Hallberg and Christian Koninckx, eds., *A Passage to China: Colin Campbell's Diary of the First Swedish East India Company Expedition to Canton, 1732–33* (Göteborg, Royal Society of Arts and Sciences, 1996).
3. Weng Eang Cheong, *The Hong Merchants of Canton: Chinese Merchants in Sino-Western Trade* (London: Curzon Press, 1997), 9–11. For a thorough discussion of the Canton Trade System, see Paul A. Van Dyke, *The Canton Trade: Life and Enterprise on the China Coast, 1700–1845* (Hong Kong University Press, 2005).
4. For a short biography of Puankhequa I and Puankhequa II, see Ch'en Kuo-tung Anthony, "Pan Youdu (Pan Qiguan er shi): Yiwei chenggong de yanghang shangren" [Pan Youdu (Puankhequa II): A Successful Hong Merchant], in his *Dongya Haiyu Yiqian nian* [A Thousand-Year History of the East Asian Waters] (Taibei: Caituan Faren Cao Yonghe Wenjiao Jijinhui, Yuanliu Chuban Shiye Gufen Youxian Gongsi, 2005), 419–65.
5. William Hickey, *Memoirs of William Hickey 1749–1775*, ed. Alfred Spencer (London, Hurst & Blackett, Ltd., Paternoster House, E.C., 1913), Vol. 1, 223–4.
6. ———, 224.
7. See Zhao Rongguang, *Man-Han Quanxi Yuanliu Kaoshu* (Beijing: Kunlun chubanshe, 2003), 135–6.
8. For Staunton's account, see George Thomas Staunton, *Notes of Proceedings and Occurrences during the British Embassy to Pekin in 1816* (1824 by Havant Press; London: Routledge, 2000), 49–50. For Abel's account, see Clarke Abel, *Narrative*

of a Journey in the Interior of China, and of a Voyage to and from that Country, in the Years 1816 and 1817; containing an account of the most interesting transactions of Lord Amherst's Embassy to the Court of Pekin, and Observations on the Countries which is visited (London: Printed for Longman, Hurst, Rees, Orme, and Brown, Paternoster-Bow, 1818), 84.

9. See, for example, Gugong Bowuyuan, ed., *Qingdai Waijiao Shiliao* [Jiaqing chao] (Beijing: Gugong Bowuyuan, 1932), Vol. V.
10. For a groundbreaking study of the American traders in Canton in the eighteenth and nineteenth centuries, see Jacques M. Downs, *The Golden Ghetto: The American Commercial Community at Canton and the Shaping of American China Policy, 1784–1844* (Bethlehem, PA: Leigh University Press; London: Associated University Press, 1997).
11. In this essay, the major reference I use to identify the Hong merchants is Liang Jiabin, *Guangdong shisanhang kao* (1937; Guangzhou: Guangdong Renmin Chubanshe, 1999).
12. Tilden 7 (Ship Canton, Third Voyage of BPT to China, 1818–1819), 39–40; in the manuscript, collection of the Philips Library, Peabody Essex Museum, Salem, Massachusetts. Throughout the journal, spellings and punctuations are not strictly consistent. In most cases Puankhequa is spelled "Paunkeiqua." The italics indicate Tilden's own emphasis.
13. ———, 40–1.
14. ———, 43–4.
15. ———, 45.
16. For a brief history of Madeira wine, see http://en.wikipedia.org/wiki/Madeira_wine (accessed June 26, 2009).
17. Robert Morrison, *Vocabulary of the Canton Dialect* [廣東省土話字彙] (Macao: Printed at the Honorable East India Company's Press, 1828).
18. Tilden 7, 45–6.
19. ———, 48.
20. ———, 48–9.
21. However, whether this practice should be considered "Western" needs more documentation. Harvey Levenstein suggests "serving *à la Russe* had swept the dining table of the British and French elites in the 1850s and 1860s and became fashionable in the United States in the 1870s. Instead of placing a goodly number of dishes on the table at once, with the host carving and serving them while guests helped themselves from other dishes placed around the table, a butler carved and served each course at a sideboard, arranging it attractively on individual plates or platters from which servants would then serve the guests." See Harvey Levenstein, *Revolution at the Table: The Transformation of the American Diet* (New York and Oxford, Oxford University Press, 1988), 16.
22. Henry Charles Sirr, *China and the Chinese: Their Religion, Character, Customs, and Manufactures* (London: Wm. S. Orr & Co., 1844), 155–8.

23. William Hunter, *The Fan Kwae at Canton: Before Treaty Days 1825–1844* (London 1882), 40. Hunter noted that the best quality of birds' nests was brought from Java and that this "whimsical luxury" was worth 4,000 Spanish dollars per picul of 133 1/3 pounds.
24. Walter William Mundy, *Canton and the Bogue: The Narrative of an Eventful Six Months in China* (London, Samuel Tinsley, 1875), 152, 154.
25. Sirr, 155, 157.
26. John Reeves's letter to Joseph Banks (27 December 1812) from Canton, *Banks Correspondence*, manuscript, collection of the British Library.
27. Charles T. Downing, *The Fan-Qui or Foreigner in China*. 3 vols. (London: Henry Colburn, Publisher, 1840), Vol. 3, 119.
28. Mundy, 152.
29. Sirr, 156.
30. See Neville John Irons, *Silver & Carving of the Old China Trade* (London: House of Fans, 1983).
31. Mundy, 152–3.
32. Charles T. Downing, *The Fan-Qui or Foreigner in China*, Vol. 3, 82–6. Downing happened to be in Canton on the day when the new Hoppo was installed in his office, and had the opportunity of seeing him attending the feast.
33. William Hunter, *Bits of Old China* (London: Kegan Paul, Trench, & Co., 1885) 38–9.
34. See Roy Strong, *Feast: A History of Grand Eating* (London: Jonathan Cape, 2002), 291–2. One of my reviewers suggests that in pre-electricity times, dinner had to be started earlier so that good food could be seen in proper daylight. But Puankhequa II's chopstick dinner did not end until 9:00 or 10:00 p.m. One can imagine that a luxurious residence such as his must have been equipped with enough lanterns and candles to light up the later courses.
35. Ida Preiffer, *A Woman's Journey Round the World* (London, 1850), 96
36. Samuel Wells Williams, *Easy Lessons in Chinese* [拾級大成] (Macau: Xiangshan Shuyuan, 1842), 96.
37. Tilden 7, 109.
38. For more details about this Chinese theatre, see May-bo Ching, "A Preliminary study of the theatres built by Cantonese merchants in the late Qing," *Frontiers of History in China*, 5.2 (2010).
39. "Inauguration of the New Chinese Theatre 'Hing Chuen Yuen'; Grand Banquet at the Hang Heong Low Restaurant," *Daily Alta California* (January 28, 1868).
40. *The Visit of the Royal Highness: The Duke & Duchess of Connaught to Hong Kong,* May 21, 1890 (Government Records Service, PRO, Hong Kong).
41. In Gansu Province, as a consequence of the outbreak of SARS in 2003, there was a promotion of "food distribution practice" (*fencan zhi*) that looks so atypical that the *People's Daily* (Overseas edition) pays a brief tribute to it. See the illustrated report of *People's Daily* (Overseas edition), June 14, 2003.

Chapter 6

1. Harriett Low, *Light and Shadows of a Macao Life: The Journal of Harriett Low, Travelling Spinster*, 2 vols, ed. Nan P. Hodges and Arthur W. Hummel (Woodinville, WA; The History Bank, 2002), Vol. 1, 67.
2. "Macau nos anos (18)30: o diário de Caroline Hyde Butler Laing (1837)," *Revista portuguesa de estudos chineses (Zhongguo yanjiu)* 1.2 (2007): 71–112.
3. Edith Nevill Smythe Ward, *Caroline Hyde Butler Laing (1804–1892). A Family Heritage: Letters and Journals of Caroline Hyde Butler Laing, 1804–1892* (East Orange, NJ: Abbey Printers, 1957), 1–31, 75.
4. I will be quoting from the typescript version of the "Journal of Caroline Hyde Butler (Laing) on Trip to China 1836–1837," [Journal of a voyage to China in the year 1836–7 on the ship *Roman*, Capt. Benson], 198 pages (New York Historical Society: "Papers of the Butler-Laing Family 1804–1892, bulk 1865–1871").
5. Ward, 46.
6. J. N. Reynolds, *Voyage of the United States Frigate Potomac, under the Command of Commodore John Downes, during the Circumnavigation of the Globe in the Years 1831, 1832, 1833, and 1834* (New York: Harper & Brothers, 1835), vi.
7. ———, 336–7, 341, 353.
8. See Rogério Miguel Puga, "A Vivência Social do Género na Macau Oitocentista: O Diário de Harriet Low (Hillard). *Administração: revista de administração pública de Macau.* 15.56 (2002): 605–64; "Imagens de Macau Oitocentista: A Visão Intimista de Uma Jovem Americana. O Diário de Harriet Low (Hillard) (1829–33)," *Estudos sobre a China V*, ed. Ana Maria Amaro. Lisbon: Centro de Estudos Chineses-Instituto Superior de Ciências Sociais e Políticas (2003): Vol. 2, 713–67; "'A Gem of a Place': Macau Após a Guerra do ópio: O Diário de Rebecca Chase Kinsman." *Estudos sobre a China VI*, ed. Ana Maria Amaro. Lisbon: Centro de Estudos Chineses-Instituto Superior de Ciências Sociais e Políticas (2004): Vol. 2, 903–55; "Images of nineteenth-century Macau in the journals of Harriett Low (1829–1834) and Rebecca Chase Kinsman (1843–1847)," *Oriente* 14 (April 2006): 90–104.
9. Butler, 108.
10. ———, 109.
11. ———, 108; For more, see Rogério Miguel Puga, "O Primeiro Olhar Norte-Americano sobre Macau: Os Diários de Samuel Shaw (1754–1794)," *Intertextual Dialogues, Travel & Routes: Actas do XXVI encontro da APEAA*, ed. Ana Gabriela Macedo et al. (Braga: University of Minho, 2007): 227–51.
12. ———, 109.
13. ———, 110.
14. ———, 109, 111.
15. Rebecca Chase Kinsman, "The Daily Life of Mrs. Nathaniel Kinsman in Macao, China. Excerpts from Letters of 1844," *The Essex Institute Historical Collection*. LXXXVI (October 1950): 311–30.
16. ———, 324.

17. See Puga, 2004.
18. Rogério Miguel Puga, *A World of Euphemism: Representações de Macau na Obra de Austin Coates: City of Broken Promises enquanto Romance Histórico e Bildungsroman Feminino* (Lisbon: Fundação para a Ciência e a Tecnologia-Ministério da Ciência, Tecnologia e Ensino Superior/Fundação Calouste Gulbenkian, 2009), 141.
19. Butler, 121.
20. Monkey Island (*Maliuzhou*) is the Chinese name for the Island(s) of the Bugios.
21. Butler, 127–8.
22. ———, 121.
23. William C. Hunter, *Bits of old China* (London: Kegan Paul, Trench, 1885), 73–77.
24. Harriett Low, Vol. 1, 74–5; George Bennet, *Wanderings in New South Wales, Batavia, Pedir Coast, Singapore, and China. Being the Journal of a Naturalist in those Countries, during 1832, 1833, and 1834*, 2 vols. (London: Richard Bentley London, 1834), Vol. 2, 36–52; W.S.W. Ruschenberger, *Narrative of a Voyage Round the World during the Years 1835, 36, and 37; including a Narrative of an Embassy to the Sultan of Muscat and the King of Siam*. 2 vols. (London: Richard Bentley, 1838), Vol. 2, 199–201; Cyrille-Pierre Theodore LaPlace, *Voyage Autour du Monde par les Mers d'Inde et de la Chine Exécuté sur La Corvette de L'état la Favorite pendant les Années 1830, 1831 et 1832 sous Le Commandement de M. Laplace Capitaine de Frégate*. 5 vols. (Paris: Imprimerie Royale, 1833–39), Vol. 2, 269; Charles Toogood Downing, *The Fan-qui in China, in 1836–7*. 3 vols. (London: Henry Colburn, 1838), 38–9.
25. Butler, 124–5.
26. ———, 179.
27. Padre Manuel Teixeira, *A Gruta de Camões em Macau* (Macao: Fundação Macau-Instituto Internacional de Macau, 1999), 52.
28. Butler, 168.
29. ———, 153.
30. ———, 117.
31. ———, 117–8.
32. ———, 154.
33. ———, 118.
34. See Rogério Miguel Puga, "Macau and Timor in 1929: The Journal and the Unpublished Drawings of Lucy Cleveland," *Oriente* 18 (2007): 3–33.
35. For the descriptions of the rich Chinese residents, see Butler, 118–9; the Chinese beggars who make New York beggars look like kings, 132; the local monks, 118; and, the Tanka or boat women, 123–4.
36. Butler, 123–4.
37. Rebecca Chase Kinsman, "Life in Macao in the 1840's: Letters of Rebecca Chase Kinsman to Her Family in Salem. From the Collection of Mrs. Rebecca Kinsman Munroe," *The Essex Institute Historical Collection* LXXXVI (April 1950), 139, my italics.

38. Yen-Ping Hao, *The Comprador in Nineteenth-century China: Bridge between East and West* (Cambridge, MA: Harvard University Press, 1970), 1–77, 154–223,
39. Butler, 126–7.
40. Christina Miu Bing Cheng, *Macau: A Cultural Janus* (Hong Kong University Press, 1999).
41. Butler, 155
42. ———, 155.
43. ———, 131. These same fields and the poor people's houses in the fields visited by Caroline Butler during her frequent strolls are also described by a Portuguese author, José Manuel de Castro Sampaio, in *Os Chins de Macau* [*The Chinese of Macao*] (Hong Kong: Tipografia Noronha e Filhos, 1867), 6–7.
44. See the "Journal of Rebecca Chase Kinsman kept on her voyage to China in 1843," Typescript 1958, by Mrs. Storer P. Ware (Boston, MA: Baker Library, Harvard Business School [call number: WPBK56]), 1–2; and, "Life in Macao in the 1840's: Letters of Rebecca Chase Kinsman to her Family in Salem, from the Collection of Mrs. Rebecca Kinsman Munroe, *The Essex Institute Historical Collection* LXXXVI (January 1950), 17, 20, 15; Kinsman (April 1850), 137; Kinsman (October 1850), 317.
45. On the "Cameons [*sic*] Cave," see Butler, 165–70; on the "beautiful Garden at Macoa" (Thomas Beale's garden), 171–5; on "The Penha," 176–80; and on "Life of Foreign Ladies at Macoa," 186–9.
46. Butler, 186.
47. Robert Bennet Forbes asks: "You have never been in a Catholic Town have you?—the bells are going all day & half the night—ding dong–ding dong—this is a great annoyance." In *Letters from China: The Canton-Boston Correspondence of Robert Bennet Forbes, 1838–1840,* ed. Sarah Forbes Hughes (Mystic, CT: Mystic Seaport Museum, 1996), 165.
48. Butler, 187.
49. Mary Louise Pratt, *Imperial Eyes: Travel Writing and Transculturation* (London: Routledge, 1992), 6–7.

Chapter 7

1. Adapted from S.Y. Teng and John K. Fairbank, *China's Response to the West: A Documentary Survey, 1839–1923* (Cambridge, MA: University of Harvard Press, 1954), 38–40.This memorial is now housed at the Public Records Office, National Archives, Kew, London, accession number: FO 931/484. This article was made possible by a grant from the General Research Fund, Hong Kong.
2. This portrait was later hung in the East India Company base in Canton, and a smaller full-size portrait of Lord Amherst hung opposite.
3. Public Records Office, National Archives, Kew London, accession number: FO 1048/29/9, dated to Daoguang 9th year, 1829, 9th day of the 5th month.
4. See Teng Ssu-yu, *Chang-Hsi and the Treaty of Nanking 1842* (University of Chicago Press, 1944), 80.

5. There is a long history of tribute rituals, and textual records of the ceremonies are carefully detailed in early Chinese texts such as the *Yi li* and the *Zuo chuan*. They include the ceremonial reception, rules governing the privileges of envoys, alliances, customs, access, warfare, etc.
6. Marcel Mauss's concept of the inalienable gift (that differentiates the object from a commodity because it contains a part of the donor's spiritual essence) and Annette B. Weiner's theme of inalienable possessions have informed this paper's central theme of gifting practices. See Annette B. Weiner, *Inalienable Possessions: The Paradox of Keeping-While-Giving*, (Berkeley: University of California Press, 1992); and Marcel Mauss, *Essai sur le don* (London: Cohen & West, 1954).
7. Philip Henry Stanhope, Fifth Earl Stanhope (1805–75), first introduced the idea of a national portrait institution to the House of Commons in 1846. He introduced it again in 1852, and he finally succeeded in 1856. He made a plea for the establishment of a "Gallery of original portraits, such portraits to consist as far as possible who are most honorably commemorated in British history as warriors, or as statesmen, or in arts, in literature or in science."
8. There are numerous books that can further elucidate these various positions, including Marcia Pointon, *Hanging the Head: Portraiture and Social Formation in 18th Century England* (New Haven and London: Yale University Press, 1993); Marcia Pointon and Kathleen Adler, eds., *The Body Imagined: The Human Form and Visual Culture Since the Renaissance* (Cambridge, MA: Cambridge University Press, 1993); Richard Brilliant, *Portraiture* (London: Reaktion Books, 1991).
9. For an excellent introduction to ancestral portraits, see Jan Stuart and Evelyn S. Rawski, *Worshipping the Ancestors: Chinese Commemorative Portraits* (Washington, DC: Smithsonian Institute, 2001).
10. A third type of portraiture, and the one least researched, is that of famous worthies and emperors, which were made as replicas in printed or rubbing forms. An example of printed images of emperors is from the *Sancai tu hui*, an encyclopedia that contains extensive illustrations of historic rulers up to the Jiajing Emperor (r.1522–66); see Craig Clunas, *Pictures and Visuality in Early Modern China* (Princeton, NJ: Princeton University Press, 1997), 98–9.
11. Richard Vinograd's pioneering work, *Boundaries of the Self: Chinese Portraits, 1600–1900* (Cambridge, MA: University of Cambridge Press, 1992), explores issues of identity and individuality in portraiture and underscores the importance of the portrait event; see in particular pages 2–11. Identity plays are also explored by Wu Hung in "Emperor's Masquerade—Costume Portraits of Yongzheng and Qianlong," *Orientations* (July 1995), 25–41. In this article, Wu examines portrait-masquerades as examples that confirmed the universality of emperor with portraits made for historical posterity rather than public consumption.
12. Vinograd, 2–11.

13. Natasha Eaton, "Between Mimesis and Alterity: Art, Gift and Diplomacy in Colonial India, 1770–1800," *Comparative Studies in Society and History* 46 (2004), 816–44.
14. ———, 824.
15. Some indication of Chinnery's movements can be traced from his dated works. He was in Guangdong in the late summer and autumn of 1826, 1827, 1828, 1829, and again in 1832, when he stayed from mid-April to December.
16. Although the difference between the Chinese ancestor portrait and Chinnery's oil painting is stark, there is a crucial if subtle feature seen in both: Wu's gesture. His left hand is slightly raised and his fingers are delicately holding a large bead on a court necklace. The pictorial roots of this gesture can be traced to portraits of the Chinese Imperial Court, in which the pictorial language of prestige utilized the necklace as a symbol of contemplative authority. Court necklaces were worn with ceremonial robes by men and women at the court. It follows the form of Buddhist rosaries, made up of 108 beads with 4 large beads (known as "Buddha heads" or "beads of four seasons") of contrasting colors and placed between each group of 27 beads. See Stuart, 56.
17. Versions of Chinnery's portraits of Wu Bingjian were sold as mementos to traders and their shipping crews as a form of tourist art. Many of these portraits are similar, and it may be that Chinnery and his followers made several versions, based on Chinnery's sketches of Howqua, and adapted them for different customers. There is also a sketch of the painting by Chinnery in pen and ink that has on the back the words "December 26th, 1827, Canton." This painting is now believed to be the one in the Hong Kong Shanghai Bank Collection.
18. Jules Itier, *Journal d'un Voyage en Chine en 1843, 1844, 1845, 1846* (Paris: Chez Duvin et Fontaine, 1848), 2 vols, 74.
19. Qiying was in charge of investigating corruption cases in Jiangxi and Guangdong in 1836–37, which was the only time he was involved in work south of the capital. As an imperial commissioner, he could exercise power equal to that of the emperor, within the limits of his commission. This satisfied the British demand for negotiating with representatives with "full powers."
20. Qi Shan had ceded Hong Kong to the British and agreed to diplomatic equity and an indemnity of $6 million. See Frederic Wakeman, Jr., *Strangers at the Gate: Social Disorder in South China, 1839–1861* (Berkeley: University of California Press, 1966), 81–2.
21. Public Records Office, National Archives, Kew, London, accession number: FO 17/68 (no.74). Please note that the transliteration of Qiying's name is Keying after the Cantonese pronunciation.
22. Whether knowingly or not, Qiying's request was particularly fitting because miniatures were part of the sentimental and social life of "institutionalized separation": mementos of loved ones taken on lengthy tours, naval campaigns, and maritime trading of eighteenth- and nineteenth-century Western expansionism.

23. Public Records Office, National Archives, Kew, London, accession number: FO 682/137/13.
24. Teng and Fairbank, 40–1.
25. There are many examples of this usage found in the correspondence between the two men. For case in point, see the Public Records Office, National Archives, Kew, London, accession number: FO 682/68/3.
26. See John Rogers Haddad, "The Cultural Fruits of Diplomacy," in *The Romance of China: Excursions to China in U.S. Culture: 1776–1876* (New York: Columbia University Press, 2008). See "Chapter 7: The Cultural Fruits of Diplomacy: A Chinese Museum and Panorama," http://www.gutenberg-e.org/haj01/haj08.html (site accessed May 22, 2011).
27. Caleb Cushing Papers, Library of Congress, Washington, DC, Box 40, Macau, July 3, 1844. The final signing of the treaty was at the Buddhist Temple of the Goddess of Mercy, located in the settlement of Wangxia or Wang-Hsia in Macao, which was then a Portuguese colony. Caleb Cushing of Newburyport, Massachusetts, a United States representative prior to his mission to China, successfully negotiated this first treaty between the United States and China. Signed on July 3, 1844, it won the same concessions that the British had gained in the Treaty of Nanjing following the conclusion of the Opium War in 1842.
28. Cushing. Minutes of meeting taken by Peter Parker.
29. The McCartney Mission in 1793 included gifts of scientific objects that demonstrated, in their eyes, technological advances that also by extension represented the possibilities of free trade. However, the Qianlong Emperor deemed the objects tributary gifts and, using the rhetoric of tributary relations, dismissed the mission. Simon Schaffer, "The Instruments of Cargo in the China Trade," *History of Science* 44 (2006), 216–46.
30. Ronald J Zboray and Mary Saracino Zboray, "Between 'Crockery-dom' and Barnum: Boston's Chinese Museum, 1845–47," *American Quarterly* 56.2 (June 2004), 271–307.
31. Lydia Liu suggests that the connotations of fear and hatred behind the popular use of the term "fan gui" to designate foreigners stemmed from the Sanyuanli Incident in 1841, when the local militias defeated a small group of British Army men. Lydia Liu, *Clash of Empires: The Invention of China in Modern World Making* (Boston, MA: Harvard University Press, 2004), 101–8.
32. Ye Cha and Luo Cha were two fearsome ghosts.
33. Pan Shicheng, *Guiqu tu yong ti*, 73a/b, manuscript dated 1851. For translation and further information about this painting, see Yeewan Koon, "Lives and Afterlives: Luo Ping's Guiqu tu," *Orientations* 40 (September 2009).

Chapter 8

1. The work of Lisa Lowe at the University of California, San Diego, exemplifies but does not exhaust this development. See, for example, *Immigrant Acts: On Asian American Cultural Politics* (Durham, NC: Duke University Press, 1996). The

Duke University Press journal, *Positions*, under the editorship of Tani Barlow, has done much to develop the same sort of interests, deepening the applicability of Western critical categories and systems to Asian and Chinese realities. See, for example, Tani Barlow's edited volume, "Alain Badiou and Cultural Revolution," 13.1.

2. The Society for Historians of American Foreign Relations have supported the journal *Diplomatic History* since 1976, but recently have added cultural materials to inflect their own discourses. See, for example, Joan Huff, "American Diplomacy from a Postmodern Perspective," 33.3 (2009): 512–6.
3. Andy Xie, "If China Loses Faith the Dollar Will Collapse," *The Financial Times* (May 4, 2009), http://www.ft.com/cms/s/0/2f842dec-38d8-11de-8cfe-00144feabdc0.html?nclick_check=1 (accessed May 16, 2009).
4. See the informative and challenging book by *The New Yorker* writer Peter Hessler, *Oracle Bones: A Journey Between China's Past and Present* (New York: HarperCollins, 2006).
5. The State is not a subject and we should not attempt to interpret it psychologically or in any way that suggests it is available for analysis and description in terms derived from theories of subjectivity. Those who approach the state in this way are guilty of anthropocentrism and commit the same faults as those who anthropomorphize a divinity. In essence, such an error is metaphysical and at worst magical thinking that substitutes its own discursive fantasies for the hard details of state operations. Scholars of the weak US state, with its divisions of government, and its highly regionalized and fragmented economic interests, especially within large capital formations, should especially understand the inapplicability of subject-based theories to thinking about the state. For an understanding of the basic errors involved in such anthropomorphism, see David Hume, *Dialogues Concerning Natural Religion,* 2nd ed. (New York: Hackett Publishing Co., 1998).
6. "The Opening to China Part I: the First Opium War, the United States, and the Treaty of Wangxia, 1839–1844," *Timeline of U. S. Diplomatic History*, produced by the office of the Under Secretary of State for Public Diplomacy and Public Affairs, at http://www.state.gov/r/pa/ho/time/dwe/82011.htm (accessed May 16, 2009).
7. See, for example, David Gedalecia, "Letters from the Middle Kingdom: The Origins of American's China Policy," *Prologue Magazine*, 34.4 (Winter 2002). *Prologue* is a publication of the US State Department.
8. Implicit in my discussion and in the State Department's history stands an important fact that I cannot treat in this space. In a way that Henry Adams later theorizes in his letters on China and John Hay, we come to see that the Europeans, especially the British, operated to impose on China a form of international and internal order parallel to that established by the Treaty of Westphalia. Just as China and Russia were themselves outside this order by virtue of what Europeans would call "under-development," so America was outside it,

self-defined as uniquely exceptional it could not understand itself nor act on itself as a Westphalian state.

9. "The Burlingame-Seward Treaty, 1868," at http://www.state.gov/r/pa/ho/time/gp/82013.htm (accessed May 19, 2009).
10. *Letters of John Hay and Extracts from Diary*, Vol. 3 (New York: Gordian Press, 1969; printed in 1908 but not published), 139f. These volumes were edited by Henry Adams but redacted by Hay's widow. Adams's name does not appear.
11. Cf. "Henry Adams and the 'American System,'" translated in Hindi as "Henry Adams O Markini Byabosthya," *Abobhash* 3.2 (July–September 2003).
12. Garry Wills, *Henry Adams and the Making of America* (Boston, MA: Houghton Mifflin, 2003).
13. Henry Adams, *The Education of Henry Adams* (New York: The Library of America, 1983), 1077.
14. ———, 1077.
15. ———, 1020.
16. ———, 1120–1.
17. ———, 1121.
18. ———, 1121.
19. *Letters of John Hay*, 153.
20. ———, 171.
21. ———, 192–3.
22. ———, 142–3.
23. ———, 195.
24. Adams, 1077.
25. ———, 1078.
26. ———, 1078.
27. ———, 1078.
28. Alfred Thayer Mahan, *The Influence of Sea Power Upon History* (New York: Dover Publications, 1987; originally published in 1894).
29. H. J. Mackinder, "The Geographical Pivot of History," a paper presented in 1904 to the Royal Geographical Society, meeting in London. For a record of the meeting, see *The National Geographic Magazine* 15 (1904), especially pages 331ff.
30. Mackinder, quoted in *The National Geographic*, 331.
31. ———, 332.
32. ———, 334.
33. ———, 333.
34. ———, 333.
35. Adams, 1078.

Chapter 9

1. We are grateful to Bryan Philips, who assisted in collecting data from the Ma-Tsu Temple in San Francisco in April 2009.

2. See J. Bosco and P. P. Ho, *Temples of the Empress of Heaven* (Hong Kong: Oxford University Press, 1999); and H.X. Jiang, "Mingqing shiqi mazu xinyang chuantai guocheng ji yingxiang xunzong (The process of Mazu belief spreading to Taiwan in Ming and Qing Dynasty)," *Dongnan Chuanbo* (Southeast Media) 1 (2008): 24–5.
3. Bosco and Ho, 46–7.
4. Q.Y. Wu, *Mazu xinyang yu haiwai minnanren de "shenyuan": yi xinjiapo tianfugong weili* (Beijing: Zhongyang wenxian chubanshe. 2003): http://www.fjql.org/qszl/xsyj39.htm. (accessed June 11, 2009)
5. Y. L. Wang and M. R. Deng. "Mingqing shiqi hainandao de mazu xinyang" ("A Study of the Worship of Mazu in Hainan Island during Ming and Qing Dynasties") *Humanities and Social Sciences Journal of Hainan University* 22.4 (2004): 382.
6. J. H. Lin, J. Q. Fu, and L. L. Zhuang. "Shangmao fazhan yu mazu xianghuo wangluo kuozhan de guanxi" ("The relationship between the commerce and trade development and the expansion of Mazu incense networks") *Journal of Putian University* 14.6 (2007): 91.
7. The Confucian hierarchy places the scholar, *shi* (士), in the top place, followed by the farmer, *nong* (农), artisan, *gong* (工), and merchants, *shang* (商), the lowest of the four categories.
8. See Wu; and Khun Eng Kuah-Pearce, "Cultural and Network Capitals: Chinese Women and the 'Religious' Industry in South China," in *Chinese Women and Their Social and Network Capitals*, ed. Khun Eng Kuah-Pearce (Singapore: Marshall Cavendish International, 2004), 121–43.
9. Bosco and Ho, 10.
10. J.B. Jacobs, *Local Politics in a Rural Chinese Cultural Setting: A Field Study of Mazu Township, Taiwan* (Canberra: Contemporary China Centre, Research School of Pacific Studies, Australian National University, 1980), 96.
11. Wu, 254.
12. Bosco and Ho, 41.
13. Young Kil Zo, *Chinese Emigration into the United States, 1850–1880*, Ph.D dissertation, Columbia University, 1971 (Imprint: Ann Arbor, MI: University Microfilms, 1971), 60.
14. Yong Chen, "China in America: A Cultural Study of Chinese San Francisco, 1850–1943" (Ph.D. dissertation, Cornell University, 1993) (Ann Arbor, MI: University Microfilms International Imprint, 1994), 37.
15. Jonathan H. X. Lee, "Creating a Transnational Community: The Empress of Heaven and Goddess of the Sea, Tianhou/Mazu, from Beigang to San Francisco," in *Religion at the Corner of Bliss and Nirvana: Politics, Identity, and Faith in New Migrant Communities*, ed. Lois Ann Lorentzen et al. (Durham, NC: Duke University Press, 2009), 169.
16. Zo, 3, 56.
17. ———, 56.
18. Lee, 169.

19. Zo, 57.
20. M. Hsu, "Trading with Gold Mountain: *Jinshanzhuang* and Networks of Kinship and Native Place," in *Chinese American Transnationalism: The Flow of People, Resources, and Ideas between China and America during the Exclusion Era,* ed. Sucheng Chan (Philadelphia, PA: Temple University Press, 2006), 22.
21. Hsu, 22.
22. Yong Chen, "Understanding Chinese American Transnationalism during the Early Twentieth Century: An Economic Perspective," in *Chinese American Transnationalism: The Flow of People, Resources, and Ideas between China and America during the Exclusion Era,* ed. Sucheng Chan (Philadelphia, PA: Temple University Press, 2006), 163.
23. Hsu, 25.
24. ———, 26.
25. ———, 26.
26. ———, 27.
27. ———, 27.
28. Y. Chen, 1993, 130.
29. Lee, 170.
30. *The California Illustrated Magazine* (June–Nov 1982): 728–41.
31. Y. Chen, 1993, 134.
32. ———, 135.
33. ———, 135.
34. ———, 136.
35. ———, 136.
36. Erika Lee, "Defying Exclusion: Chinese Immigrants and their Strategies during the Exclusion Era," *Chinese American Transnationalism: The Flow of People, Resources, and Ideas between China and America during the Exclusion Era*, ed. Sucheng Chan (Philadelphia, PA: Temple University Press, 2006), 10–11.
37. Zo, 57.
38. Lai, 2004, 49–50.
39. Hsu, 31.
40. E. Lee, 10–11.
41. See Sucheng Chan, "Against All Odds: Chinese Female Migration and Family Formation on American Soil during the Early Twentieth Century," in Chan, 34–135.
42. Shehong Chen, "Republicanism, Confucianism, Christianity, and Capitalism in American Chinese Ideology," in Chan, 185–6.
43. Chen, 186.
44. Ginger Chih, "Immigration of Chinese Women to the U. S. A. 1900–1940" (M.A. Thesis, Sarah Lawrence College, 1977), 33.
45. ———, 34.
46. Chan, 72.
47. Y. Chen, 1993, 35.

48. Him Mark Lai, *The Chinese of America, 1785–1980: An Illustrated History and Catalog of the Exhibition* (San Francisco: Chinese Culture Foundation, 1980), 65. Also see Him Mark Lai, *Becoming Chinese American: A History of Communities and Institutions* (Walnut Creek, CA: AltaMira, 2004).
49. Lai, 1980, 65.
50. ———, 65.
51. Y. Chen, 2006, 164.
52. ———, 164.
53. S. Chen, 181–2.
54. Y. Chen, 2006, 167–70.
55. Information derived from the printed brochure of Ma-Tsu Temple U.S.A., provided by the temple caretaker.
56. Jonathan H. X. Lee, "Transnational Goddess on the Move: Meiguo Mazu's Celestial Inspection Tour and Pilgrimage as Chinese American Culture Work and Vernacular Chinese Religion" (Ph.D. dissertation, University of California Santa Barbara; UMI Microform 3375556, 2009), 154.
57. Lee, 166–83.
58. Printed brochure of Ma-Tsu Temple U.S.A.
59. Lee, *Transnational Goddess on the Move*, 155.
60. ———, 163.
61. ———, 163.
62. ———, 163.
63. ———, 163.

Bibliography

Abeel, David. *Journal of a Residence in China, and the Neighboring Countries, from 1829 to 1833*. New York: Leavitt, Lord & Co., 1834.

Adams, John Quincy. "December 1841, Lecture on the War with China, Delivered before the Massachusetts Historical Society." *Chinese Repository* 11.5 (May 1842): 274–89.

Adams, Henry. *The Education of Henry Adams*. New York: The Library of America, 1983. First published in 1918.

Aldridge, Alfred Owen. *The Dragon and the Eagle: The Presence of China in the American Enlightenment*. Detroit, MI: Wayne State University Press, 1993.

Ahern, E.M. *Chinese Ritual and Politics*. Cambridge: Cambridge University Press, 1981.

Ahmad, Diana L. *The Opium Debate and Chinese Exclusion Laws in the Nineteenth-Century American West*. Reno and Las Vegas: University of Nevada Press, 2007.

Anon. "Christian Missions in China." *Chinese Repository* 3 (April 1835): 559–68.

———. "Free Intercourse with China." *Chinese Repository* 3 (July 1833): 128–37.

———. "Free Trade." *The Chinese Repository* 1 (December 1833): 355–73.

———. "Intercourse with the Chinese." *The Chinese Repository* 1 (August 1832): 141–7.

———."Opium and the China Question." *Blackwood's Edinburgh Magazine* CCXCVI (June 1840): 717–38.

———. "Postscript to the Opium and the China Question." *Blackwood's Edinburgh Magazine* CCXCVI (June 1840): 847–53.

———. "Promulgation of the Gospel in China." *Chinese Repository* 3 (January 1835): 428–37.

———. Review of *The Journals of Major Samuel Shaw, The First American Consul at Canton: With a Life of the Author, by Josiah Quincy*. Boston, MA: Crosby & Nichols. 1847. *North American Review* CXXXVIII (January 1848): 250–3.

———. "Treaty with the Chinese," *Chinese Repository* 4 (February 1835): 441–9.

———. "Universal Peace," *Chinese Repository* 3 (March 1835): 516–27.

———. "War with China, and the Opium Question." *Blackwood's Edinburgh Magazine* CCXCIII Vol. XLVII (March 1840): 368–83.

Anthony, Robert J. *Like Froth Floating on the Sea: The World of Pirates and Seafarers in Late Imperial South China*. Berkeley, CA: Institute of East Asian Studies, 2003.

Arrighi, Giovanni. *Adam Smith in Beijing: Lineages of the Twenty-first Century*. London: Verso, 2007.

———. *The Long Twentieth Century: Money, Power, and the Origins of Our Times*. London: Verso, 1994.

Barneby, W. Henry. *The New Far West and the Old Far East: Being Notes of a Tour in North America, Japan, China, Ceylon, Etc*. London: Edward Stanford, 1889.

Belohlavek, John M. *Broken Glass: Caleb Cushing and the Shattering of the Union*. Kent, OH: Kent State University Press, 2005.

Bennet, George. *Wanderings in New South Wales, Batavia, Pedir Coast, Singapore, and China. Being the Journal of a Naturalist in those Countries, during 1832, 1833, and 1834*. 2 vols. London: Richard Bentley, 1934.

Bentley, Anne E. "The Columbia-Washington Medal." *Massachusetts Historical Society Proceedings* 101 (1989): 123–6.

Blussé, Leonard. *Visible Cities: Canton, Nagasaki, and Batavia and the Coming of the America*. Cambridge, MA: Harvard University Press, 2008.

Bosco, J. & P.P. Ho. *Temples of the Empress of Heaven*. Hong Kong: Oxford University Press, 1999.

Bowra, C.A.V. "Hosea Ballou Morse." *The Journal of the Royal Asiatic Society of Great Britain and Ireland* 2 (April 1934): 425–30.

Braudel, Fernand. *Civilization and Capitalism, 15th–18th Century*. 3 vols. New York: Harper & Row, 1982–84.

Bridgman, Eliza J. *Daughters of China: Or, Sketches of Domestic Life in the Celestial Empire*. New York: Robert Carter & Brothers, 1953.

———, ed. *The Pioneer of American Missions in China: The Life and Labors of Elijah Coleman Bridgman*. New York: Anson D.F. Randolph, 1864.

Butler (Laing), Caroline Hyde. "Journal of Caroline H. Butler (Laing) on a trip to China (1836–1837)" [Journal of a voyage to China in the year 1836–37 on the ship *Roman*, Capt. Benson]. Typescript (198 pp.). New York: New York Historical Society, 1836–37.

Callahan, James Morton. *American Relations in the Pacific and the Far East, 1784–1900*. Baltimore, MD: Johns Hopkins University Press, 1901.

Carroll, John M. *A Concise History of Hong Kong*. Lanham, MD: Rowman & Littlefield Publishers, Inc., 2007.

Chan, Sucheng. "Against All Odds: Chinese Female Migration and Family Formation on American Soil during the Early Twentieth Century." In *Chinese American Transnationalism: The Flow of People, Resources, and Ideas between China and America during the Exclusion Era*, edited by Sucheng Chan, pp. 34–135. Philadelphia, PA: Temple University Press, 2006.

———, ed. *Chinese American Transnationalism: The Flow of People, Resources, and Ideas between China and America during the Exclusion Era*. Philadelphia, PA: Temple University Press, 2006.

Chang, Hsin-pao. *Commissioner Lin and the Opium War.* Cambridge, MA: Harvard University Press, 1964.

Chaudhuri, K.N. *The Trading World of Asia and the English East Indian Company, 1600–1760.* Cambridge: Cambridge University Press, 1978.

Chatterjee, Partha. *Nationalism Thought and the Colonial World.* Minneapolis: University of Minnesota Press, 1993.

Ch'en, Anthony Kuo-tung. *The Insolvency of the Chinese Hong Merchants, 1760–1843.* Taipei: The Institute of Economics, Academia Sinica, 1990.

———. "Pan Youdu (Pan Qiguan er shi): Yiwei chenggong de yanghang shangren" (Pan Youdu [Puankhequa II]: A successful Hong merchant). In *Dongya Haiyu Yiqian nian* (A Thousand-Year History of the East Asian Waters), pp. 419–65. Taibei: Caituan Faren Cao Yonghe Wenjiao Jijinhui, Yuanliu Chuban Shiye Gufen Youxian Gongsi, 2005.

Chen, Shehong. "Republicanism, Confucianism, Christianity, and Capitalism in American Chinese ideology." In *Chinese American Transnationalism: The Flow of People, Resources, and Ideas between China and America during the Exclusion Era,* edited by Sucheng Chan, pp. 174–93. Philadelphia, PA: Temple University Press, 2006.

Chen, Yong. *China in America: A Cultural Study of Chinese San Francisco, 1850–1943.* Ph.D. Dissertation, Cornell University, 1993. Ann Arbor, MI: University Microfilms International Imprint, 1994.

———. "Understanding Chinese American Transnationalism during the Early Twentieth Century: An Economic Perspective." In *Chinese American Transnationalism: The Flow of People, Resources, and Ideas between China and America during the Exclusion Era,* edited by Sucheng Chan, pp. 156–73. Philadelphia, PA: Temple University Press, 2006.

Cheng, Christina Miu Bing. *Macau: A Cultural Janus*. Hong Kong University Press, 1999.

Cheong, W.E. *Hong Merchants of Canton: Chinese Merchants in Sino-Western Trade.* London: Curzon Press, 1997.

Cheung, King-kok and Stan Yogi. *Asian American Literature: An Annotated Bibliography*. New York: Modern Language Association of America, 1988.

Cheyfitz, Eric. *The Poetics of Imperialism: Translation and Colonization from The Tempest to Tarzan*. Philadelphia: University of Pennsylvania Press, 1997. First published 1991.

Christman, Margaret C.S. *Adventurous Pursuits: Americans and the China Trade 1784–1844*. Washington DC: Smithsonian Institution Press, 1984.

Chih, Ginger. *Immigration of Chinese Women to the U. S. A. 1900–1940*. M.A. Thesis, Sarah Lawrence College, 1977.

Cleland, Robert G. *Asiatic Trade and the American Occupation of the Pacific Coast.* American Historical Association Reports, Vol. 1 (1914). Washington, 1916.

Clunas, Craig. *Pictures and Visuality in Early Modern China.* Princeton: NJ: Princeton University Press, 1997.

Clyde, Paul. H., ed. *United States Policy Toward China: Diplomatic and Public Documents, 1839–1939*. New York: Russell and Russell, 1964.

Coates, Austin. *Macao and the British, 1637–1842: Prelude to Hong Kong*. University of Hong Kong Press, 2009. First published 1966.

Coe, Andrew. *Eagles & Dragons: A History of Americans in China & the Origins of the American Club Hong Kong*. Hong Kong: The American Club, 1997.

Cohen, Warren I. "American Perceptions of China, 1789–1911." In *China in the American Political Imagination*, edited by Carola McGiffert. Washington, DC: CSIS Press, Center for Strategic International Studies, 2003.

———. *America's Response to China: An Interpretative History of Sino-American Relations*. New York: John Wiley & Sons, 1971.

Conner, Patrick. *The Hongs of Canton: Western Merchants in South China, 1700–1900, as Seen in Chinese Export Paintings*. London: English Art Books, 2009.

Cook, Alexandra. "Linnaeus and Chinese Plants: A Test of the Linguistic Imperialism Thesis." *Notes and Records of the Royal Society* 64 (2010): 121–38.

Danton, George H. *The Culture Contacts of the United States and China: The Earliest Sino-American Culture Contacts, 1784–1844*. New York: Barnes & Noble, 1963. First published 1931.

Davids, Jules, ed. *American Diplomatic and Public Papers: The United States and China*. Series 1: *The Treaty System and the Taiping Rebellion, 1842–1860*. 21 vols. Wilmington, DE: Scholarly Resources, 1973.

Davis, Nancy Ellen. *The American China Trade, 1784–1844: Products for the Middle Class*. Ph.D. Dissertation, George Washington University, 1987.

Delano, Amasa. *Narratives of Voyages and Travels in Northern and Southern Hemispheres*. Boston, 1817.

———. *Delano's Voyages of Commerce and Discovery: Amasa Delano in China, the Pacific Islands, Australia, and South America, 1789–1807*, edited by Eleanor Roosevelt Seagraves. Stockbridge, MA: Berkshire House Publishers, 1994. First published 1871.

Dennett, Tyler. *Americans in Eastern Asia: A Critical Study of United States' Policy in the Far East in the Nineteenth Century*. New York: Barnes & Noble, 1963. First published 1922.

Desmond, Jane C. and Virginia R. Domínguez. "Resituating American Studies in a Critical Internationalism." *American Quarterly* 48.3 (September 1996): 475–90.

Dirlik, Arif. "Bringing History Back In: Of Diasporas, Hybridities, Places, and Histories." In *Beyond Dichotomies: Histories, Identities, Cultures, and the Challenge of Globalization*, edited by Elisabeth Mudimbe-Boyi, pp. 93–127. Albany: State University of New York Press, 2002.

———. "Chinese History and the Question of Orientalism." In *Genealogies of Orientalism: History, Theory, Politics*, edited by Edmund Burke III and David Prochaska, pp. 384–413. Lincoln: University of Nebraska Press, 2008.

———. *Chinese on the American Frontier*. Editor, with the assistance of Malcolm Yeung. Lanham, MD: Rowman & Littlefield Publishers, 2001.

———. "Dialogue on Post-Capitalism." *boundary 2* 35 (Fall 2008): 133–87.

———. "The End of Colonialism? The Colonial Modern in the Making of Global Modernity." *boundary 2* (Spring 2005): 1–31.

———. "Global Modernity, Spatial Reconfigurations, and Global Health: Perspectives from the People's Republic of China." *boundary 2* 33 (Spring 2006): 99–122.

———. "Introduction." *boundary 2* 35 (Summer 2008): 1–13.

———. "Postmodernism and Chinese History." *boundary 2* 28 (Fall 2001): 19–60.

———. "Timespace, Social Space, and the Question of Chinese Culture." *boundary 2* 35 (Spring 2008): 1–22.

Doerflinger, Thomas M. *A Vigorous Spirit of Enterprise: Merchants and Economic Development in Revolutionary Philadelphia*. Chapel Hill: University of North Carolina Press, 1986.

Downs, Jacques. *The Golden Ghetto: The American Commercial Community at Canton and the Shaping of American China Policy, 1784–1844.* Bethlehem, PA: Lehigh University Press, 1997.

Downing, Charles Toogood. *The Fan Qui in China in 1836–1837*. 3 vols. London, 1838.

Drake, Francis S. *Tea Leaves: Being a Collection of Letters and Documents Relating to the Shipment of Tea to the American Colonies in the Year 1773, by the East Indian Tea Company*. Detroit, MI: Singing Tree Press, 1970.

Dulles, Foster Rhea. *The Old China Trade*. Boston, MA: Houghton Mifflin, 1930.

Dunn, Nathan. *Ten Thousand Chinese Things: A Descriptive Catalogue of the Chinese Collection in Philadelphia, with Miscellaneous Remarks Upon the Manners, Customs, Trade, and Government of the Celestial Empire*. Philadelphia, 1839.

Du Halde, Jean Baptiste. *The General History of China. Containing a Geographical, Historical, Chronological, Political and Physical Description of the Empire of China, Chinese-Tartary, Corea and Thibet. Including an Exact and Particular Account of their Customs, Manners, Ceremonies, Religion, Arts and Sciences. The Whole Adorn'ed with Curious Maps, and Variety of Copper Plates*. From the French of Du Halde [by R. Brookes]. 3rd ed. corrected. 4 vols. London: Printed for J. Watts and Sold by B. Dod at the Bible and Key in Ave-Mary Lane, near Stationers-Hall, 1741. 1735; London: Printed for J. Watts, 1741.

———. *A Description of the Empire of China and Chinese-Tartary, Together with the Kingdoms of Korea and Tibet: Containing the Geography and History (Natural as well as Civil) of those Countries. Enrich'd with General and Particular Maps, and Adorned with a Great Number of Cuts*. From the French of P.J.B. Du Halde, Jesuit: With Notes Geographical, Historical, and Critical; and Other Improvements, particularly in Maps, by the Translator [R. Brookes]. 2 vols. London: Printed by T. Gardner in Bartholomew-Close, for Edward Cave, at St. John's Gate, 1738, 1741.

Edwards, Randle. "The Old Canton System of Foreign Trade." In *Law and Politics in China's Foreign Trade*, edited by Victor H. Li, pp. 360–78. Seattle: University of Washington Press, 1978.

Ellis, William. *An Authentic Narrative of a Voyage Performed by Captain Cook and Captain Clerke, in His Majesty's Ships* Resolution *and* Discovery, *During the Years 1776,*

1777, 1778, and 1780; in Search of a North-West Passage Between the Continents of Asia and America. Including a Faithful Account of All Their Discoveries, and the Unfortunate Death of Captain Cook. 2 vols. London: Printed for G. Robinson, Pater-noster Row; J. Sewell, Cornhill; and J. Debrett, Picadilly, 1783.

Fabian, Johannes. *Time and the Other: How Anthropology Makes Its Object.* New York: Columbia University Press, 1983.

Fay, Peter Ward. *The Opium War 1840–1842: Barbarians in the Celestial Empire in the Early Part of the Nineteenth Century and the War by Which They Forced Her Gates Ajar.* Chapel Hill: University of North Carolina Press, 1975.

Fairbank, John K. *China Perceived: Images and Policies in Chinese-American Relations.* New York: Knopf, 1974.

———. *Chinese-American Interactions: A Historical Summary.* New Brunswick, NJ: Rutgers University Press, 1975.

———. *The Great Chinese Revolution, 1800–1985.* New York: Harper & Row, 1986.

———. *Late Ch'ing, 1800–1911.* Cambridge: Cambridge University Press, 1978.

———. *Trade and Diplomacy on the China Coast: The Opening of the Treaty Ports, 1842–1854.* Cambridge, MA: Harvard University Press, 1953.

———. *The United States and China.* Cambridge, MA: Harvard University Press, 1948.

Fichter, James. *American East Indies, 1772–1815.* Ph.D. Dissertation, Harvard University, 2006.

———. "American History on Other Continents." *Common-Place* 7.1 (October 2006); http://www.historycooperative.org/journals/cp/vol-07/no-02/tales/ (accessed May 20, 2010).

———. *So Great a Profit: How the East Indies Trade Transformed Anglo-American Capitalism.* Cambridge, MA: Harvard University Press, 2010.

Fleischacker, Samuel. "Adam Smith's Reception among the American Founders, 1776–1790." *The William and Mary Quarterly* 59.4 (October 2002): 897–924.

Fontenoy, Paul E. "An Experimental Voyage to China, 1785–1787." *The American Neptune* (1996); http://www.pem.org/neptune/voyage1.htm (accessed June 20, 2010).

———. "Ginseng, Otter Skins, and Sandalwood: The Conundrum of the China Trade." *The Northern Mariner /Le Marin du nord* 7.1 (January 1997): 1–16.

Forbes, Crosby. *Hills and Streams: Landscape Decoration on Chinese Export Blue and White Porcelain.* International Exhibition Foundation, 1982.

Forbes, John Murray. *Letters and Recollections of John Murray Forbes,* edited by Sarah Forbes Hughes. 2 vols. Boston: 1899.

———. *Reminiscences of John Murray Forbes.* 3 vols. Boston, MA: George H. Ellis, 1902.

Forbes, Robert Bennet. *Letters from China: The Canton-Boston Correspondence of Robert Bennet Forbes, 1838–1840,* edited by Sarah Forbes Hughes. Mystic, CT: Mystic Seaport Museum, 1996.

———. *Remarks on China and the China Trade.* Boston, MA: Samuel N. Dickinson, 1844.

Foster, John W. *American Diplomacy in the Orient*. Boston and New York: Houghton, Mifflin and Company, 1903.

Fox-Genovese, Elizabeth and Eugene D. Genovese. *The Mind of the Master Class: History and Faith in the Southern Slaveholders' Worldview*. Cambridge: Cambridge University Press, 2005.

Freedgood, Elaine. *The Ideas in Things: Fugitive Meaning in the Victorian Novel*. Chicago, IL: University of Chicago Press, 2006.

Fuess, Claude M. *The Life of Caleb Cushing*. 2 vols. New York: Harcourt, Brace, 1923.

Gallagher, John and Ronald Robinson. "The Imperialism of Free Trade." *Economic History Review*. 2nd series. 6.1 (1953): 1–15.

Garrett, Valery M. *Heaven Is High, the Emperor Far Away: Merchants and Mandarins in Old Canton*. New York: Oxford University Press, 2002.

Gibson, James R. *Otter Skins, Boston Ships, and China Goods: The Maritime Fur Trade of the Northwest Coast, 1785–1841*. Seattle: University of Washington Press, 1992.

Goldsmith, Oliver. *A History of the Earth and Animated Nature*. 4 vols. Philadelphia, PA: Printed for Mathew Carey, 1773.

———. *A History of the Earth and Animated Nature*. 5 vols. Philadelphia, PA: Thomas T. Ash, 1823.

Goldstein, Jonathan. *Philadelphia and the China Trade, 1682–1846*. University Park: Pennsylvania State University Press, 1978.

———. Review of *The Golden Ghetto: The American Community at Canton and the Shaping of American China Policy, 1784–1844* by Jacques M. Downs. *The Journal of Asian Studies* 58 (February 1999): 159–61.

Goldstein, Jonathan, Jerry Israel, and Hilary Conroy, eds. *America Views China: American Images of China Then and Now*. Bethlehem, PA: Lehigh University Press, 1991.

Grant, Frederic Delano. "Hong Merchant Litigation in the American Courts." *Proceedings of the Massachusetts Historical Society* 99 (1988): 44–62.

Green, John. "Receipts, Canton in China, 1784–1786." Rare Book and Manuscripts Library: Van Pelt Library, University of Pennsylvania (Ms. Coll. 499).

Greenberg, Michael. *British Trade and the Opening of China, 1800–42*. Cambridge: Cambridge University Press, 1951.

Greenbie, Sydney and Marjorie Barstow. *Gold of Ophir, or The China Trade in the Making of America*. New York: Wilson-Erickson, 1937. First published as *Gold of Ophir: The Lure that Made America*.

Griffin, Katherine H. and Peter Drummey. "Manuscripts on the China Trade at the Massachusetts Historical Society." *Proceedings of the Massachusetts Historical Society*. 3rd series. 100 (1988): 128–39.

Griffin, Martin I. J. *Commodore John Barry, Father of the American Navy: The Record of His Services for Our Country*. Published by the author: Philadelphia, 1903.

Gulick, Edward V. *Peter Parker and the Opening of China*. Cambridge, MA: Harvard University Press, 1973.

Gurn, Joseph. *Commodore John Barry, Father of the American Navy*. New York: P.J. Kennedy & Sons, 1933.

Haddad, John Rogers. *The Romance of China: Excursions to China in U.S. Culture: 1776–1876*. New York: Columbia University Press, 2008.

Hao, Yen'ping. "Chinese Teas to America: A Synopsis." In *America's China Trade in Historical Perspective: The Chinese and American Performance*, edited by Ernest R. May and John K. Fairbank, pp. 11–31. Cambridge, MA: Harvard University Press, 1986.

———. *The Commercial Revolution in Nineteenth-Century China: The Rise of Sino-Western Mercantile Capitalism*. Berkeley: University of California Press, 1986.

———. *The Comprador in Nineteenth-Century China: Bridge between East and West*. Cambridge, MA: Harvard University Press, 1979.

Hay, John. *Letters of John Hay and Extracts from Diary*, edited by Henry Adams. Vol. 3. New York: Gordian Press, 1969. Printed in 1908 but not published.

He, Sebing. "Macao in the Making of Sino-US Relations." In *Bridging the Sino-American Divide*, edited by Priscilla Roberts, pp. 332–61. Newcastle, UK: Cambridge Scholars, 2007.

———. "Russell and Company and American Trade with Canton in the Nineteenth Century" (Qichang Yanghang yu shijiu shiji Meiguo dui Guangzhou maoyi). *Academic Research* (Xueshu yanjiu) 6 (2005): 109–16.

Howard, David Sanctuary. *New York and the China Trade*. The New York Historical Society, 1984.

Howay, Frederic William, ed. *Voyages of the "Columbia" to the Northwest Coast 1787–1790 and 1790–93*. Oregon Historical Society Press, in cooperation with The Massachusetts Historical Society, 1990. First published 1941.

Hsu, M. "Trading with Gold Mountain: *Jinshanzhuang* and Networks of Kinship and Native Place." In *Chinese American Transnationalism: The Flow of People, Resources, and Ideas between China and America during the Exclusion Era*, edited by Sucheng Chan, pp. 22–33. Philadelphia, PA: Temple University Press, 2006.

Huang Zisheng and Sibing He. *Feilübin Huaqiao Shi* (*History of the Philippine Chinese*). Rev. and enlarged ed. Guangzhou: Guangdong Gaodeng Jiaoyü Chubanshe (Guangdong Higher Education Press), 2009, 262–3.

Hummel, Arthur W., ed. *Eminent Chinese of the Ch'ing Period (1644–1912)*. 2 vols. Washington, DC: U.S. Government Printing Office, 1943–44.

———. *Bits of Old China*. London: Kegan Paul, Trench, & Co., 1885.

Hunt, Freeman. *Lives of American Merchants*. New York: Derby & Jackson; Cincinnati, OH: H. W. Derby & Co., 1857.

Hunt, Michael H. *The Making of a Special Relationship: The United States and China to 1914*. New York: Columbia University Press, 1983.

Hunter, William C. *The "Fan Kwae" at Canton*. Taiwan: Ch'eng-Wen Publishing Company, 1970. First published 1882.

———. *Bits of Old China*. London: Kegan Paul, Trench, & Co., 1885.

Isaacs, Harold. *Scratches on Our Minds: American Images of China and India*. New York: J. Day, 1958.

Itier, Jules. *Journal d'un Voyage en Chine en 1843, 1844, 1845, 1846*. 2 vols. Paris: Chez Duvin et Fontaine, 1848.

Jacobs, J.B. *Local Politics in a Rural Chinese Cultural Setting: A Field Study of Mazu Township, Taiwan*. Canberra: Contemporary China Centre, Research School of Pacific Studies, Australian National University, 1980.

Jansen, Marius B. "Obituary: John King Fairbank (1907–1991)." *The Journal of Asian Studies* 51.1 (February 1992): 237–42.

Jiang, H.X. "Mingqing shiqi mazu xinyang chuantai guocheng ji yingxiang xunzong" ("The Process of Mazu belief spreading to Taiwan in Ming and Qing Dynasty") *Dongnan Chuanbo* (Southeast Media) 1 (2008): 24–5.

Johannson, Kristin. *Ginseng Dreams: The Secret World of America's Most Valuable Plant*. Lexington: University of Kentucky Press, 2006.

Johnson, Rossiter, ed. and John Howard Brown, managing ed. *The Twentieth Century Biographical Dictionary of Notable Americans*. 10 vols. Boston, MA: The Biographical Society, 1904.

Jorge, Cecília. "Rebecca Chase: An American in Macau." *MACAU* 11 (2002): 38–53.

Jung, Moon-Ho. *Coolies and Cane: Race, Labor, and Sugar in the Age of Emancipation*. Baltimore, MD: Johns Hopkins University Press, 2006.

———. "Outlawing 'Coolies': Race, Nation, and Empire in the Age of Emancipation. *American Quarterly* 57.3 (September 2005): 677–701.

Keliher, Macabe. "Anglo-American Rivalry and the Origins of U.S. China Policy." *Diplomatic History* 31.2 (April 2007): 227–57.

Kuah-Pearce, Khun Eng. "Cultural and Network Capitals: Chinese Women and the 'Religious' Industry in South China." In *Chinese Women and Their Social and Network Capitals*, edited by Khun Eng Kuah-Pearce, pp. 121–43. Singapore: Marshall Cavendish International, 2004.

Khun, Philip A. *Origins of the Modern Chinese State*. Stanford, CA: Stanford University Press, 2002.

King, Caroline Howard. *When I Lived in Salem, 1822–1866*. Brattleboro, VT: Stephen Daye Press, 1937.

Kinsman, Rebecca Chase. "Daily Life of Mrs. Nathaniel Kinsman in Macao, China. Excerpts from letters of 1844." *The Essex Institute Historical Collection*. LXXXVI (October 1950): 311–30.

———. "Journal of Rebecca Chase Kinsman Kept on Her Voyage to China in 1843." *Essex Institute Historical Collection* 90.3 (July 1954): 289–308; and *EIHC* 90 4 (October 1954): 389–409.

———. "Journal of Rebecca Chase Kinsman Kept on her Voyage to China in 1843." Typescript [1958, by Mrs. Storer P. Ware]. Boston, MA: Baker Library, Harvard Business School. Call number: WPBK56 (1843).

———. "Life in Macao in the 1840's: Letters of Rebecca Chase Kinsman to her family in Salem. From the collection of Mrs. Rebecca Kinsman Munroe." *Essex Institute Historical Collection*. LXXXVI (January 1950): 15–40.

———. "Life in Macao in the 1840's: Letters of Rebecca Chase Kinsman to her Family in Salem. From the Collection of Mrs. Rebecca Kinsman Munroe." *Essex Institute Historical Collection* LXXXVI (April 1950): 106–43.

Kirker, James. *Adventures to China: Americans in Southern Oceans, 1792–1812*. New York: Oxford University Press, 1971.

Knox, Jerry Bradley. *History, Geography, and Economics of North American Ginseng*. Ann Arbor: UMI, 2000.

Koo, Yi Kyuin Wellington. *The Status of Aliens in China*. New York: Columbia University Press, 1912.

Koon, Yeewan. "Lives and Afterlives: Luo Ping's Guiqu tu." *Orientations* 40 (September 2009).

Krafft, Herman Frederick and Walter B. Norris. *Sea Power in American History*. New York: The Century Co., 1920.

Lai, Him Mark. *The Chinese of America, 1785–1980: An Illustrated History and Catalog of the Exhibition*. San Francisco, CA: Chinese Culture Foundation, 1980.

———. *Becoming Chinese American: A History of Communities and Institutions*. Walnut Creek, CA: AltaMira Press, 2004.

———. *The Chinese of America, 1785–1980: An Illustrated History and Catalog of the Exhibition*. San Francisco, CA: Chinese Culture Foundation, 1980.

Lai, Walton Look. *Indentured Labor, Caribbean Sugar: Chinese and Indian Migrants to the British West Indies, 1838–1918*. Baltimore, MD: Johns Hopkins University Press, 1993.

Lamas, Rosmarie W.N. *Everything in Style: Harriet Low's Macau*. Hong Kong University Press, in conjunction with Instituto Cultural do Governo da R.A.E. de Macau, 2006.

LaPlace, Cyrille-Pierre Theodore. *Voyage autour du monde par les mers d'Inde et de la Chine exécuté sur la corvette de l'état la Favorite pendant les années 1830, 1831 et 1832 sous le commandement de M. Laplace capitaine de frégate*. 5 vols. Paris: Imprimerie Royale, 1833–39.

Larson, John Lauritz. *Bonds of Enterprise: John Murray Forbes and Western Development in America's Railway Age*. Expanded ed. Iowa City: University of Iowa Press, 2001. First published 1984.

Latourette, Kenneth Scott. *The History of Early Relations between the United States and China, 1784–1844*. New Haven, CT: Yale University Press, 1917.

Laurence, Keith and Floyd Cheung. *Recovered Legacies: Authority and Identity in Early Asian American Literature*. Philadelphia, PA: Temple University Press, 2005.

Layton, Thomas N. "The Voyage of the 'Frolic': New England Merchants and the Opium Trade." *Journal of Asian Studies* 57.2 (May 1988): 501.

Lazich, Michael. "American Missionaries and the Opium Trade in Nineteenth-Century China." *Journal of World History* 17 (Spring 2006): 197–223.

Legarda, Benito J. *After the Galleons: Foreign Trade, Economic Change and Entrepreneurship in the Nineteenth-Century Philippines.* Quezon City: Ateneo de Manila University Press, 1999.

Le Pichon, Alain, ed. *China Trade and Empire: Jardine, Matheson & Co. and the Origins of British Rule in Hong Kong, 1827–1843.* Oxford: Published for the British Academy by Oxford University Press, 2006.

Ledyard, John. *A Journal of Captain Cook's Last Voyage to the Pacific Ocean.* New Haven: CT, 1783.

Lee, Erika. "Defying Exclusion: Chinese Immigrants and their Strategies during the Exclusion Era." In *Chinese American Transnationalism: The Flow of People, Resources, and Ideas between China and America during the Exclusion Era,* edited by Sucheng Chan, pp. 1–22. Philadelphia, PA: Temple University Press, 2006.

Lee, Benjamin. "Critical Internationalism." *Public Culture* 7 (1995): 559–92.

Lee, Jean Gordon. *Philadelphians and the China Trade, 1784–1844.* Philadelphia Museum of Art, 1984.

Lee, Jonathan H. X. "Creating a Transnational Community: The Empress of Heaven and Goddess of the Sea, Tianhou/Mazu, from Beigang to San Francisco." In *Religion at the Corner of Bliss and Nirvana: Politics, Identity, and Faith in New Migrant Communities,* edited by Lois Ann Lorentzen et al., pp. 166–83. Durham, NC: Duke University Press, 2009.

———. *Transnational Goddess on the Move: Meiguo Mazu's Celestial Inspection Tour and Pilgrimage as Chinese American Culture Work and Vernacular Chinese Religion.* Ph.D. Dissertation (Religious Studies), University of California Santa Barbara. UMI Microform 3375556 (2009).

Levenstein, Harvey. *Revolution at the Table: The Transformation of the American Diet.* New York and Oxford: Oxford University Press, 1988.

Liang Jiabin, *Guangdong Shisanhang Kao.* Guangzhou: Guangdong Renmin Chubanshe, 1999. First published 1937.

Lin, J.H., J.Q. Fu, and L.L. Zhuang. "Shangmao fazhan yu mazu xianghuo wangluo kuozhan de guanxi" ("The relationship between the commerce and trade development and the expansion of Mazu incense networks") *Journal of Putian University* 14.6 (2007): 87–92.

Linton, Derek S. "Asia and the West in the New World Order—From Trading Companies to Free Trade Imperialism: The British and Their Rivals in Asia, 1700–1850." In *Asia in Western and World History,* edited by Ainslie T. Embree and Carol Gluck, pp. 83–116. New York: M.E. Sharpe, 1997.

Lipsey, Robert E. "U.S. Foreign Trade and the Balance of Payments, 1800–1913." In *The Cambridge Economic History of the United States.* Vol 2. Edited by Stanley L. Engerman and Robert E. Gallman, pp. 685–732. Cambridge: Cambridge University Press, 2000.

Liu, K.C. *Anglo-American Steamship Rivalry in China, 1862–1874.* Cambridge, MA: Harvard University Press, 1962.

Liu, Lydia H. *Clash of Empires: The Invention of China in Modern World Making.* Cambridge, MA: Harvard University Press, 2004.

———, ed. *Tokens of Exchange: The Problem of Translation in Global Circulation.* Durham, NC: Duke University Press, 1999.

Loines, Elma, ed. *The China Trade Post-Bag of the Seth Low Family of Salem and New York.* Manchester, ME: Falmouth Publishing House, 1953.

Lossing, Benson J. *Pictorial Field-Book of the Revolution; or, Illustrations, by Pen and Pencil, of the History, Biography, Scenery, Relics, and Traditions of the War for Independence.* 2 vols. 1853; New York: Harper & Brothers, 1859.

Low, Harriett. *Light and Shadows of a Macao Life: The Journal of Harriett Low, Travelling Spinster.* 2 vols. Edited by Nan P. Hodges and Arthur W. Hummel. Woodinville, WA: The History Bank, 2002.

———. *My Mother's Journal: A Young Lady's Diary of Five Years Spent in Manila, Macao, and the Cape of Good Hope from 1829-1834,* edited by Katherine Hilliard. Boston, MA: G. H. Ellis, 1900.

Lowe, Lisa. *Immigrant Acts: On Asian American Cultural Politics.* Durham, NC: Duke University Press, 1996.

Lum, Raymond. "Ko K'un-hua: The Brief Life of Harvard's First Chinese Instructor: 1838–1882." *Harvard Magazine* (March–April 2008): 44–5.

Lyman, Theodore, Jr. *Diplomacy of the United States.* Boston, MA: Wells and Lilly, 1828.

McGrath, Tim. *John Barry: An American Hero in the Age of Sail.* Yardley, PA: Westholme Publishing, 2010.

McCusker, John J. *How Much is That In Real Money?* Worcester, MA: American Antiquarian Society, 2001.

Mackinder, H. J. "The Geographical Pivot of History." Paper presented in 1904 to the Royal Geographical Society meeting in London. For a record of the meeting, see *The National Geographic Magazine* 15 (1904).

Mahan, Alfred Thayer. *The Influence of Sea Power Upon History.* New York: Dover Publications, 1987. First published 1894.

Malcolm, Elizabeth. "The Chinese Repository and Western Literature on China 1800 to 1850." *Modern Asia Studies* 7.2 (1972): 165–78.

May, Ernest R. *American Imperialism: A Speculative Essay.* Chicago, IL: Imprint Publications, 1991. First published 1868.

May, Ernest R. and John K. Fairbank. *America's China Trade in Historical Perspective: The Chinese and American Performance.* Committee on American-East Asia Relations, in collaboration with the Council on East Asian Studies, Harvard University. Cambridge, MA: Harvard University Press, 1986.

Mayer, Brantz. "China and the Chinese." *Southern Quarterly Review* 12.23 (July 1847): 1–51.

———. *History of the War between Mexico and the United States, with a Preliminary of its Origin.* New York and London: Wiley and Putnam, 1848.

———. *Mexico as It Was and as it Is.* New York: J. Winchester, 1844.

———. *Mexico, Aztec, Spanish and Republican: A Historical, Geographical, Political, Statistical and Social Account of that Country from the Period of the Invasion by the Spaniards to the Present Time: With a View of the Ancient Aztec Empire and Civilization; A Historical Sketch of the Late War; and Notices of New Mexico and California.* Hartford, CT: S. Drake and Company, 1853.

———. *A Nation in a Nutshell.* Philadelphia, PA: Brown, Bicking, & Guilbert, 1841.

Mazumdar, Sucheta, Vasant Kaiwar, and Thierry Labica. *From Orientalism to Postcolonialism: Asia, Europe and the Lineages of Difference.* London: Routledge, 2009.

Meany, William Barry. *Commodore John Barry, the Father of the American Navy: A Survey of Extraordinary Episodes in His Navel Career.* New York: Harper and Brothers Publishers, 1911.

Meyer, David R. *Hong Kong as Global Metropolis.* Cambridge: Cambridge University Press, 2000.

Millard, Thomas F. *America and the Far Eastern Question: An Examination of the Modern Phases of the Far Eastern Question, Including the New Activities and Policy of Japan, the Situation of China, and the Relation of the United States of America to the Problems Involved.* New York: Moffat, Yard and Company, 1909.

Miller, David Hunter. *Treaties and Other International Acts of the United States of America.* 8 vols. Washington DC: Government Printing Office, 1931–34.

Miller, Stuart Creighton. *The American Trader's Image of China, 1785–1882. The Pacific Historical Review* 36.4 (November 1967): 375–95.

———. "Ends and Means: Missionary Justification of Force in Nineteenth Century China." *The Missionary Enterprise in China and America.* Edited by John K. Fairbank, pp. 249–82. Cambridge, MA: Harvard University Press, 1974.

———. *The Unwelcome Immigrant: The American Image of the Chinese, 1785–1882.* Berkeley: University of California Press, 1969.

Molloy, William M., ed. *Treaties, Conventions, International Acts, Protocols and Agreements between the United States of America and Other Powers, 1776-1909.* 2 vols. Washington DC: Government Printing Office, 1910.

Morse, Hosea Ballou. *The Gilds of China: With an Account of the Gild Merchant or Co-Hong of Canton.* London: Longmans, Green, 1909.

———. *The International Relations of the Chinese Empire.* 3 vols. London: Longmans, Green, 1910–18.

———. *The Trade and Administration of the Chinese Empire.* Shanghai: Kelley and Walsh, 1908.

Moore, John Bassett. *American Diplomacy, Its Spirit and Achievements.* New York: Harper & Brothers, 1905.

Morrison, Mary. *Memoirs of the Life and Labours of Robert Morrison.* London: n.p., 1839.

Morrison, Robert. *Vocabulary of the Canton Dialect* (廣東省土話字彙). Macao: Printed at the Honorable East India Company's Press, 1828.

Mundy, William Walter. *Canton and the Bogue: The Narrative of an Eventful Six Months in China*. London: Samuel Tinsley, 1875.

Munn, Christopher. *Anglo-China: Chinese People and British Rule in Hong Kong, 1841–1880*. Richmond, Surrey: Curzon, 2001.

———. "The Hong Kong Opium Revenue, 1845–1885." *Opium Regimes: China, Britain, and Japan, 1839–1952*, edited by Timonty Brook and Bob Tadashi Wakabayashi. Berkeley: University of California Press, 2000.

Nye, Gideon. *British Opium Policy and Its Results to India and China*. Macao, 1874.

———. *The Gage of Two Civilizations: Shall Christendom Waver?* Macao, 1860.

———. *The Morning of My Life in China*. Canton, 1873 and 1877.

———. *The Rationale of the China Question*. Macao, 1857 and 1873.

———. *Tea and the Tea Trade*. Canton: 1850. First published in *Hunt's*, January and February 1850.

Oliphant, Margaret ("Mrs. Oliphant"). *Annals of a Publishing House: William Blackwood and His Sons, Their Magazine and Friends*. 3 vols. Edinburgh and London: William Blackwood and Sons, 1897.

Parsons, Chris. "Ginseng in Canada?" August 2008, http://brown.edu/Facilities/John_Carter_Brown_Library/I%20found%20it%20JCB/august08.html (accessed January 17, 2011).

Perdue, Peter C. "Rise & Fall of the Canton Trade System- I: China in the World (1700-1860s)." MIT Visualizing Cultures. http://ocw.mit.edu/ans7870/21f/21f.027/rise_fall_canton_01/index.html (accessed May 23, 2011).

———. "Rise & Fall of the Canton Trade System- II: Macau & Whampoa Anchorage." MIT Visualizing Cultures. http://ocw.mit.edu/ans7870/21f/21f.027/rise_fall_canton_02/index.html (accessed May 23, 2011).

———. "Rise & Fall of the Canton Trade System- III: Rise & Fall of the Canton Trade System." MIT Visualizing Cultures. http://ocw.mit.edu/ans7870/21f/21f.027/rise_fall_canton_03/index.html (accessed May 23, 1969).

Perry, John Curtis. *Facing West: Americans and the Opening of the Pacific*. Westport, CT: Praeger, 1994.

Peters, John R. *Miscellaneous Remarks Upon the Government, History, Religions, Literature, Agriculture, Arts, Trades, Manners, and Customs of the Chinese, as Suggested by an Examination of the Articles Comprising the Chinese Museum*. New York: John F. Trow, 1849.

Pickowicz. "William Wood in Canton: A Critique of the China Trade Before the Opium War." *Essex Historical Collections* 107 (1971): 3–32.

Pomeranz, Kenneth. *The Great Divergence: China, Europe, and the Making of the Modern World Economy*. Princeton: Princeton University Press, 2000.

Porter, David. *Journal of a Cruise Made to the Pacific Ocean by Captain David Porter, in the United States Frigate* Essex, *in the years 1812, 1813, and 1814*. 2 vols. New York: 1822.

Pratt, Mary Louise. *Imperial Eyes: Travel Writing and Transculturation*. London: Routledge, 1992.

Preble, George. *The First Cruise of the United States Frigate* Essex. Salem, MA: 1870.

Puga, Rogério. "A gem of a place": Macau após a guerra do ópio: o diário de Rebecca Chase Kinsman. *Estudos sobre a China VI*. Vol. 2. Edited by Ana Maria Amaro. Lisbon: Centro de Estudos Chineses-Instituto Superior de Ciências Sociais e Políticas (2004): 903–55.

———. "Imagens de Macau oitocentista: a visão intimista de uma jovem americana. O diário de Harriet Low (Hillard) (1829–33). *Estudos sobre a China V*. Vol. 2. Edited by Ana Maria Amaro. Lisbon: Centro de Estudos Chineses-Instituto Superior de Ciências Sociais e Políticas (2003): 713–67.

———. "Images of Nineteenth-century Macau in the Journals of Harriett Low (1829–1834) and Rebecca Chase Kinsman (1843–1847)." *Oriente* 14 (April 2006): 90–104.

———. "Interpreting Macau through the Journals of Harriett Low and Rebecca Chase Kinsman." *Journal of Sino-Western Cultural Studies* 6.1 (June 2008): 605–64.

———. "Macau nos anos (18)30: o diário de Caroline Hyde Butler Laing (1837)." *Revista portuguesa de estudos chineses (Zhongguo yanjiu)*. 1.2 (2007): 71–112.

———. "Macau and Timor in 1929: The Journal and the Unpublished Drawings of Lucy Cleveland." *Oriente* 18 (2007): 3–33.

———. "O primeiro olhar norte-americano sobre Macau: os diários de Samuel Shaw (1754–1794)." *Intertextual dialogues, travel & routes: actas do XXVI encontro da APEAA*, edited by Ana Gabriela Macedo et al., pp. 227–51. Braga: University of Minho, 2007.

———. *A World of Euphemism: Representações de Macau na obra de Austin Coates: City of Broken Promises enquanto Romance Histórico e Bildungsroman Feminino*. Lisbon: Fundação para a Ciência e a Tecnologia-Ministério da Ciência, Tecnologia e Ensino Superior/Fundação Calouste Gulbenkian, 2009.

———. "A vivência social do género na Macau oitocentista: o diário de Harriet Low (Hillard). *Administração: revista de administração pública de Macau*. 15.56 (2002): 605–64.

Qiao, Mingshun, *The First Page of Sino-US Relations: The Signing of the Wangxia Treaty of 1844*. (Zhongmei guangxi de diyi ye: 1844 nian wangxia tiaoyue qianding de qianqian houhou). Beijing: Shehui kexue wenxian chubanshe (Social Sciences Documentation Press), 1991.

Quintner, David. *Willow! Solving the Mystery of Our 200-year Love Affair with the Willow Pattern*. Burnstown, ON: General Store Publishing House, 1997.

Reynolds, Jeremiah N. *Voyage of the United States Frigate* Potomac, *under the Command of Commodore John Downes, During the Circumnavigation of the Globe in the Years 1831, 1832, 1833, and 1834*. New York, 1835.

Richards, Rhys. "United States Trade with China, 1784–1814." *The American Neptune* 54 (Special Supplement) Salem, MA: Peabody Essex Museum, 1994.

Rickman, John. *Journal of Captain Cook's Last Voyage to the Pacific Ocean on* Discovery; *Performed in the Years 1776, 1777, 1778, 1779*. London: Printed for E. Newberry, the Corner of St. Paul's Church-Yard, 1780.

Ride, Lindsay and May Ride. *An East India Company Cemetery: Protestant Burials in Macao*, edited by Bernard Mellor. Hong Kong University Press, 1995.

Rifkin, Mark. "Debt and the Transnationalization of Hawai'i." *American Quarterly* 60.1 (March 2008): 43–66.

Roberts, Edmund and W.S.W. Ruschenberger. *Two Yankee Diplomats in 1830s Siam*. Bangkok: Orchid Press, 2002.

Roberts, Priscilla. *Sino-American Relations since 1900*. Hong Kong: Center of Asian Studies, University of Hong Kong, 1991.

Rubinstein, Murray A. *The Origins of the Anglo-American Missionary Enterprise in China, 1807–1848*. Metuchen, NJ: Scarecrow Press, 1996.

Ruschenberger, W.S.W. *Narrative of a Voyage round the World during the Years 1835, 36, and 37; Including a Narrative of an Embassy to the Sultan of Muscat and the King of Siam*. Vol. 2. London: Richard Bentley, 1838.

Ruskola, Teemu. "Canton Is Not Boston: The Invention of American Imperial Sovereignty." *American Quarterly* 57.3 (September 2005): 859–84.

Said, Edward. *Orientalism*. New York: Vintage Books, 1979.

———. "Orientalism Reconsidered." In *Literature, Politics and Theory: Papers from the Essex Conference, 1976-84*, edited by Francis Barker, Peter Hulme, Margaret Iversen, and Diana Loxley, pp. 210–29. London: Methuen, 1986.

Sampaio, Manuel de Castro. *Os Chins de Macau*. Hong Kong: Tipografia Noronha e Filhos, 1867.

Sanchez-Eppler, Karen. "Copying and Conversion: An 1824 Friendship Album 'from a Chinese Youth.'" *American Quarterly* 59.2 (June 2007): 301–39.

Schuyler, Eugene. *American Diplomacy and the Furtherance of Commerce*. London: Sampson Low, 1886.

Semmel, Bernard. *The Rise of Free Trade Imperialism: Classical Political Economy, the Empire of Free Trade and Imperialism, 1750–1850*. Cambridge: Cambridge University Press, 1970.

Shaw, Samuel. *The Journals of Major Samuel Shaw, The First American Consul at Canton: With a Life of the Author by Josiah Quincy*, edited by Josiah Quincy. Boston, MA: Wm. Crosby and H.P. Nichols, 1847.

———. Letter to John Jay, 19 May 1785. *American Museum* I (March 1787): 194–7.

———. "Remarks on the Commerce of America with China." *American Museum* 7 (March 1790): 126–8.

———. "Statement of the Ships Employed in the Trade to Canton." *American Museum* 7 (March 1790): 128.

Shavit, David. *The United States in Asia: A Historical Dictionary*. New York: Greenwood Press, 1992.

Shewmaker, Kenneth E. "Forging the 'Great Chain': Daniel Webster and the Origins of American Foreign Policy Toward East Asia and the Pacific, 1841–1852." *Proceedings of the American Philosophical Society* 129.3 (1985): 225–59.

Shuck, Henrietta Hall. *A Memoir of Mrs. Henrietta Hall Shuck, the First American Female Missionary to China,* edited by Jeremiah Bell Jeter. Boston, MA: Gould, Kendall, and Lincoln, 1850.

Sirr, Henry Charles. *China and the Chinese: Their Religion, Character, Customs, and Manufactures.* London, Wm. S. Orr & Co., 1844.

Smith, Adam. *Inquiry into the Nature and Causes of the Wealth of Nations.* New York: Prometheus Books, 1991. First published 1776.

Smith, Philip Chadwick Foster. *The Empress of China.* Philadelphia Maritime Museum, 1984.

Souza, George Bryan. *The Survival of Empire: Portuguese Trade and Society in China and the South China Sea, 1630–1754.* Cambridge: Cambridge University Press, 1986.

Speer, William. *The Oldest and the Newest Empire: China and the United States.* Cincinnati, OH: National Publishing Co., 1870.

Spence, Jonathan. *The Search for Modern China.* New York: W.W. Norton, 1999.

Stelle, Charles Clarkson. *Americans and the China Opium Trade in the Nineteenth Century.* New York: Arno Press, 1981.

Stuart, Jan and Evelyn S. Rawski, *Worshipping the Ancestors: Chinese Commemorative Portraits.* Washington DC: Smithsonian Institute, 2001.

Swift, John W., P. Hodgkinson, and Samuel W. Woodhouse. "The Voyage of the Empress of China." *The Pennsylvania Magazine of History and Biography* 63.1 (January 1939): 24–36.

Swisher, Earl. *China's Management of the American Barbarians: A Study of Sino-American Relations, 1841–1861, with Documents.* New Haven, CT: Far Eastern Publications, Yale University Press, 1951, 1953.

Takaki, Ronald. *A Different Mirror: A History of Multicultural America.* Boston, MA: Little Brown, 1993.

Taylor, David A. *Ginseng, the Divine Root.* Chapel Hill, NC: Algonquin Books of Chapel Hill, 2006.

Taylor, Fitch W. *The Flag Ship or A Voyage Around the World in the United States Frigate Columbia.* 2 vols. New York, 1840.

Tchen, John Kuo Wei. *New York Before Chinatown: Orientalism and the Shaping of American Culture, 1777–1882.* Baltimore, MD: Johns Hopkins University Press, 1999.

Teixeira, Padre Manuel. *A Gruta de Camões em Macau,* Macao: Fundação Macau-Instituto Internacional de Macau, 1999.

Teng Ssu-yü and John K. Fairbank, eds. *China's Response to the West: A Documentary Survey, 1839–1923.* 1954; New York: Antheneum, 1963.

Thomas, Brook. "China Men, United States v. Wong Kim Ark, and the Question of Citizenship." *American Quarterly* 50.4 (December 1998): 689–717.

Ticknor, Benajah. *The Voyage of the Peacock: A Journal,* edited by Nan Powell. Ann Arbor: University of Michigan Press, 1991.

Tiffany, Osmond Jr. *The Canton Chinese: Or, the American's Sojourn in the Celestial Empire.* Boston and Cambridge, MA: James Munroe and Company, 1849.

Tilden, Joseph. *Ship Canton, Third Voyage of BPT to China, 1818–1819*. Manuscript in collection of the Philips Library, Peabody Essex Museum, Salem, Massachusetts.

Todd, David. "John Bowring and the Global Dissemination of Free Trade." *The Historical Journal* 51.2 (2008): 373–97.

Tong, Te-kong. *United States Diplomacy in China, 1844–60*. Seattle: University of Washington Press, 1964,

United States Department of State. *Despatches from United States Consuls in Macao, 1849–1869*. Record group 59. Microcopy no. 109. Washington, DC: National Archives, 1947.

Urban Council. *Scenes of Two Cities: Hong Kong & Macau*. Hong Kong: Urban Council, 1983.

Van Dyke, Paul A. *The Canton Trade: Life and Enterprise on the China Coast, 1700–1845*. Hong Kong University Press, 2005.

———. "Operational Efficiencies and the Decline of the Chinese Junk Trade in the Eighteenth and Nineteenth Centuries: The Connection." In *Shipping Efficiency and Economic Growth 1350-1800*, edited by Richard Unger. Forthcoming.

——— and Cynthia Viallé. *The Canton-Macao Dagregisters, 1762*. Macau: Macau Cultural Institute, 2006.

———. *The Canton-Macao Dagregisters, 1763*. Macau: Macau Cultural Institute, 2008.

Ver Steeg, Clarence L. "Financing and Outfitting the First United States Ship to China." *Pacific Historical Review* 22.1 (1953): 1–12.

Vinograd, Richard. *Boundaries of the Self: Chinese Portraits, 1600–1900*. Cambridge: University of Cambridge Press, 1992.

Wakeman, Frederic, Jr. *Strangers at the Gate: Social Disorder in South China, 1839–1861*. Berkeley: University of California Press, 1966.

———. "The Canton Trade and the Opium War." In *The Cambridge History of China*. Vol. 10, *Late Ch'ing*, 1800–1911. Part 1. Edited by Denis Twitchett and John K. Fairbank, pp. 163–212. Cambridge: Cambridge University Press, 1978.

Waln, Robert Jr. *China*. Philadelphia, PA: 1823.

Wang, Jinwei. *Limited Adversaries: Post-Cold War Sino-American Mutual Images*. Oxford: Oxford University Press, 2000.

Wang, Y.L. and M.R. Deng. "Mingqing shiqi hainandao de mazu xinyang" ("A Study of the Worship of Mazu in Hainan Island during the Ming and Qing Dynasties") *Humanities and Social Sciences Journal of Hainan University* 22.4 (2004): 381–6.

Ward, Edith Nevill Smythe. *Caroline Hyde Butler Laing (1804–1892). A Family Heritage: Letters and Journals of Caroline Hyde Butler Laing, 1804–1892*. East Orange, NJ: Abbey Printers, 1957.

Williams, Samuel Wells. *Easy Lessons in Chinese* (*Shiji Dacheng*). Macau: Xiangshan Shuyuan, 1842.

———. *The Middle Kingdom*. 2 vols. 1848; New York: Charles Scribner's Sons, 1883.

Williams, William A. "The Age of Mercantilism: An Interpretation of American Political Economy, 1763–1828." *William and Mary Quarterly* 15.4 (October 1958): 419–37.

Wills, Garry. *Henry Adams and the Making of America*. Boston, MA: Houghton Mifflin, 2003.

Wills, John E. *Pepper, Guns, and Parleys: The Dutch East India Company and China, 1662–1681*. Cambridge, MA: Harvard University Press, 1974.

———. "Tribute, Defensiveness, and Dependency: Uses and Limits of Some Basic Ideas about Mid-Qing Dynasty Foreign Relations." *American Neptune* 48.4 (Fall 1988): 225–9.

Wines, E. C. *A Peep at China, in Mr. Dunn's Chinese Collection; with Miscellaneous Notices Relating to the Institutions and Customs of the Chinese and the Commercial Intercourse with Them*. Philadelphia, PA: Printed for Nathan Dunn, 1830.

Wood, William W. *Sketches of China*. Philadelphia, PA: 1830.

Wong, K. Scott and Sucheng Chan, eds. *Claiming America: Constructing Chinese American Identities during the Exclusion Era*. Philadelphia, PA: Temple University Press, 1998.

———. "The Transformation of Culture: Three Chinese Views of America." *American Quarterly* 48.2 (June 1996): 201–32. Reprinted in *Locating American Studies: The Evolution of a Discipline*. Baltimore, MD: Johns Hopkins University Press, 1998.

Woodhouse, Samuel W. "The Voyage of the Empress of China." *Pennsylvania Magazine of History and Biography* 63.1 (1939): 24–36.

Wu, Q.Y. *Mazu xinyang yu haiwai minnanren de "shenyuan": yi xinjiapo tianfugong weili*. Beijing: Zhongyang wenxian chubanshe (2003): 252–61. http://www.fjql.org/qszl/xsyj39.htm (accessed June 11, 2009).

Yin, Xiao-huang. *Chinese American Literature since the 1850s*. Chicago: University of Illinois Press, 2000.

Zboray, Ronald J. and Mary Saracino Zboray. "Between 'Crockery-Dom' and Barnum: Boston's Chinese Museum, 1845–47." *American Quarterly* 56.2 (June 2004): 271–307.

Zheng, Yangwen. *The Social Life of Opium in China*. Cambridge and New York: Cambridge University Press, 2005.

Zhu, X.F. *The Study of the Coastwise Fishermen in Fujian Province since the Ming and Qing Dynasties*. M.Phil Thesis, Fujian Shifan University, 2007.

Zo, Young Kil. "Chinese Emigration into the United States, 1850–1880." Ph.D. Dissertation, Columbia University, 1971. Imprint: Ann Arbor, MI: University Microfilms, 1971.

Zug, James. *American Traveler: The Life and Adventures of John Ledyard, the Man Who Dreamed of Walking the World*. New York: Basic Books, 2005.

Index